April 17 1983
To Fred,
Happy Birthday!
Bill

P.S. May this be the forerunner of the reel thing!

MG: THE SPORTS CAR SUPREME

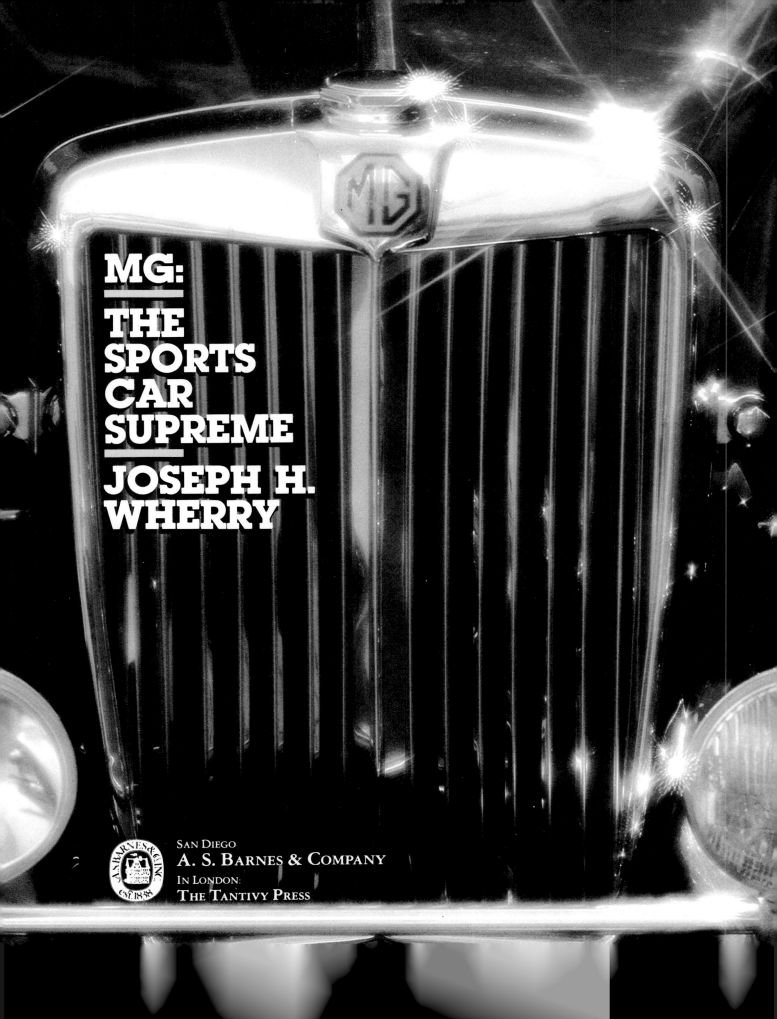

MG:
THE SPORTS CAR SUPREME

JOSEPH H. WHERRY

San Diego
A. S. Barnes & Company
In London:
The Tantivy Press

To David, my son.

Composition Design by Joseph Holland
Page Layouts by Gary Williams
Halftones by Ocean Graphics

Text Set in 11/13 Memphis Light by
Printed Page Graphics

Printed on 60# Moistrite Matte by
Publishers Press
Smythe Bound by Mountain States Bindery

MG: The Sports Car Supreme copyright © 1982 by Joseph H. Wherry.

First Edition
Manufactured in the United States of America

For information write to:

A. S. Barnes & Company, Inc.
P.O. Box 3051
La Jolla, California 92038

Library of Congress Cataloging in Publication Data

Wherry, Joseph H.
  MG

  Bibliography: p.
  Includes index.
  1. M.G. automobile.   I. Title.
TL215.M2W39   629.2'222   81-3633
ISBN 0-498-02565-9   AACR2

1 2 3 4 5 6 7 8 9   85 84 83 82

Contents

Also by Joseph H. Wherry

Economy Car Blitz (1956)
The MG Story
The Jaguar Story
The Alfa Romeo Story
Automobiles of the World
Concours d'Elegance
The Totem Pole Indians
Indian Masks and Myths of the West

Acknowledgments

The Author hastens his most cordial thanks to the many people around the world who have been so helpful through the years. Until "Black Friday" was approaching, another book about *MG: The Sports Car Supreme* had not been contemplated. Clearly, however, my old *The MG Story* (1967) was passé despite success in three languages.

Letters were dispatched to MG Car Club Centres on four continents, with varied degrees of success, and more than one overseas telecon came through at the oddest hours. The object was a search for photographs of some of the more obscure, less numerous Types of the world's most popular sports car.

Centres secretaries and newsletter editors sent out the word and *the faithful* responded valiantly. The fruits of this much-appreciated, cooperative endeavor are manifested in many of the cars shown on these pages. Those who entrusted the author with precious photographs—some very old—are credited in captions. Where appropriate and when time permitted—delays in mail deliveries have been a problem—some owner/restorers are mentioned in the text.

My special thanks are extended to the many MG owners and restorers who have gone beyond the call of duty by making their cars available for photography, not only during the preparation of this title but throughout the past quarter century. All of these *faithful* are cited with the photographic reproductions of their MGs. Particular salutations are deserved by MGCC Centres officers, so the crests of their organizations are shown in Chapter XV, the Epilogue.

To Mr. MG, John W. Thornley, the author extends particular thanks for his encouraging correspondence and kindness in providing the exact text of what will become an increasingly famous letter; this letter provides most of the text in the Afterword.

Special thanks, also, to Michael L. Cook of British Leyland in Leonia, New Jersey, and to his predecessors in the old M.G. Car Company in Abingdon, The Nuffield Organization, and British Motor Corporation, with whom the author has had sporadic contact for many years.

The author must also mention *the faithful* organizers of the annual *British Field Day* in Portland, Oregon, and *GoF West '81* in Spokane, Washington. Completion of this book made impossible the author's attendance, as invited, at these two festive events.

The wives of authors deserve unusual acknowledgment, too. Bettye's management of our home is made more difficult when this author is on the final third of a book. Bettye manages magnificently, does indispensable proofreading, types the manuscript, and puts up with the peculiarities and eccentricities of this author who, after all, does not think of himself as eccentric at all. Thanks, also, to my daughter Carol, who has permitted the publishing of her lovely visage in the 1966 MGs in the chapters concerned, and son David, who assisted in photography for this volume.

To everyone at my publisher's, special thanks, too; they have held up magnificently.

Finally, thanks to all of *the faithful*, and *viva* MG.

Author's Preface

MG, the feisty fun car that introduced motoring sports to America after the Second World War, was a healthy and vigorously youthful 56 years old on "Black Monday."

"Black Monday" was September 10, 1979, when MG's annual sales were greater than the combined sales of the other three British Leyland cars exported to North America.

On that day, the worldwide announcement of the British Leyland Motor Corporation really "kicked the hive" as John W. Thornley, OBE, eloquently wrote in a special editorial in the December 1980 issue of *Safety Fast*, the independent and official journal of the MG Car Club, a widespread band of enthusiasts with whom he had been associated for many years.

Thornley—"J.W.T.," as he's known by MG enthusiasts on every continent—began working in the factory in Abingdon-on-Thames in 1931 and was Managing Director from late 1952 until his retirement in July 1969.

The dismally ludicrous announcement by BLMC nabobs in their Piccadilly headquarters was that MG was doomed—notwithstanding the loyal organization of dealers and the marque's worldwide sports car sales supremacy. Production of the world's best-selling sports car, which had brought the cost of motor sports participation within reach of the average person, was scheduled to be ended within one year.

The Abingdon works closed on "Black Monday II," which fell on October 27, 1980, when the international MG fraternity was larger and more enthusiastic than at any time since the car's genesis in 1923.

Writing a *preface* is usually a pleasant task. This time the chore is difficult, and especially so in the light of a poignant letter recently received from John Thornley.

In November 1980, John Thornley resigned the chairmanship of the MG Car Club (MGCC), which he helped found, "after fifty years non-stop, active association with the marque." He did this after attending the October 27 closing ceremonies at Abingdon with two other ex-MG personalities of note: Sydney Enever, who designed many of the post-war Types, including the MGA and the MGB; and Wilson McComb, who labored in publicity.

Fifty years is a long time to be influentially associated with a successful product, so when J.W.T. writes that "*they* have destroyed 'my' factory," his disappointment is understandable.

With an impressive proportion of the more than one-million post-war MGs still on the roads, and with parts still in abundance—and, in fact, being made in several places—and with the Club still active, MG will live on for many years.

The corporate mergers beginning in 1952, which made matters difficult for true enthusiasts such as Thornley and others, will be dealt with later. Of greater interest to enthusiasts everywhere is the story of the genesis of the *marque* MG, and the dozens of Types and variants which have carried the "Sacred Octagon" to fame around the world—and which will continue to do so for as long as we are able to enjoy motor cars.

Joseph H. Wherry
Pierce County, Washington

Genesis and the Morris Connection

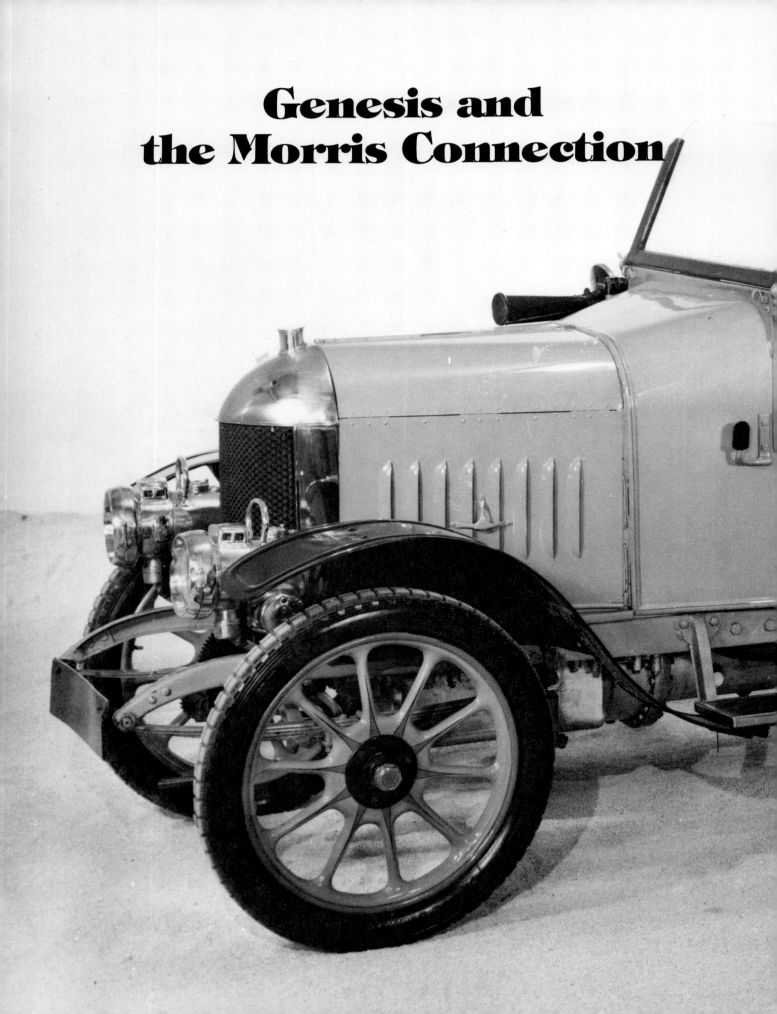

Chapter I

Direct ancestor of the first MG was this "Bullnose" Morris Oxford of 1913. (British Motor Corporation)

Genesis is creation, which means there was a creator. Where the *marque* MG is concerned, the creator was Cecil Kimber. To this man, well over a million owners have been indebted from 1923 to the present. Kimber, who died in a war-related train wreck in February 1945, had the imagination, organizing genius and a degree of engineering know-how to change a reliable (albeit humdrum) car into a scrappy and exciting machine, which was capable of engaging in competitive events.

Frangas non flectes, the Kimber family motto meaning "Break but not bend," certainly indicated the stubborn character of the MG's creator. When Kimber believed he was right, he would not compromise. Kimber always persevered; he made certain that MG cars would be designed and engineered properly, so they would be able to survive when the going became tough. That MGs have done that is the reason for the *marque's* being synonymous with "sports cars" around the world. Since World War II, the MG has led all other makes of sports cars in sales.

But the beginning was humble and somewhat obscure, with characteristics of a puzzle.

The Eden of the MG was in the ancient university city of Oxford, where several automobile sales and service facilities—which ul-timately went by the name of The Morris Garages—had their origin in 1893. In that year, 15-year-old William Richard Morris (later the Viscount Nuffield [1878– 1963]) began doing odd jobs in an Oxford bicycle repair shop for the paltry remuneration of five shillings a week (barely enough to purchase a cup of coffee today). The young Morris had found his vocation and, in less than a year, he started his own repair shop in his father's woodshed in Cowley, a town near Oxford.

Reckoning that he could build better bicycles than the ones he was repairing, Morris purchased parts and components and, late in 1894, he assembled the first Morris bicycle. Already known in the Oxford-Cowley area as a fine mechanic, Morris sold his first bicycle to a local vicar and soon had several orders for more. Forced to expand, he rented larger facilities at 48 High Street in Oxford, along with a salesroom and additional space for a repair shop in Queens Lane. In 1901 Morris purchased rough engine castings which he machined and built up into a 1.75-horsepower motorcycle engine. This he installed in a frame of his own design, and entered the motorcycle business.

To gain capital, Morris formed a partnership with another bicycle dealer named Cooper. In a livery stable in Holywell Lane,

The American-made Hupmobile was one of the several car makes sold by W. R. Morris in his garages before he began building his own cars. This 1909 Hupmobile runabout is owned by Edward Kiely. (Joseph H. Wherry photo)

Morris and Cooper built two motorcycles and displayed them in a 1902 motor show. However, a disagreement over the potential future of motor vehicles in general, and motorcycles in particular, caused a dissolution of the young partnership. This was disappointing for Morris, who was determined to manufacture motorcycles. Fortunately, a newly wealthy Oxford student with a desire to enter the motor vehicle business teamed with an experienced businessman of good repute. They contacted Morris, whose own reputation as a creative mechanic was already widespread, and businessman F. G. Barton, Morris and the wealthy student joined forces. The latter invested a considerable amount of money but was a silent partner. Barton invested some funds and his own cycle sales firm, which had branches in Oxford, Abingdon and one or two other towns, and became general manager and sales director. Morris had the technical experience and some money to invest, and was the

manager of manufacturing—the works manager, as the British say.

The new enterprise, the Oxford Automobile & Cycle Agency, put the Morris motorcycle into production in 1903. The air-cooled, one-cylinder, 2.75 HP de Dion-type engine had a mechanically operated inlet valve—rare at that date—and a newly patented carburetor of Morris's own design. The special frame, also an original Morris design, was curved to avoid contact with the crankcase, and the handlebars mounted a Bowden cable that operated the clutch, another Morris innovation. This arrangement has been standard on most motorcycles for decades.

In spite of encouraging sales, the three-way partnership lost money and the principals went their separate ways some time in

1905. Morris re-established himself near his old premises in High Street and in the old repair shop in Holywell Lane. Again doing business as The Oxford Garage, Morris managed to continue manufacturing his motorcycles, which rapidly earned a reputation for reliability and durability. A new venture into automobile sales and servicing enabled Morris to dispose of his bicycle and motorcycle businesses in 1908.

Franchises for a number of makes of cars—the British-made Humber, Singer, Standard and others; the Scottish Arrol-Johnson; and the sporty, American-made Hupmobile—brought Morris prosperity. Expanding existing facilities in Longwall Street with an impressive new two-story building in 1910, he registered a new firm name, The Morris Garage. The name would be pluralized in 1913 to The Morris Garages, W. R. Morris, Proprietor, when further expansion required the purchase and rebuilding of the Queens Hotel in Oxford and acquiring more facilities in Cross Street.

With several new car salesrooms and his successful repair garages, Morris naturally began to consider manufacturing automobiles, as had many other motorcycle makers. Because of his extensive experience in selling and servicing cars, Morris reasoned that quantity sales could be combined with quality

The Humber roadster was sold by The Morris Garages in the early days. The 1909 roadster cost £290 "complete with Side and Tail Lamps, Horn, Tools and Hood." (Courtesy: Rootes Motors, Ltd.)

by purchasing engines, transmissions, chassis frames and suspensions built to his specifications from established components manufacturers. This would permit fairly rapid production of distinctive cars for the low-priced market. He also reasoned that he would publicize the origin of the components, which he would assemble and equip with bodies of his own design. These would be acquired from experienced coachbuilders with good reputations. (Most light car makers kept secret the origins of their components, which they purchased from external sources.)

During the 1910–1912 period, while The Morris Garages were expanding, Morris secured the interest of the Earl of Macclesfield, who approved his ideas about quality, quantity production, and catering to the demand for low-priced cars. In 1912, with the Earl's financial backing assured, Morris registered W.R.M. Motors, Limited, and designed his first car, subsequently marketed as the Morris Oxford. Aimed at the market being filled by the Humber, Singer and Standard (which he was still selling in the Garages), Morris decided to make his new car price competitive with that ubiquitous American import, the Model T Ford. However, Morris was determined to make *his* car just a bit more stylish.

The Oxford was designed around a 4-cylinder, T-head, 60 x 90 mm. engine and a 3-speed gearbox operated by a gear shift lever instead of pedals like Henry Ford's famous T. White & Poppe, Ltd., makers of the engines of a dozen makes including Singer, agreed to supply the power train, while the axles and steering mechanism were E. G. Wrigley, Ltd., products. Raworths, Ltd., of Oxford, supplied the hardwood-framed, metal-sheathed bodies to Morris's own designs. Most other parts were bought in from firms which were known the length and breadth of Britain. The rounded "bullnose" radiator grille was to be the hallmark. All engineering and assem-

bly work was headquartered in Cowley, in the old military college buildings Morris had purchased.

The new Morris Oxford, with wheelbase and tread of 84 and 40 inches respectively, was introduced early in the summer of 1913. Almost immediately, four hundred cars were ordered by the prestigious London sales firm of Stewart & Ardern, and eager buyers snapped up the Oxfords as rapidly as Morris could deliver them. The first few Oxfords suffered universal joint troubles but this was soon corrected.

Morris was a sharp promoter, too, and although initial purchasers pronounced their approval and proved to be excellent references, Morris improved the new Oxfords by increasing the wheel tread to 42 inches to rem-

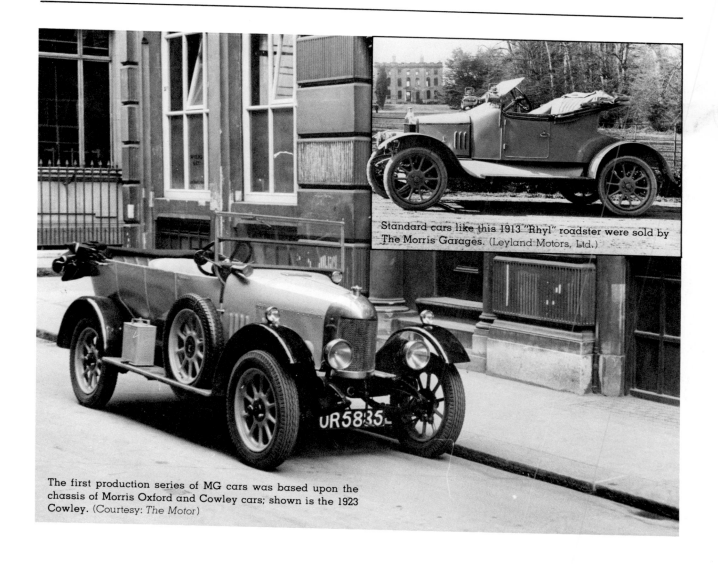

Standard cars like this 1913 "Rhyl" roadster were sold by The Morris Garages. (Leyland Motors, Ltd.)

The first production series of MG cars was based upon the chassis of Morris Oxford and Cowley cars; shown is the 1923 Cowley. (Courtesy: *The Motor*)

edy some minor steering problems. He also redesigned the clutch by reducing the number of plates from 36 to 34 to decrease sticking tendencies in cold weather.

The Cyclecar, a popular light car and motorcycle journal, tested the new bullnosed Oxford and pronounced approval in its August 6, 1913, issue. First gear, the road testers affirmed, took the car to 20 mph-plus, while second and third gears provided over 38 and a bit over 50 mph. For a light economy car, 50-plus was considered fairly fast and definitely sporting. "Keen motorists" of competitive bent were quick to realize the Oxford's potential, and a brand new car won a Gold Medal for performance in the 1913 London to Edinburgh to London Trial. Another Oxford captured *first place* in the grueling Dutch Reliability Trials, a six-day ordeal in which many more expensive and powerful cars were entered.

Morris produced a total of 393 cars during the last half of 1913, a respectable number in those days and particularly so in the case of a new motorcar maker. Production continued in 1914 with the tread again increased—to 45 inches—for even better steering and cornering stability. When the Great War of 1914–1918 erupted in August, The Morris Garages kept busy with repair work on all makes and Morris Motors continued to produce cars. A new model, the 102-inch wheelbase Cowley (of importance in the MG saga, as will be seen), was introduced. The Morris version of the White & Poppe engine was exceptionally high-revving for the time—3,800 revolutions per minute being claimed. For the best and most reliable performance, the German-made Bosche spark plug seemed to be required, but patriotic owners who fitted fairly expensive Lodge plugs claimed their Morris cars performed just as well with the British variety.

In 1919, after the war, Morris restyled his automobile works as Morris Motors, Ltd., and began manufacturing some engines of his own design while continuing to buy in chassis components from Wrigley. During a 1921 business appointment in the Wrigley factory, Morris met Cecil Kimber (1888–1945), a motorcycle and light car sports racer whose talents included design and engineering skills. Kim-

ber's long suit, however, was in production and management, and Morris hired him into The Morris Garages.

By mid-1922, Cecil Kimber had become the general manager of The Morris Garages. He was given authority to sell cars (Morris cars, of course), expand the repair business, and to exercise his initiative by exploring the potentialities of new automotive enterprises. A prewar motorcycle accident had left him with one leg considerably shorter than the other. Consequently, Kimber had not been accepted for military service, but his adventurous spirit and love of fast vehicles had made him a keen motor sports enthusiast.

The Morris Garages business was made for Kimber's creative energy because one of the established enterprises was the production of a special line of "Bullnose" Morris Cowley two-seaters, which were powered by 1,548 cc. Hotchkiss engines. Separate and independently functioning, The Morris Garages bought in 102-inch wheelbase Cowley chassis and fitted them with sporty, lightweight coachwork produced by Raworths of Oxford, or by Carbodies, Ltd., of Coventry. The result was known as the Morris Cowley Chummy.

With an eye to the future, Kimber had a Chummy fitted with a "tuned" or reworked engine with polished exhaust ports and a few other small refinements such as special aluminum pistons which were calculated to increase the output. (Chummy roadsters were so named because the hood [or top as we call it] covered the two occasional passengers, who sat over the rear axle in the "dickey" [rumble seat].) Tests proved that Kimber's modifications improved the car's performance. Kimber thereupon entered his new Morris Cowley Chummy Special in the 1923 London to Land's End Trial, run over the Easter weekend.

Some 275 miles west-southwest of London, Land's End is the rugged, windblown tip of Cornwall near the town of Penzance. The roads traversed by the entrants—scarcely more than trails in places—crossed moors and low mountains, and the route was by no means a straight line. A traditional British sporting event, the Trials had been the Waterloo of many large and powerful motorcars.

Surmounting all handicaps, Kimber and his Morris Garages Morris Cowley Chummy Special won a Gold Medal. To this day, that car has been acclaimed by some as "the first MG."

Compounding the confusion over which model was the first MG is the fact that The Morris Garages also marketed distinctive Morris Oxford Sports models with special coachwork. As with the Cowley Chummy, the Oxford Sports are said to have been based upon Oxford chassis which, in small numbers, were bought in from the related but separate Morris Motors factory. That no photographs of the Oxford Sports are on record as being avail-

"Old Number One" is still in top-notch running order, as this picture proves. Taken in 1975 in England, the car is on one of the special stages it ran on in the 1925 London To Land's End Trial. The car won a gold medal with Cecil Kimber driving in this event. (British Leyland Motors, Inc.)

able—nor do any seem to have been published—causes the mystery to deepen.

Early in 1924, Cecil Kimber directed the construction of another special sporting car; according to some accounts, this one was based upon an Oxford chassis. On the other hand, a Cowley chassis is favored by John W. Thornley—who should know if anyone does. At any rate, the tail end of the chassis frame of Kimber's new special was cut off and mod-

Just one headlight and all muscle, that was "Old Number One." (M.G. Car Company, Ltd.)

ified by new rails, which curved up and over the axle to secure the modified and outward-splayed rear leaf springs.

Work on the Kimber special proceeded slowly—as shop time permitted. Large Oxford-type drum brakes were fitted to all four wheels, according to another former MG ad-ministrative staffer, Wilson McComb. Early in 1925, Carbodies built the very narrow, boat-tailed, two-seater body. Mudguards were scanty and, in cross-section, looked like tents.

The seats were staggered to reduce the width. The power plant was an overhead-valve 11.9 HP (tax rating) Hotchkiss engine of 1,548 cc. displacement. This had Morris Garages modifications, including balanced pistons and connecting rods; it also included a larger SU carburetor with leather bellows, polished exhaust ports and a higher pressure oil pump. By some means, probably by fitting a new and shorter stroke, balanced crankshaft, Kimber reduced the displacement to less than 1,500 cc., thus permitting registry in the "Light Car" class. Tall wire wheels were secured to the hubs by three lug bolts each, and there were small cowl lamps and a single headlight. The usually high Cowley steering wheel was lowered by raking the column. Instruments were more numerous than on any of the parent Morris cars; they included, besides the usual speedometer and ammeter, a tachometer, plus fuel and oil pressure gauges. Completed late in March of 1925, the car was registered FC.7900. The shortened semi-elliptic springs were tightly snubbed, and test runs proved Kimber's special to handle precisely at speed and to be capable of exceeding 80 mph with ease.

FC.7900, in more recent years, has been officially stated to be *the first MG*.

Kimber drove FC.7900 in the 1925 Land's End Trial and won another Gold Medal for First Place in the Light Car racing class. Strangely, Kimber sold FC.7900 for around £300 shortly after winning the Land's End Trial. Thereafter, it suffered numerous indignities—serving as prime mover for a butcher's cart, undergoing various other calamities, and finally nearly expiring in a junkyard—before being rescued in 1932 by the MG works. Hauled back to Abingdon, the forlorn FC.7900 was restored, designated as "Old Number One," and displayed in the factory museum for a time. Said to have been warehoused in Cowley during the 1939–1945 war, FC.7900 was displayed in the 1969 London Motor Show, has visited the USA, and is now somewhere in the United Kingdom.

FC.7900 barely made it as *the first MG*, though, because there were two other Gold Medal-winning, Morris Garages-built cars competing in the 1925 Land's End Trial. One

was driven by R. V. Saltmarsh and the other by Russell Chiesman, and they were acknowledged in The Morris Garages advertising, but whether they ran in the Light Car class is not known. For some unexplained reason, Kimber's FC.7900 and "their" Gold Medal were never publicly mentioned. Oddly enough, Kimber's "riding mechanic" in the 1923 Trial had been the same Russell Chiesman, a restaurant owner.

There is yet another ghostly reference to merit attention: Morris Garages advertisements in the motoring press during early 1924 showed cars called "The M. G. Super Sports Morris." The initials "MG" were contained inside an octagon, apparently Kimber's idea. In fact, this line is quoted from an advertisement in the March 1924 issue of the *Morris Owner* magazine, about 12 months before FC.7900— "Old Number One"—was completed.

Perhaps one day new light will be shed on the mystery surrounding "Old Number One."

More certainty attends the acknowledged and documented first production MG cars, some of which still exist in England. The 1924–1933 large MGs were elegant cars indeed.

"Old Number One" at the Library of the California Institute of Technology during its 50th Anniversary Tour of the USA. (Courtesy: S. Peter Thelander)

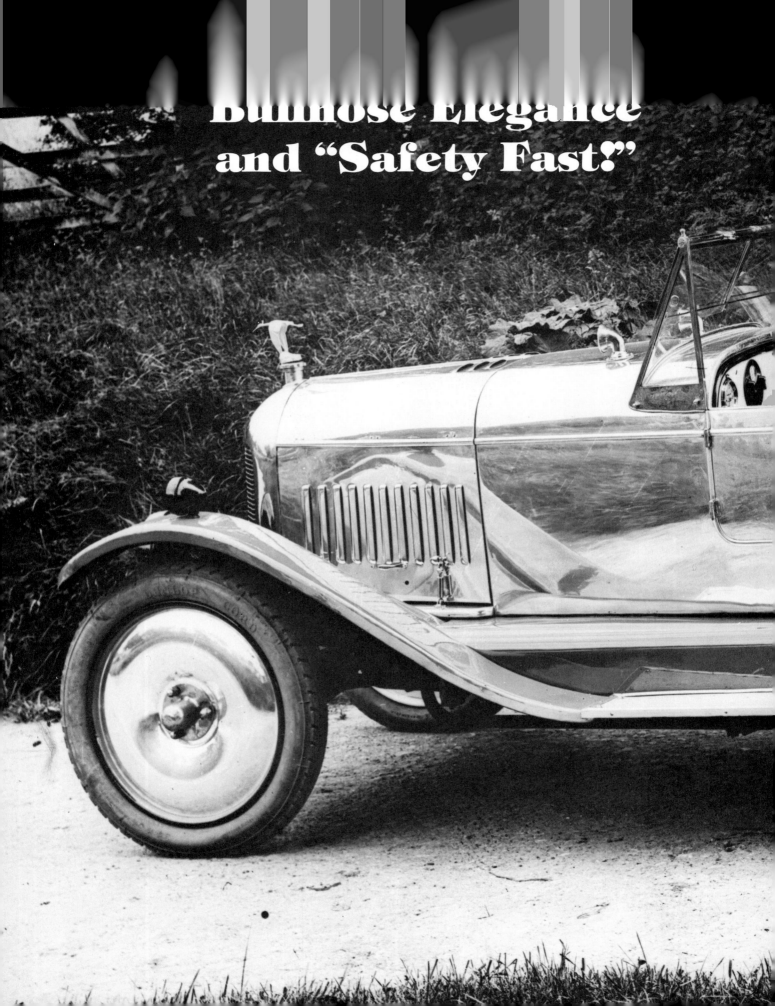

Bullnose Elegance and "Safety Fast!"

Chapter II

Louvres atop the bonnet and polished aluminum coachwork made the Type 14/28 a sparkling beauty. (British Motor Corporation)

At least six Kimber-designed Morris Garages Cowley sports roadsters emerged during 1923 and into 1924. These were two-seaters, not Chummies, and were in addition to Kimber's personal Special which he drove in the 1923 Land's End Trial. The stock Cowley chassis wheelbase of 102 inches was retained, but the front and rear tread was increased to 48 inches. The Cowley L-head, Hotchkiss 1,548 cc. engine was fitted with a single horizontal 30 mm. SU carburetor and balanced pistons and connecting rods, so the tax rating of 11.9 horsepower was unchanged. The usable output was increased, but by how much is not known. Three-speed gearboxes and torque tube-enclosed propeller shafts were utilized.

To accommodate a lower, sporting profile, the steering columns were raked to permit low facia panels—"dashboards" on this side of the Atlantic. Kimber specified decreased camber springs, which were snubbered tightly by Hartford shock absorbers; in addition, the steering gear ratio is believed to have been modified for fewer lock-to-lock turns of the wheel. The bodies, designed by Kimber, were built by Raworths coachworks, but the familiar Bullnose of the Morris cars was retained. Some of the Raworths bodies were painted bright yellow; the mudguards were black. The price out of the showrooms of the Morris Garages was about £350—around $1,540 in those carefree days—not too bad for a low roadster with an 80 mph Smiths speedometer, which could reach somewhere between 60 and 65 mph on a long straight, but too much for mere two-wheel brakes (only on the rear wheels) and no self-starter. Kimber persevered, but nearly a year passed before he managed to sell all six of the Raworths-bodied sports roadsters. Very likely the two other "MGs" which won Gold Medals in the 1925 Land's End Trial were from this small series.

Clearly something had to be done. Kimber's solution was to buy in a 13.9 horsepower Morris Oxford chassis. The more powerful 1,802 cc. engine was in a frame nearly identical to that of the Cowley; the wheelbase was the same 102 inches but the 12-inch diameter brake drums were larger by 3 inches, although still fitted to the rear wheels only. After the usual polishing of the cylinder head and ports, balancing of the crankshaft, and the like, Kimber's crew fitted rather somber four-door saloon coachwork to the Oxford chassis. The car was completed in January or February of 1924. Definitely not sporting with artillery spoke wheels, the center-split, V-type windshield was about the only distinguishing feature. Even more unfortunate was the price of £460 because, at almost the same time, Morris Motors was introducing the factory's own new Oxford Saloon for just under £400.

Quite obviously communications were not the best between The Morris Garages and the parent, though separate, Morris Motors organization, or such a faux pas would not have occurred. Nevertheless—not one to *bend*, you know—Kimber advertised this unexciting Morris Garages Oxford Saloon in the March 1924 issue of *The Morris Owner*. (The reasoning behind the stately but dull Saloon is not known. This one-off effort is believed to be in lonely contrast to the smart, small, closed saloons of the next decade and the large saloons heralded by the advent, in 1936, of the successful and exceptionally stylish, almost sporting SA-types, which would remain in production nearly four years.) Fortunately several other one-off coupe, carbriolet and other experimental models, built on the 14/28 Oxford chassis, went little further than prototypes at the time.

Never any more ready to *break* than to *bend*, though, Kimber was determined to produce relatively low-priced, high-performance sporting cars which would prove worthy of the MG name. His creative instincts soon received the necessary nudge when a well-known competition motorcyclist, Reg Brown, called on him in his office. Brown worked for John Marston, Ltd., the manufacturers of Sunbeam motorcycles, and The Morris Garages sold Sunbeams. Whether Brown came to see Kimber on business or to show off a flashy new car is obscure. But the nudge to Kimber's psyche was the car, which the motorcyclist had built on a new Morris Oxford chassis. Wire wheels were suspended on flat springs and the low, sporty touring coachwork was sheathed in polished aluminum. From the Bullnose back, Brown's car was striking in appearance.

Losing no time, Kimber designed a body and ordered it to be built for installation on a new 14/28 Oxford chassis, which had been purchased by a Morris Garages salesman named Gardiner. Unspecified engine and chassis "tuning" was undertaken, but the Oxford-type spoked artillery wheels were retained. The new four-seat tourer coachwork

was delivered promptly and installed on the modified 14/28 chassis. This was accomplished in time for registration as FC.6333 before the middle of March, and the subject car was featured in an advertisement in the April 1924 issue of *The Morris Owner*, a magazine owned by the parent Morris Motors, Ltd. (Today such periodicals are called "house organs," and their contents generally reflect the policy preferences of the firms in whose interests they are published.)

The new Morris Garages Super Sport, as designed by Kimber for Gardiner and advertised as being available to the public at £395, featured a steeply raked steering column, attractively slanted windscreen, and polished aluminum coachwork by Carbodies of Coventry. Only the Bullnose radiator grille evidenced relationship to the Morris Oxford. Kimber's new design for Gardiner was undoubtedly influenced by the car Reg Brown had built on his Oxford chassis. As the young MG program developed, Gardiner's car could be considered to be the logical prototype of the first production series of MG cars, which were introduced in the autumn of 1924. Prior to the introduction of the new 14/28 MG, however, the parent Morris Motors, Ltd. seems to have recognized the MG as a specific *marque*. This was indicated by the May 1924 issue of *The Morris Owner*. That issue—the third in sequence to advertise MG cars—carried a large display advertisement for the previously discussed Raworths-bodied Morris Garages MG Super Sports roadsters, the small, hard-to-sell series concocted by Kimber on the Chummy chassis.

One might wonder whether William R. Morris, who owned *The Morris Owner* magazine, was pushing Kimber or whether the latter was getting ahead of his allegedly remote employer. Readers who still find themselves confused about the elusive *first* MG will be comforted to know that such confusion among enthusiasts has been part and parcel of the history of the *marque* for many years. Once all of the evidence is sifted, however, we are forced to the conclusion that the winner of the Gold Medal in the 1925 Land's End Trial is as good a candidate for MG Number One as any of the early Morris Garages cars. As we have seen—and this is what counts in the chronological order of the MG line—construction began very early in 1923 on "Old Number One."

That 1924 series of advertisements, running from March through June, certainly suggested that MG cars would soon be available to the public. Inquiries were already coming to The Morris Garages, so Kimber arranged for the promotional effort to continue and began to buy in Oxford chassis for the new series. One of the earliest of these cars was built for Billy Cooper, a nationally known competition driver who had done well with Morris Cowley two-seaters in cross-country trials and hill climbs. Cooper's 14/28 was much like the one built for Gardiner, but with a few changes: the body was even lower and the fenders—"mudguards" or "wings" in the King's English—were painted blue. The finishing touch was to fit the artillery wheels with Ace discs, and the vehicle was delivered to Cooper on May 31, 1924. *The Motor* featured the new sports car in an illustrated article in its June 1924 issue.

Thus launched with editorial recognition in that popular and independent motoring journal, the 14/28 MG Super Sports, as Kimber described the car in a brochure, was in production and went on sale in the autumn of 1924. Aft of the Bullnose radiator grille, the hallmark of Morris cars since the first 1913 roadsters, the polished aluminum coachwork by Carbodies gave an unbroken horizontal line and a hint of streamlining. The four-piece windscreen was sharply slanted and 11 louvres on each side of the bonnet aided engine cooling. Most numerous among the first offerings were open two-seaters and four-seat tourers with two doors. An unusual—perhaps exclusive—feature was the canvas hood, which is said to have been designed to permit raising and fastening quickly without the occupants leaving the car in the event of a sudden downpour. A third body type was soon to be available, a two-door Salonette with a V-windscreen, a stubby boat-tail luggage boot and a small rear seat to accommodate two smaller people.

Genuine leather upholstery was standard and this was dyed blue or claret with the gracefully shaped wings painted to match the interiors. For £350 and £375 for the two-seater and the four-seater, respectively (including insurance), the customer received an outstanding car on a 102-inch wheelbase chassis, which was admitted to have originated on the Morris Oxford assembly line. The Salonette, listed in 1925, was fairly expensive at £475. According to Wilson McComb, just six Salonettes were sold (along with about 25 "assorted closed bodies") during the first 12 months of production. The steering column was raked even more steeply than on Gardiner's car. This was accomplished by means of raising the steering gear box and fitting a longer drop arm, which provided quicker steering. With due credit to the parent firm, the longer drop arm actually was a Morris Motors' improvement on their standard Oxford which, however, retained the stodgy, high steering wheel common on most passenger cars of the time.

As on the car built for Cooper, the leaf springs were flattened and "balloon" tires were used, but the rod-operated 12-inch drum brakes still were fitted only to the front wheels. The customary "special tuning" of the 1,802 cc. Oxford engine raised the output sufficiently to justify advertising the new MG Super Sports as a 14/28. The "14" was a reference to the tax rating of 13.9 horsepower while the "28" probably was Kimber's estimate of the brake horsepower.

After a few dozen 14/28 MGs were built in late 1924, Kimber's natural aggressiveness was encouraged by the parent company's achieving a bit over 40 percent of the British motorcar market. Kimber now decided to enter the "better" car field by building larger cars on the newly available 108-inch wheelbase Oxford chassis for the 1925 and 1926 seasons. The 6 inches added to the wheelbase allowed correspondingly longer coachwork and, hence, even more elegant lines. Upper body surface and bonnets were now made of steel and painted to match the leather interiors and the wings. Colors other than the standard blue or claret became available on special order for the painted body parts and wings. Also, for the first time, there were external door latch handles. Three-lug, bolt-on Dunlop wire wheels, rather than the artilleries, accentuated the "Super Sports" in the name of the

1925 MG. Another practical improvement was the increased radiator capacity for better cooling. Four-wheel brakes made driving safer for those sporting motorists (and seizure less likely for their more sedate passengers) who were stimulated by the 65-mph performance.

For the 1926 models, a Dewandre vacuum-servo system required less foot pressure during operation of the mechanical, rod-operated brakes, and was a welcome assist to racing and long-distance trials competitors. A few complaints about the car's narrow confines influenced Kimber to instruct Carbodies to widen the coachwork by about 2 inches. Until 1926, the octagon was used discreetly in an attempt to establish MG as a distinct *marque*: the famous symbol appeared only on the body beneath the doors. From the first 1926 models, however, the octagon was etched delicately on the front of the glass Colormeter, which graced the top of the Bullnose radiator. The front of the latter, if marked at all, displayed the Morris Oxford badge through 1926: the coat of arms of the city of Oxford encircled by a band containing the words, M.G. Super Sports. Most 14/28 MGs also carried a badge on the facia panel—also an Oxford component—and this displayed the combined coats of arms of the city of Oxford and Oxford University.

A fine car at a moderate price was the 1924–1926 MG 14/28 sports tourer with the bullnose radiator shell. (M.G. Car Company, Ltd.)

Approximately 400 MG 14/28 Super Sports cars were sold during the 1925–1926 period. Many owners compared their 14/28 MGs to the Bentley and other fine cars. At a fraction of the price of such prestige cars, the MG was an excellent buy. Royal personages were among Kimber's customers; one of them was the heir to the Spanish throne, the Prince of Asturias. The prince's open four-seater was delivered in Spain's royal colors of purple, gold and red. The Spanish prince had inherited the love of fine cars from his father, King Alfonso XIII, who did much to spread the fame of the incomparable Hispano-Suiza.

Morris Motors, Ltd., underwent a major corporate change around mid-1926 when stock was issued. The conversion from private to public company by the parent firm had no effect on MG, however, which remained independent and wholly owned by W. R. Morris. Kimber's status as general manager was likewise unaffected. Morris Motors' mainstay car, however, did change and Kimber was consequently forced to take new measures to maintain the increasing popularity of his *marque*.

To begin with, the famed Bullnose was gone; in its place was a flat radiator which simply was not conformable with the elegantly long lines of the MG 14/28. This was not the only problem. The new Morris Oxford for the 1927 season featured a new, heavier frame with the wheelbase reduced by 1½ inches. Although the reduction of chassis length seems slight, it was enough, combined with the loss of the Bullnose radiator shape, to require the complete redesigning of the body. Furthermore, the increase of the new Oxford's chassis weight was not accompanied by a new, more powerful engine. This meant, Kimber feared, that performance would suffer. Performance and style were, after all, the MG's reason for being. Altogether, Kimber's efforts to establish the MG as a completely independent and distinct car were made all the more difficult.

In response, Kimber hastily designed a completely new body and Carbodies again received the contract for coachwork. The rounded Bullnose of all MGs to date had caused the sleek coachwork to appear to be even lower than it was. The vertical plane of the new flat-fronted radiator had further complicated design because it was almost flat across the top when viewed from the front. Though handicapped by the shorter chassis and the necessity of complimenting a radiator and engine bonnet shape less distinctive than the old Oxford's Bullnose, Carbodies still managed to execute Kimber's drawings with boldness. A straight trim line ran horizontally from a point on each side of the radiator—about level with the tops of the headlights—to the rear of the four-seater models. On the two-seaters, this trim line arced gracefully downward, from directly above the rear axle, to the rear.

Below the trim line, the aluminum sheathing was either polished or decorated with the engine-turning motif so popular in those days. Above the trim line, the upper body and engine bonnet were painted in colors matching the leather upholstery, thus continuing the dual tone scheme that had proven so popular on the Bullnose models. Wheels were wire Dunlops, with the spare side-mounted. The Oxford engine was modified to maintain the 65 mph performance, a tough assignment in view of the weight increase of some 200 pounds. A single horizontal Solex carburetor became standard on the 1927 flatnosed 14/28, which was introduced late in 1926—before the last Bullnose was sold.

Acceptance of the new model was good despite Kimber's inability to afford a stand in the annual Fall Motor Show in Earl's Court. If performance suffered, the loss was slight because Morris Garages mechanics were very proficient in squeezing out every bit of power possible by head and valve port polishing, balancing crankshafts, matching pistons and rods, tuning of ignitions and carburetors, and various diverse modifications. Reasoning, therefore, that the new flat radiator 14/28 was actually the third MG type produced to date—the first and second series being, respectively, the few Raworths-bodied Chummy roadsters and the 1924 through 1926 Bullnose 14/28 models—Kimber decided that the time was ripe to upgrade MG with a new Type designation. Already an excellent image had been established.

The 14/28 won two First Class awards in the 1925 MCC High Speed Trial at Brooklands, and won another First Class award in the same event in 1926. Even more impressive, a 14/28 roadster driven by Alberto Sanchiz Cires won first place overall in a circuit race at the San Martín autodrome near Buenos Aires, Argentina. This October 30, 1927, event brought MG its first international victory, a portent of things to come. Engine modifications were clearly able to provide considerably more power; therefore, the 14/28 designation for the engine had become obsolete. MG had gained some international fame.

For the 1928 season and on until late 1929, the 1,802 cc. MG was designated the 14/40 Mark IV. The "40" indicated the engineering department's estimate of 40-brake horsepower (bhp). Subsequent information indicates that 35 bhp would have been more realistic. The 14/40 remained in production until late 1929 and was *the first* MG of any type to be decorated with the famed chocolate-brown and cream *octagon* as a radiator nameplate badge. About seven hundred 14/40s were built and all of them found ready buyers. With the letters MG inside the octagon on the 1928 model, Kimber finally had succeeded in marking his *marque* without any reference to Morris Motors or the Oxford. The octagon marked the rear of 14/40 bodies between the springs and wherever else such identification was applicable.

Spread all over Oxford, various facilities of The Morris Garages were busy developing several other new MG types during the 1927–1928 period. One of these was the M-Type Midget, which will be detailed in a later chapter about the early members of that numerous tribe. Another type, an outgrowth of the continuing relationship with Morris Motors, also saw the light late in 1928 and would present customers with a larger 6-cylinder alternative to the 14/40.

The nucleus of the new MG 18/80 Six was

a sophisticated overhead-camshaft engine developed by Frank Woollard and an engineer named Pendrell who were, respectively, manager and head of engineering in the Morris Engines works in Coventry. W. R. Morris had purchased the factory from Hotchkiss in 1923 and had continued the plant's manufacture of 4-cylinder engines, which were based upon the previous firm's designs. Up to this time, all MG engines were Hotchkiss derivatives. Cecil Kimber had much to do with the development of the new 6-cylinder engine; However, this was first tried in some new Morris cars.

Early in 1928, The Morris Garages shop in

The 1927–1928 Morris Oxford was the first with a flat radiator, and was the basis for the 1926 MG 14/28. (Society of Motor Traders & Manufacturers)

Edmund Road in Oxford began the design and construction of a completely new chassis frame on a wheelbase of 114 inches. Front and rear tread measured 48 inches. For this new car, Kimber designed the classic radiator that was to be used, with little alteration, on all MG types until the mid-1950s. A distinguishing feature of this successful innovation was the slender vertical rib, which was topped with the brown and cream MG octagon. When the new MG 18/80 Six was introduced—along with the above-mentioned first Midget—in the 1928 Motor Show (W. R. Morris had approved MG's presence in the display with other Morris-owned marques), motoring enthusiasts discovered that the editors of *The Autocar* had not exaggerated in their pre-introduction feature in the August 17 issue. The engine block contained the induction passages for the pair of horizontal SU carburetors, and polished aluminum ports were employed in impressive locations, many of them marked with the MG octagon cast thereon. Bearings were pressure-fed, as was the clutch. The overhead camshaft was chain-driven and double breakers were used in the specially designed distributor.

If the transmission was still a three-speed unit, the fly-off hand brake lever provided a proper sporting feel and, again for a first on any production MG, center-locking (knock-off) wire wheels of Rudge-Whitworth design were specified as standard. On the forward side of the firewall (bulkhead in England) were reserve supply tanks for fuel and oil. Inside, on a black panel, were matched Jaeger instruments and, to satisfy discriminating motorists, the steering column and foot pedals were adjustable. Clearly here was a car for the most fastidious, with prices to match. The cost ran from £480 for a drop-head two-seater to around £550 or more for a saloon—depending upon the coachwork specified by the buyer. (The pound was then worth a bit more than $4.50.)

The Motor published the first road test of the new car in their March 1929 issue. Waxing eloquent, the editors stated that the maximum speed of nearly 80 mph, and the attendant acceleration, placed the 18/80 Six in a league with the Lagonda, Alvis and other fine cars. Approximately 60 bhp was developed at a re-laxed 3,200 rpm of the long-stroke engine which, smooth as silk, actually provided the advertised 8 to about 80 mph maximum speed in top gear.

Sir Francis Samuelson took the saloon prototype 18/80 Six to the Continent for the Monte Carlo Rally in January 1929; there the car placed first in coachwork and a respectable third in speed in the Mont des Mules hill climb. Some five hundred of the 18/80 Six Mk. I were produced, their manufacture lasting until the middle of 1931. A man's car *par excellence*, coachwork ran the gamut from Weymann fabric-covered tourers to aluminum-bodied roadsters with dickey seats, coupes and saloons. Meanwhile, The Morris Garages car factory had been gathered into a single location, much to Kimber's relief. Morris, who had become Sir William, purchased the old Pavlova Leather Company works in Abingdon-on-Thames; this was the Berkshire factory, which became a Mecca for MG enthusiasts around the world. About the same time, Morris purchased Singers Union, Ltd., makers of SU carburetors. The complex move was made in September 1929, and The Morris Garages were reorganized as The M. G. Car Company, Ltd., with Cecil Kimber as the managing director. The office telephone number was 251.

When Motor Show time arrived in the autumn of 1929, Kimber's ambitions began to be manifested. Alongside the Midget (of which, more later) was an improved 18/80 Six, the Mark II. This was also called Type A, and was based upon a new chassis that owed nothing to Morris Motors. Heavier than the Mark I chassis by about 300 pounds, the tread was increased to 52 inches to decrease a skidding tendency, and larger 14-inch diameter finned brake drums were fitted. The steering system, final drive and rear axle were made heavier, as were all frame components. A foot-operated automatic Tecalemit chassis lubrication system—which simplified maintenance on the new 18/80 Mk. II—and a new 4-speed gearbox were other major improvements. Few, if any, engine changes were made, but the chassis refinements did increase the curb weight of the new Mk. II by some 400 pounds—making the average weight about 3,000

Coachwork by Carbodies of Coventry distinguished many of the Type 14/40 Mark IV roadsters—like this one with the distinctive rear deck. (British Motor Corporation)

The aluminum-sheathed coachwork of the Type 14/40 Mark IV was finished with an engine-turning motif on some models—like this two-seater sports model. (British Motor Corporation)

The 14/40 Mark IV Tourer was a prestige car for families with sporting proclivities. (British Motor Corporation)

Fine fabric-covered coachwork was a mark of distinction on this MG 18/80 Mark I. (British Motor Corporation)

The MG 18/80 Mark I two-seater. (British Motor Corporation)

pounds. The price rose to £625, placing the car well into the fine car field. Despite the weight increase, Mk. II buyers got a car easily capable of a true 80 mph maximum due to much better gearing, and the suspension changes are said to have improved the handling remarkably. Mark II was a superb road machine, and the new model soon demonstrated this by winning a medal for a "perfect run" in the 1930 Monte Carlo Rally.

The 18/80 Six Mark II went on sale late in 1929 and, by the end of production in mid-1933, some 236 had been sold. This does not seem to be many cars by American standards, but two factors must be remembered: per capita ownership of cars in Great Britain was nowhere near as high as in the USA, and this MG Type was a luxury car. It was always fitted with the finest coachwork and appointments, which competed most respectably with other fine car makes—many of which had preceded the MG offering by a number of years.

The MG 18/80 Six Mk. II Type A also firmly established a new MG tradition. While a few preceding MG types had been assigned exclusive MG chassis serial numbers, this car was the first production series to be engineered and produced totally, from chassis up, as an MG; hence the Type A alphabetical designation in addition to the model nomenclature of 18/80 Six. The serial number affixed to the chassis, therefore, was A.0251. Just how "251" became a part of chassis serial numbers of prototypes of each new MG type has incited numerous debates among *aficionados*. As mentioned, when the MG works was established beneath one roof in Abingdon, the office telephone number was 251, and would remain so until the end of 1980. Consequently, prototype chassis numbers would, henceforth, begin with the Type letter designation followed by 0251. The first digit "0" indicated prototype. The 18/80 Six Mk. II prototype was given the first letter Type designation, A, ever accorded an MG. Hence, the prototype chassis was numbered A.0251 and the tradition was established.

Several other traditions were established as the new factory in Abingdon increased MG prestige. Up until this time, the old slogan,

"Faster Than Most," had sufficed, but something happened late in 1929 that called this slogan into question. From George Tuck, MG publicity manager from 1929 to 1939, and a Kimber intimate now living in South Africa, comes this story. The anecdote was passed on to the author through Norman Ewing of Johannesburg. (There's a bit more to this than was published in the December 1978 issue of *Safety Fast*, the MG Car Club journal.)

Norm Ewing and his wife, Pat, had purchased a 1960 MGA coupe which had belonged to the Tucks. "Armed with a tape recorder," they drove to the Cape of Good Hope to meet George. Several copies of the MGCC journal were in evidence and, during the visit, George Tuck suddenly remarked, "Why is there no exclamation mark at the end of *Safety Fast?* It was always *Safety Fast!*"

Pat Ewing then asked "the only man alive" who'd know the answer, "Where did it come from?"

Whereupon, George Tuck taped the story of the origin of the famous slogan, a subject of much speculation in recent decades. Here's Tuck's straight information, as related by Ewing:

"Ted Colgrove, advertising manager at that time, was driving through Oxford (probably in October or November 1929) behind a new bus. To warn people behind that it could stop quicker than the old buses because it had brakes fitted to all wheels—a new innovation in those days—it had a triangle painted on the back and a slogan which said 'Safety First!'

"Ted thought if it was changed to *Safety Fast!* it would be a great slogan, and he rushed back to tell Kimber. When he arrived, Kimber was fuming as he had, in front of him, an ad with the old slogan 'Faster Than Most' onto which someone had added 'Bicycles' so that it read, 'Faster Than Most Bicycles.' He [Kimber] saw that *Safety Fast!* could not be tampered with and changed it immediately to become the new slogan."

Yet another MG tradition has survived to this day, with or without the official blessing of the factory. Responsibility for this other tradition belongs to Kimber and, to a certain extent, to his magnificent 18/80 Mk. II Type A.

The Golden Age of Racing

Chapter III

With gauze windscreen folded flat and high-riding Brooklands exhaust sounding off, the MG Type C Montlhéry racing Midget was the machine that sensitized the sporting fraternity in 1931. (M.G. Car Company, Ltd.)

With the reorganized MG Car Company firmly ensconced in Abingdon, and the 18/80 Mk. I and Mk. II Type A showing the octagon in the ranks of luxury cars, Kimber took serious aim at racing. Between January 1930 and mid-1935, six types built specifically for racing influenced MG philosophy for two decades.

MG's golden age began with a project to build a road-racing, International Class, four-seat sports car. Kimber had assembled an excellent senior staff, among whom were George Propert as general manager and H. N. Charles as head of engineering. Charles, an engineer of repute with a track record in Royal Air Force development projects, Zenith carburetors and other assignments, joined MG via Morris Motors. Sydney Enever, an ingenious designer who began his career as a shop laborer in Morris Motors; publicity director George Tuck; and Reg Jackson, an artist with overhead camshaft engines, were others who assisted Kimber in devising policy and projects as well as implementing them.

Everyone in management level agreed that successful racing competition was an open sesame to market penetration. They also agreed that they had a vehicle in hand which merited development toward those goals, the 18/80 Six Mk. II (the A Type).

Along with tooling the Abingdon works for production of the first Midgets, the M Type, a veritable super car was being created upon the 18/80 chassis. Modifications of the 2,468 cc. engine included a new, fully balanced crankshaft with matched connecting rods and pistons. There was a new cross-flow cylinder head with integral inlet ports (the 18/80 Marks I/II ports were in block), inclined valves and dual ignition, and the compression ratio was increased from 5.8:1 to 6.9:1. Chain drive for the overhead camshaft was retained but the camshaft was new. On the bottom of the block was a new dry sump. Dual oil pumps were mounted in front and shrouded by a louvered cover between the dumb irons, as was a 4.5-gallon oil tank. Carburetion was by a pair of specially made SU downdraft units.

Said to have developed approximately 100 bhp at somewhat more than 5,000 rpm, the sound of the free-flowing Brooklands exhaust system must have been impressive. Another change in the 18/80 Six chassis was a more steeply raked steering column, which positioned the steering wheel in a nearly vertical plane. The driver had a close ratio gearbox containing 3 pints of lubricant and a brake-adjusting system within easy reach. The finned 14-inch drums of the 18/80 were retained. Double Hartford shock absorbers and 19-inch, center-locking "knock-off" wire wheels, along with a big fuel tank (holding 28 Imperial gallons) beneath the floor in front of the rear axle comprised the other major chassis changes.

The four-seater body had a long, low, lean appearance with generous applications of louvers everywhere. A leather strap secured the engine bonnet, scanty cycle-type mudguards and a spreader bar with W-bracing supported a single huge Lucas headlamp flanked by a pair of smaller lamps. Normal road lighting was available for the "MG Six Sports Road Racing Model," as the over-the-counter machine was catalogued (the car was officially the 18/100 Six Mark III Type B). Somewhere along the line, the nickname "Tigress" was applied; often the motoring press added an "e" and called the critter "Tigresse," while there is evidence that "Tiger" was also a popular name.

MG's first all-out racing car, the 18/100 Six Mk. III, weighed in at 2,940 pounds at the curb and the price of £895—around $4,300 at the time—was just as hefty. The Viscount Rothschild purchased a "Tigress." In 1930, however, there were few takers. In some respects the 18/100 Six Mk. III was an aberration because Kimber's original intention was to build affordable sports cars for the average person. This aim was still paramount in Abingdon (as will be observed in the next chapter). The big 18/100 Mark III Type B, however, was built for a very different purpose—racing—and the debut was to be electrifying, to say the least.

The Double Twelve Hour Race at Brooklands (12 hours on each of two days) on the second weekend of May 1930 would be the debut of the mighty 18/100 Mark III. Big machinery of equally large reputations—such as the Bentley with three back-to-back Le Mans victories on record—would be the targets of opportunity and Kimber was determined to show the MG octagon to advantage. The new Midgets would be out in force to reaffirm the small car mastery they had established in 1929. Now MG would challenge the big cars with the new, 100 mph 18/100 Six.

Matters were well in hand during the first two hours of the Junior Car Club's Double Twelve Hour Race in May 1930. The mighty Mark III lapped Brooklands steadily at around 86 mph and led the field when, suddenly, things got hot beneath the bonnet. The Mark III went limp and retired from combat. Several reasons were advanced for the debacle. The fault (according to drivers Callingham and Parker, in a well-intentioned effort to pass the buck to a "bought in" component part) was the failure of one of the SU carburetors, which came apart. (SUs were made by Singers Union, a Morris Motors subsidiary.)* The Autocar went out on a limb and blamed a broken piston for the engine failure. More recent research, however, discloses that the pressure lubrication system had failed and, thus deprived of oil, the crankshaft bearings disintegrated. The 18/100 Six Mk. III never raced again. The car was really too expensive for its time, and only five were built. The Abingdon works had a more rational world to conquer: the gaggle of Type M Midgets swept the team prize and established the domain in which MG would reign supreme for the next 30 years.

Certain deficiencies in the M-Type Midgets were evident, however, so a prototype was laid down around June 1930 as the forerunner of an all-out racing Midget which would become famous as the C-Type.

Captain George E. T. Eyston and Ernest Eldridge, an engineer, caught wind of this new project, then being pursued by H. N. Charles and Reg Jackson. Eyston, a Royal Artillery veteran of the Great War who was making a name for himself as a competition driver, and Eldridge were preparing to assault the international One Hour speed record in Class H. (For years, the 747 cc. Austin Seven had been the leading car in this class.) Under consideration, as the nucleus of the record attempt, was an overhead-camshaft, 750 cc. Ratier engine. (Ratier was an impressive French sports car which, unfortunately, survived only from 1926 into 1928.) During discussions in the Abingdon works, Kimber suggested that the new prototype chassis being developed, with a suitably modified 847 cc. Midget engine, would make a proper record combination. Eyston liked the idea and Kim-

---

*The author bought this exoneration in his book, *The MG Story*, in 1967.

The extremely rare MG 18/100 Mark III. (British Motor Corporation)

The very rare MG Type 18/100 Mark III Tigress, a special 6-cylinder racing machine, had a too-brief career. This photo is believed to have been taken at the MG works shortly before the disastrous Double Twelve Race at Brooklands in 1930. (M.G. Car Company, Ltd.)

ber put Reg Jackson in charge of the project, which immediately became secret. An Eyston confidant, Jimmy Palmes, had already reworked several MG engines, so he joined the effort.

Kimber and Charles had been studying the partially underslung frame of the 1,100 cc. Rally, another French sports car of 1921—1933. Liking what they saw, they designed a new frame of parallel steel channel rails with tubular cross members. An M-Type front-axle beam was used and, along with the first Midget's 42-inch tread, was about the only fa-

miliar feature. The frame swept upward and over the front axle, but passed beneath the rear axle where the rear of each semi-elliptical spring was fitted through bronze trunnions in the rearmost cross member. Midget frames would follow this basic form into the 1950s. The wheelbase was 81 inches, a quarter-foot more than the Midget's. Wheels were center-locking wires of the Rudge type.

Instead of four engine mounts, two tubular mounts were used. The radiator was secured to the front engine mount to eliminate the usual flexing of hoses thus minimizing leaks,

The MG 18/100 Six Mark III, once owned by the Viscount Rothschild, is now owned by Christopher Barker in the United Kingdom. Only five were built. (British Motor Corporation)

a lesson H. N. Charles had learned during the war when he worked with fighter aircraft. Engines and radiators should be connected rigidly, Charles believed. The engine, which had begun as an 847 cc. Midget unit, rapidly became almost unrecognizable. A new counterbalanced crankshaft, designed by Eldridge, decreased the stroke to 81 mm. and new valve gear incorporated roller bearings in a manner similar to Bugatti practice. Cylinder sleeves decreased the bore to 54 mm., bringing the piston displacement down to 743 cc.

A hastily fabricated, lightweight aluminum body, with a cockpit opening barely large enough to allow the husky Eyston to insert himself, was fitted to the chassis. At the rear was a headrest faired into a pointed tail. Double straps secured the bonnet. The knock-off wire wheels had no mudguards, and the driver had no windscreen, although the sheet aluminum over the scuttle was raised slightly to form something of a windbreak.

The first test run occurred on a bleak November morning near Abingdon. With lookouts posted strategically to warn of approaching authorities, Eyston made a clandestine run and achieved 87 mph without attempting maximum speed. Eyston, car, and crew were then packed off to the Montlhéry track on the south side of Paris for a series of assaults on the under-750 cc. international records. On December 30, 1930, the crew shoehorned the ex-artillery captain into the cockpit of the EX.120, as the car was designated. Eyston soon shattered three international records: the 50 Kilometre with 86.38 mph, the 50 Mile at 87.11 mph and the 100 Kilometre with 87.3 mph. A broken valve prevented further record runs that day, so Eyston stored the EX.120 at Montlhéry and, with the crew, returned to Abingdon with the three new records as a belated Christmas gift for MG.

Conferences with Kimber began immediately because the word was out that Sir Malcolm Campbell was on Daytona Beach grooming a supercharged Austin Seven special for an attack on the 100 mph mark for under three-quarter litre cars. (Pathé and Fox newsreels, at the time, were giving major attention to Campbell's simultaneous preparations to crack the world land speed record

with his big Blue Bird.) In January 1931, Campbell had taken the Flying Mile for Class H at 94 mph in his Austin Seven special, and Eyston was determined to top the century mark with the MG EX.120. Kimber agreed most emphatically. Clearly a supercharger was necessary to compete, in short order, with the blown Austin. Eyston approached the Powerplus supercharger people with a bit of an advantage: he was a stockholder.

Time was of the essence. Campbell could try for 100 mph with his Austin any day, and tests with superchargers were a distinct urgency. Eldridge, Jackson and an assistant named Phillips had worked out all of the problems in a scant three weeks. Before the end of January, the supercharged EX.120 engine was ready for installation and the crew rushed back to Montlhéry where the new engine was installed. Then there was more testing. Finally, running for the 100-mph record with AIACR (later FIA) officials manning the timing equipment, the best Eyston and EX.120 could do was a disappointing 97 mph.

Numerous modifications were tried — timing changes and gear ratios. One story has it that the bitterly cold weather was causing the external SU carburetor to freeze despite alcohol in the fuel, and that a part of an old oil drum was hurriedly beaten into a new radiator cowling. In any event, late on February 16, 1931, Eyston again took the EX.120 out on the Montlhéry track. With the tachometer reading 7,000 rpm, the century mark was attained and records began to fall: Five Kilometres at 103.13 mph, Five Miles at 102.76, Ten Kilometres at 102.43 mph and Ten Miles at 101.87 mph! Kimber's MG had beaten the vaunted Austin.

Returning to England, Eyston and his crew prepared EX.120 to tackle the Flying Mile on the Brooklands circuit when the weather improved. During March 1931, Eyston won the Flying Mile record for under-750 cc. cars but he was disappointed because his best speed was just 97.07 mph. Another attempt to crack 100 mph in the Flying Mile, a couple of days later, ended abruptly when a connecting rod broke and the engine was destroyed. The secret shop in the Abingdon works, presided over by Charles and Jackson, prepared another Powerplus supercharged engine for the

EX.120. After installation and testing, car and crew returned to Montlhéry to try for 100 miles in one hour—"the Hour"—and the 100-mph Flying Mile.

After much preparation, Eyston and EX.120 were doing nicely, averaging approximately 101 mph on lap after lap, when he failed to see the signal telling him that he had completed the hour. Eyston continued at full bore into another lap and disappeared around a curve with an ominous change in the engine's sound. When he did not return to view, the crew set out to find him. When they reached the flaming wreckage of what had been the EX.120, Eyston was nowhere in sight. Before too long, the crew learned that Eyston had managed, somehow, to extricate his considerable self from the cockpit. The only superficially bruised Eyston was given a ride to a hospital by a passing test driver for one of the French car manufacturers.

Eyston and EX.120 were officially credited with the two records under assault, but the car was a charred ruin. A burned-out bearing had caused a fire in the oil sump. Thus ended the too brief career of an exciting car. The EX.120, however, accomplished its purpose: Austin was beaten!

Eyston would endure to compete later with the "Magic Midget" and the EX.135.

Originally the EX.120 was engined with the 847 cc. block of the M-Type Midget for its intended role as a prototype for the D-Type Midget.* Then a complete redesign of the engine, to relieve Austin of the weight of record holding, had resulted in a potentially potent power plant for competition sports cars. The resulting 54 × 81 mm., 743 cc. engine of the EX.120 was being modified, even during Eyston's record assaults.

Around March 1, 1931, Kimber hosted a bash in Abingdon. Drivers who had driven the Double Twelve Midgets to victory the previous year at Brooklands were guests of honor. The real object of the party, however, was a new chassis with an improved version of the EX.120 engine. With bore increased slightly to 57 mm. and stroke decreased to 73 mm., the new 746 cc. overhead camshaft engine was the nucleus, Kimber told the assembled sports car enthusiasts, of a new Montlhéry Midget.

This was envisioned as an over-the-counter production sports car, which keen drivers could take into full-bore racing on any venue in the under-750 cc. class. To be known as the Type C MG, the Montlhéry Midget would enter production immediately; 14 of them would be on tap for the May 1931 running of the Double Twelve Hour Race, said Kimber.

The guests, including the Earl of March (later the Duke of Gordon and Richmond) and other successful M-Type Midget drivers, were properly impressed. So confident was Kimber, in the glow of Eyston's record roster in the EX.120, that he had invited the director of the Austin racing organization, Captain Arthur Waite, who was also the son-in-law of Sir Herbert Austin, the target of Kimber's ambition. Even now one would wonder whether a new competition car could be placed in sufficient quantity production, in scarcely two months, to permit fielding as many as fourteen examples for a successful debut in a major race.

Kimber had handed his engineering staff and labor force—fewer than three hundred in all—a major assignment, because the M-Type Midget was in full production. Sir William Morris agreed that Eyston's successes with the EX.120 must be confirmed by an immediate string of racing victories. Not only would the new C-Type look much like the record breaker but it would be named for the site of its forerunner's triumphs and final disaster.

Brookland's grid crackled with the sounds of thirteen new C-Types when the flag dropped for the start of the Double Twelve Hour Race in May 1931. Four teams of three cars each were captained by the Earl of March, Major "Goldie" Gardner (of whom we shall hear more later on), Cecil Randall, and a lady competitor, the Honourable Mrs. Chetwynd, who was related to that famous driver of Bentleys and other "sporting lorries," Sir Henry Birkin. A single C-Type entry was mounted by Hugh Hamilton, a car salesman who became quite famous as an MG driver. The performance of the Midget M-Types had astonished the racing fraternity for the past two years and they were in for another lesson this year—the more so

---

*Chapter IV.

because the C-Type's engine was in the tiny 750 cc. class, smaller than the M-Type engines. When the two twelve-hour racing days were over, the Austin teams had been thoroughly thrashed—as had all of the "lorries," as Midget enthusiasts were inclined to call the big cars. The new C-Types garnered the Team award, the *first five* places overall, and every International Class prize. What had those people at Abingdon-on-Thames wrought?

There was much about the C-Type that the specifications table does not show. The frame was underslung in the rear, incorporating features of the EX.120. Four-wheel brakes using 8-inch drums with all cable controls protected by armored casings were used, as was a fly-off handbrake. A small adjusting device, within the driver's reach, facilitated the use of the brake pedal and the handbrake. The front shock absorbers were mounted outside the body paneling for facility during pit stops. The rear snubbers were adjustable by a knob beneath the instrument panel. As on the EX.120, the rear springs had no shackles and the front axle rode above the front springs.

The engine displacement was 746 cc., the block being basically like that of the preceding M-Type, with 57 mm. bore. The overhead camshaft actuated the valves through adjustable rockers and a new crankshaft reduced the stroke to 73 mm. Inlet and exhaust ports were on the same side. The cylinder head was the A-A Type, also common to the Type M. Without supercharging, the compression ratio was 9.0 to 1, unusually high for 1931. The output was 44 bhp at 6,400 rpm, giving a maximum speed of about 80 mph. With the 4-speed, non-synchromesh, close-ratio transmission running through a two-plate clutch, and with a rear axle ratio of 5.375 to 1, the advertised miles per hour per 1,000 rpm was quoted at 14.7, assuring high performance. The oil sump held 4 quarts and there was a 2-gallon oil reserve tank that automatically supplied oil by means of a float feed. This little detail made for happy bearings.

According to *The Autocar* of May 22, 1931, the C-Types were intended to race at 5,500 rpm maximum, or around 81 mph. It is likely, however, that several exceeded this rpm figure because some consistently lapped the

course at 70 mph and more, and there was gear changing to be done, with consequent higher engine speeds. The fuel tank held 13.5 Imperial gallons and was located where it belonged—beneath the boat-tailed rear deck. About three hundred miles between fuel stops was the goal. A single downdraft SU carburetor was used and fuel was pumped by an arrangement of two Autopulse pumps: one pump normally operated until all but 2 gallons of fuel were expended, whereupon the second pump was actuated by a switch on the facia to feed the reserve.

Dual coils were used in the 6-volt Lucas or Rotax ignition. One functioned as a spare, with a change switch on the facia which carried a full complement of instruments. The large 8,000-rpm tachometer had the appropriate portion blanked in cautioning red. On the steering column, below the wheel, was the ignition retard and advance control.

The streamlined and lightweight aluminum body was bolted to the frame cross members at three places on each side. The windshield folded flat forward of the double cowl (or "scuttle"), and deep cuts in each door and the separate bucket seats were at once comfortably efficient and properly sporting. The left seat occupant was well advised to watch his outboard arm because of the close proximity of the exhaust pipe, which terminated above the left rear cycle fender in the flaring Brooklands manner.

Costing £295 delivered (less than $1,500 at the time) and absolutely ready for racing, the Type C was bound to be a success. A C Montlhéry could be bought, over the counter, complete with a Powerplus No. 7 supercharger. This, at 12 psi, boosted the rated output to 52.5 bhp at 6,500 rpm, the top speed to 100 mph, and the price by another £180. With the blower, the supercharged type used the new AB cylinder head with opposed inlet and exhaust ports. Compression ratio was 5.8 to 1.

From May of 1931 to June 1932, the C-Types were listed in the MG catalogue and produced on order; in all, 44 were built. Today a "C" is worth a fortune. Most of them shed the Montlhéry radiator shroud in favor of the classic vertical MG shell. As potent as they were beautiful, the C-Types won the 1931 Irish

The supercharged K.3 Magnette racer. (British Motor Corporation)

Grand Prix in Dublin, the Royal Automobile Club's International Tourist Trophy at Belfast, and a host of other victories too numerous to list. All this secured the Type C a place in automotive history.

Developing specials and outright racing models was MG policy *if* they could pay their own way through sales to the public, and *if* their features were applicable to the bread-and-butter sports Midgets and other MG types. Thus it was not until very late in 1932 that two prototypes of the next racer, the K.3 Magnette, came forth. Strictly speaking, the K.3 was a racing development of the 6-cylinder Type K sports two-seaters, tourers, and saloons which entered production in October 1932.* The reasoning is supposed to have been that MG, having swept the events in the 750 cc. class, should have a go at awards in the 1,100 cc. Class G. The reasoning paid off for about a year.

Some 33 examples of this fabulous MG (including the prototypes) rolled forth between March 1933 and September 1934. Sharing basic chassis dimensions with all the 6-cylinder Type K two-seater sports cars, along with 13-inch, cable-operated finned brakes and the excellent 4-speed Wilson Preselector transmission, the K.3 Magnette was the first all-out attempt to produce an over-the-counter racing car (other than Midgets) since the ill-fated 18/100 Six Mark III. The chassis, of longitudinal steel channels with tubular cross members, was generally an enlargement of the practice followed in the growing Midget tribe. To eliminate steering problems (the Midgets tended to wander directionally), a secondary steering arm was used, with dual short track rods to each front wheel.

Like others in the K-Type series, the K.3 engine was essentially the well-proven, 57 mm. bore Midget block extended to make a 6-cylinder power plant. The new crankshaft had larger bearings and the stroke was reduced to 71 mm. producing a displacement of 1,087 cc. with overhead camshaft, adjustable rockers, and magneto ignition. The distributor shaft and oil pump drive also ran the water pump. Production cars for 1933 had a Powerplus 9 supercharger and the 1934 models a Marshall blower of the Rootes type. Either was mounted in front of the radiator and driven at three-quarters of the engine speed by a reduction gear. Running the blower through the 6.2 to 1 compression ratio head produced 120 bhp at 6,500 rpm—a lot of power in 1933 for a car weighing barely one ton.

*These models are covered in Chapter V.

Rare K.3 Magnette in Adelaide, South Australia, during the 1975 Concours d'Elegance of the MG Car Club's national Australia meeting. Owned by Frank Bett, the black K.3 captured first place in class and the Special Award for excellence. Note supercharger shroud between dumb irons. (Courtesy: Frank Bett)

The K.3 was the first production competition car to offer a pre-selector transmission as *standard* equipment. The four gearbox ratios were selected by a quadrant-mounted lever on top of the gearbox. The next desired ratio could be selected prior to the change, which was automatically made by a jab at the clutch pedal. Lightweight, aluminum-paneled bodies were of two styles: the prototype and the 1933 models had a square rear end and a 20.5 Imperial gallon slab tank, along with a filler on each side for rapid servicing. The spare wheel was mounted on the slab tank. The 1934 models had a streamlined tail with an internal-shaped tank holding 24.5 gallons.

The 1933 Mille Miglia was the competition debut for the K.3. A three-car works team was entered, with such famous racing names as George Eyston and Count Johnny Lurani on the grid. Also along were Lord Howe and Hugh Hamilton, and Bernard Rubin and Sir Henry Birkin. At times during this event, the new K.3s roared at more than 110 mph, shattering Maseratis and others to win the team prize.

The K.3 next took second, third and fourth places in the Junior Car Club International Trophy Race. The Italian ace, Nuvolari, drove a K.3 to victory in the Ulster Tourist Trials. In the British Empire Trophy Race at Brooklands,

a K.3 took third place at an average speed of 106.9 mph, and another K.3, wearing a special single-seater body and driven by R. T. Horton, broke the Brooklands outer circuit Class G lap record with 115.5 mph. In 1934, Horton took the Class G One Hour record at Brooklands at 117 mph.

K.3 entries also won at the Mannin Beg race in the Isle of Man, the Circuit of Modena in Italy, the Swiss Grand Prix and many lesser events. In the 1935 Le Mans race, a K.3 placed first in the 2-litre class, winning ninth overall against many larger cars. In later years, Horton's *mono-posto* K.3 fell under the spell of Lieutenant Colonel Goldie Gardner, who modified it vastly and used it to break the Class G Flying Mile at 148 mph. The K.3 engine, smooth and potent, was later used in the EX.135, which is discussed in a later chapter. Racing lore has it that the K.3 would have been produced longer had not the officials governing the 1934 Tourist Trials ruled out superchargers. By that time the K.3 was no more

Illustrator Ken Dallison is responsible for this poster art showing the MG K.3 Magnette. (British Leyland Motors, Inc.)

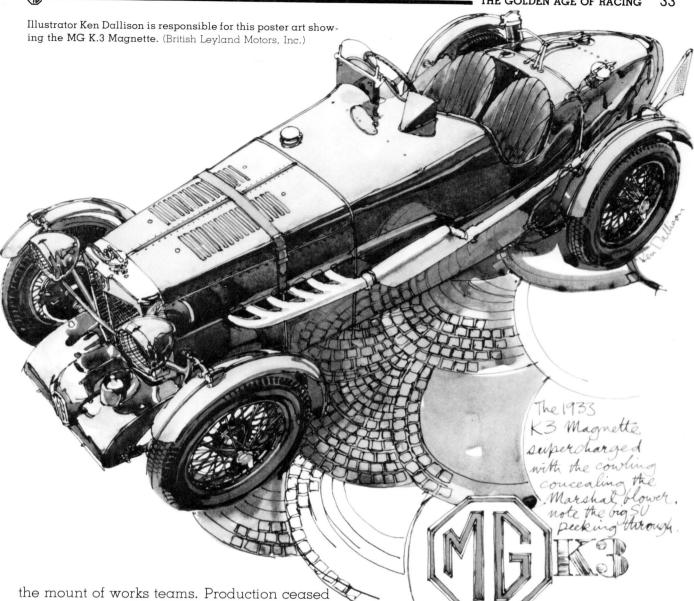

The 1933 K3 Magnette supercharged with the cowling concealing the Marshal blower. note the big SU peeking through.

the mount of works teams. Production ceased in September 1934.

The Type C Montlhéry Midget and the newer J.4 had triumphed over all comers by the end of 1933. This pleasant circumstance could not last for long, however, due to the inherent limitations of the crankshaft, which had only two main bearings. If MG success in competition was to continue in the 750 cc. class, a huskier engine was essential and this was borrowed from the new Type P Midget sports car. The result was the brief production series of eight Type Q racers built between May and October in 1934. An over-the-counter price of £550, ready to race, was good value but there were few buyers because of economic conditions.

The Type Q racing Midget engine was a version of the new, tougher, 3-main-bearing crankshaft, overhead-camshaft unit designed by H. N. Charles for the PA Midget sports cars just going into production. In effect, the PA engine was de-stroked from 83 to 73 mm. to keep the displacement at 746 cc. The Zoller Q4 supercharger was mounted in front between the dumb irons and was driven through reduction gears at 69 percent of engine speed. The boost was 25—28 pounds per square inch through one 1⅞ inch SU carburetor. This arrangement provided 113 bhp at 7,200 rpm. With an automatic slipping device in the form

Cockpit illustrations of the C-Type are seldom seen. Note short gear change lever and brake adjustment device to left of latter. (Joseph H. Wherry photo)

This MG C-Type Montlhéry Midget is owned by the Henry Ford Museum. (Joseph H. Wherry photo)

of a clutch working on the flywheel to eliminate racing stress, the quick gear-changing capabilities of the Wilson Preselector gearbox were retained without damage to the power train. Due to the available power, it was decided to increase the wheelbase for improved high-speed handling. Consequently, the Q Midget emerged on a 94³/₁₆ inch wheelbase (like the K.3) and the brakes were 12-inch finned drums. The tread, however, was 3 inches less at 45 inches.

There were no doors in the narrow, aluminum-sheathed body, and of the eight produced, none had lights or fenders. Type Q looked very much like its 6-cylinder, 1,087 cc. K.3 predecessor. The boat tail concealed 19 Imperial gallons of fuel, including 4 in reserve. Weighing in at a scant 1,500 pounds, the Q-Type set the class track record with 122.4 mph at Brooklands and consistently lapped the circuit in excess of 110 mph. The

Q raised the class standing mile to more than 85 mph and, late in 1934, this extraordinary machine averaged 76.3 mph at Montlhéry for 24 hours.

The Q Midget racer was so potent that few drivers are said to have dared to capitalize on its potential. Rigid axles and semi-elliptic springs all around, though well snubbed, caused wheelspin (because of the high torque) and some handling problems at high speeds. In October of 1934, after barely six months' production, the Type Q was discontinued. Cecil Kimber realized the traditional MG chassis designs most certainly needed improvement for big-time racing.

Chassis limitations caused Kimber and staff to decide that the four-wheel independent suspension systems, coming into racing vogue on the continent, offered the answer to high-speed safety. H. N. Charles was again handed the assignment. The Midget Type R was the answer, and it was revolutionary in every respect with the exception of the engine and drive train.

The engine was the new, proven 746 cc. unit as used in the Type Q. The compression ratio was slightly decreased from 6.4:1 to 6.2:1, and a change was made from the coil to a Lucas magneto ignition system. The Wilson Preselector 4-speed transmission was retained with the overload automatic slip device, but the gearchange quadrant and short lever was relocated to the steering column. With a Zoller 4RA supercharger running at 28 psi boost, the bhp was 110 at 6,500 rpm. With the standard 4.125 to 1 rear axle gears, 20.2 mph per 1,000 rpm was catalogued.

If the power layout was on familiar MG territory, the frame and suspension was new ground and, on this score, it is a pity that Type R was never to see complete development. The frame was beautiful. Weighing only about 57 pounds, the frame was a single unit fabricated of 16-gauge steel plates, which were welded into box sections and integrated into a Y-shape. One channel steel cross member at the front and tubular internal bracing added stiffness. Holes throughout this structure, to decrease weight, did not adversely affect the rigidity. The engine, two-plate clutch with automatic slipping device, and Wilson Preselector transmission were mounted between the forward frame arms. The open propeller shaft extended aft slightly above the wide stem of the frame. Final drive gears were straight out of the usual MG practice, and the differential

cage was securely bolted to the top of the extreme rear of the frame.

Dual wishbone brackets for each wheel, front and rear, were used instead of the familiar rigid axles of previous MG types. A longitudinal torsion bar, splined on each end, was secured on each side to the lower front wishbone near the latter's hinge point, immediately inboard of the frame. Similarly, each rear torsion bar was rigidly attached to each bottom rear wishbone. Torsion bars were then secured to the frame in brackets, permitting adjustment of the tension. Lightweight adjustable Luvax hydraulic shock absorbers, plus built-in stops to prevent undue wishbone movements, completed the radical suspension.

The steering gear was actually a dual system, each front wheel having its own drop arm operating out of the centered steering gearbox which was secured to a bulkhead at the immediate rear of the engine block. There was *no* tie rod connecting the front wheels. In the rear, the drive from the crown wheel of the differential to each wheel was by a short shaft with a universal joint on each end. Thus the vertical movement of either rear wheels or front, due to the road surface, determined the amount of movement of the associated torsion bar. Four-wheel, cable-operated, 12-inch diameter brakes filled most of the open space behind 18-inch, knock-off wire wheels. Wheel-

The supercharged racing Midget, the Type Q. (British Motor Corporation)

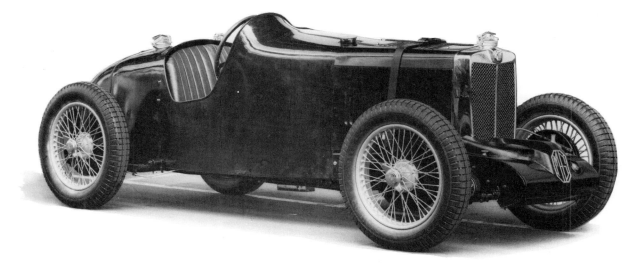

The most revolutionary MG of all time was the Type R Midget. At speed on the Accerbo course, Pescara, Italy, in 1935 with Reggie Tongue up. Note the outward lean of the wheels, characteristic of the Type R. (British Motor Corporation)

base was 90½ inches, and the tread was 46⅜ and 45½ inches front and rear, respectively.

The light alloy body was narrow and contained but one seat. Up front, the familiar MG radiator shell slanted steeply and there were external fillers atop the hood for water and the one-gallon reserve oil tank to facilitate pit stop times. There was no windscreen but the cowl swept sharply upward, and the streamlined tail concealed the 21-Imperial-gallon fuel tank; the latter included a reserve of ¾ gallon.

Type R was introduced early in April 1935 and immediately won its class in the Interna-

tional Trophy Race at Brooklands. This first-time-out performance was followed by winning the 1,100 cc. class in the French Grand Prix, a fifth place plus four other awards in the British Empire Trophy Race, and other awards at Berne, Switzerland, and at Coppa Acerbo at Pescara, Italy.

Ten Type R racers had been built by the end of June 1935. Independent suspension systems seemed to be the answer to keeping the rear wheels on the ground during the fierce acceleration of which the 1,400-pound Midget was capable, at speeds which sometimes exceeded 120 mph. Enthusiasts were looking forward to seeing MG works teams winning races during the season.

Then the bomb dropped! Sir William Morris—under whom the MG Car Company, Ltd., had thrived as a privately owned firm—sold it to Morris Motors, Ltd., which was publicly owned (and of which Morris was chairman of the board). The change in corporate ownership would have been all right, but Sir William and his board simultaneously decreed that MG works-sponsored racing would immediately cease.

Cecil Kimber, understandably, was crushed, but he stayed on until early in World War II. Chief designer H. N. Charles, however, resigned in disgust. Most likely the revolutionary single-seater Type R racing Midget—so far ahead, technologically, of traditional sports cars—had much to do with the racing ban. Type R survived in only the ten examples built; they remained in active private hands for a few years, then drifted into collections. The first all independent suspension MG, the first *mono posto* and the last, the Type R Midget was the racer that brought down the ban. Type R was also the most promising of all the Kimber-inspired all-out racers. Many have been the lamentations, during the more than four intervening decades, that this racing system was not to see maturity under the MG banner.

Shown in bare chassis, this R-Type Midget (Chassis Number R/0255) is now owned by Mr. Ralph Clarke of Cape Town, South Africa. During pre-World War II days, this rare R-Type won the 1939 Coronation 100 in Pietermaritzburg, Natal, and many other races in the capable hands of Roy Hesketh. Behind chassis is the cockpit portion of body. The unique Y-shape frame and four wheel independent suspension are seen. (Courtesy: John Watts)

The Mighty OHC Midgets

Chapter IV

The first of all MG Midgets, the M-Type. (British Motor Corporation)

The foregoing events were parallel to the rise of the MG Midgets, the first of which was being developed simultaneously with the big 18/80 Six. In fact, both size extremes of Kimber's enthusiasm were introduced to the public in the 1928 Motor Show in Earl's Court.

While the quite civilized 18/80 Six owed little to Morris Motors, the first Midget, the M-Type, had considerable Morris beneath its skin. Here's how it happened. Sir William Morris widened his empire in 1927 by purchasing Wolseley Motors, a Birmingham company with origins dating back to the 1899 outgrowth of a sheep-shearing machinery firm, which was managed by Herbert Austin. Austin built his first car—if it could be called a car—in 1895. This vehicle was a curious monstrosity with a single wheel out front, a single wheel in the rear, and another wheel amidship on each side. In plan form, the first Austin-designed Wolseley looked as if its ancestors had been South Seas outriggers, a vision not unlikely in view of Austin's early years in the sheep business in Australia. In any event, Austin's subsequent automotive successes earned him a knighthood before Morris attained that honor, and ever since around 1923, the little Austin Seven had given fits to

all of the other British car makers, including Morris.

When Morris acquired Wolseley, he obtained the nucleus for the small car he and his staff knew must be manufactured if they hoped to corner their share of the light car market, which was being dominated by Austin. The Wolseley engineers had manufactured overhead camshaft Hispano-Suiza engines during the Great War and they had used this experience to develop small and successful 4-cylinder OHC engines for their postwar cars. The newly acquired 57 × 83 mm. bore and stroke engine had a displacement of 847 cc., and a drive mechanism for the overhead camshaft which would serve the yet unborn Midget tribe from 1928 to 1936. A vertical shaft formed the armature of the generator (dynamo). Bevel gears at the top of the shaft drove the camshaft, a fairly simple and straightforward arrangement that eliminated the customary chain drive.

The engine block was so short that only two main bearings supported the crankshaft, but the entire assembly proved sufficiently rigid to rule out any need for main bearing caps. The Morris shop refined the little engine and tooled for production. The little 8 horsepower (taxable) engine proved so powerful,

The 1928 Morris Minor proved a suitable basis for the first Midget. (Society of Motor Traders & Manufacturers)

when tested in the new Morris Minor chassis, that detuning was deemed advisable to tame the engine before turning loose the new baby Morris on an unsuspecting public, which was accustomed to no more than 50 mph in their light cars. Kimber, true to form, got hold of a Minor prototype and decided that he had a potential world-beating engine for a new line of low-cost sports cars.

While the automotive press was publishing their customary forecasts of new models for the 1929 season, Kimber's people were testing the engine and re-engineering everything about the new Morris Minor except the body. The latter was set aside and a quickly designed, ash-framed, plywood body covered with fabric was produced by Carbodies of Coventry during the first week of September 1928. Somewhat spartan but light in weight, the body terminated in a racy duck tail. Timing was beautiful: the mid-August announcement of the 18/80 Six in *The Autocar* was followed a month later with a story about a forthcoming "Morris Midget," which was to be produced by the MG Car Company. Such semantic antics by the press were frustrating to people like Kimber. Actually, he was repeating the formula followed several years earlier, before the letters "MG" surrounded by an oc-

tagon had become the emblem of a distinctive *marque*, but he must have done some of his famous "fuming" in such trying moments.

When the Earl's Court Motor Show opened, a new red MG Midget shared space with the new 18/80 Six and the familiar 14/40. That the display Midget lacked an engine did not matter. Not far away was the Morris Motors stand where the centerpiece was the new Morris Minor at £125. At just £50 more, the MG Midget was the lowest-priced sports car in the 8 horsepower class.

(The tax rating for registration was based upon the Royal Automobile Club [RAC] formula: the cylinder bore [in inches] squared, times the number of cylinders, divided by two and one-half. Converting the 57 mm. bore to 2.25 inches, we have $2.25^2 \times 4 \div 2.5$ which computes to 8.1 horsepower. The registration tax collectors calculated the horsepower rating to the nearest whole number.)

The new Midget, at £175, came to market well under Kimber's previously established theory: that a car could sell for half again as much as the model from which it was developed *if* performance was increased by at least 10 percent. This was the manner in which MG had been launched. For MG purposes, the engines bought in from Morris Motors required little doctoring to develop 20 bhp at 4,000 rpm. The Morris Minor's channel steel frame was changed only slightly. New mountings for the springs permitted lowering the suspension. The steering column was also lowered and the 54 inches overall height, with canvas hood erected, was noticeably less than that of the related Morris Minor. Ground clearance was a scant 6 inches. The Minor's wheelbase of 78 inches was retained and standard Morris wire wheels were graced with special hub caps bearing MG in the octagon. The spare wheel and tire shared space with the folded hood in the duck tail, and there were cycle type mudguards. Louvres on the lower sides of the body, a sloping, V-shaped windscreen, and a reduced rendition of Kimber's classic radiator design combined to give the proper sporting appearance.

The new Midget was an immediate success; sales soon eclipsed the Triumph Super Seven two-seater and the Austin Seven sports car. (A statistic worth noting is that 3,235 of the first MG Midgets were sold during the production period, compared to about 700 Austin Seven sports cars and even fewer Triumph Super Sevens.) The M-Type brought MG international fame; one early customer was Henry Ford's son, Edsel.

With an appropriate disregard for the alphabet, the new Midget was christened Type M—no other letter would fit the Midget—and so it was recorded in the works record books. It is not recorded that anyone, not even Kimber, prophesied that this tiny vehicle, with its cloth-covered plywood body, would be the first of a long line of the world's most popular sports cars. Not underslung as later Midgets would be, the forerunner of the tribe weighed exactly 1,134 pounds sopping wet and ready to run at the curb. Whether anyone outside of the works knew that the universal joints had fabric discs, or whether they speculated about the fact that the 5-gallon fuel tank was situated beneath the bonnet and almost in the driver's lap, is not known. Certainly such an arrangement would not delight us today, nor would a two main bearing crankshaft fit an ideal specification.

The .388 brake horsepower per cubic inch, the overall light weight and small dimensions,

though, were right for the time. Those of the sports car fraternity who were close to Kimber, therefore, were duly impressed by what they saw. With the 1929 High Speed Trials—a feature of the Junior Car Club's annual Members Day at Brooklands—scheduled for May, Kimber decided to sponsor a factory team of three Type-M Midgets to be driven by the Earl of March, Leslie Callingham and H. D. Parker. The MG works would supply the riding mechanics, in accordance with the custom and racing regulations of the day.

Despite a minimum of time for car preparation and driver practice, the three new Midgets won the team award and three Gold Medals. As a not-unexpected result, various enthusiasts approached Kimber at the works with the next year's Double Twelve Hour Race in mind. Because both he and Morris saw eye-to-eye on the necessity to humble the Austin Sevens, agreement was reached to extract more power from the 847 cc. engine. H. N. Charles took on the assignment, along with development of the 18/100 Mark III racing project, to devise some modifications to increase the output. The compression ratio was raised to 5.4 to 1, and the crankshaft was strengthened and balanced, as were the connecting rods. Inlet and exhaust ports were polished, and tougher valve springs and additional support to the rocker arm shaft raised the outside maximum safety limits to well over 5,000 rpm. Valve timing was improved by allowing about 7 degrees of overlap at top dead center, and bench tests revealed a satisfying gain in output, which was now 27 bhp at a safe 4,500 rpm. Stronger wheels, a vastly improved braking system, folding gauze windscreens and deeply cut doors were other special changes.

In the Double Twelve Hour Race on May 9–10, 1930, the re-worked M-Type Midgets—raced by the works team of Edmondson, Randall and Montgomery, and including two independent entries, one piloted by a lady—upset the Austin Sevens, which were running with superchargers. Midget average speeds for the 24 hours of racing, 12 hours each day, ranged from 57.7 to 60.23 mph against a 62 mph handicap. Most remarkable, the admittedly inadequate transmission had only three

To the surprise of many, the fabric-bodied Type M Midget proved a first-class competition sports car. (British Motor Corporation)

Virtually unchanged since 1923, the Austin Seven racing sports cars dominated Class H until the onslaught of the MG Midgets. (British Motor Corporation)

This expertly restored M-Type MG, a later example with metal-sheathed body, is owned by Flip Scholten of Arnhem, The Netherlands. (Jan Scholten photos)

speeds, but the Midgets won their class team award and placed variously from 14th to 20th overall. For a time after this event, the special 27 bhp Midget was called the M 12/12.

The next big victory for the Midgets came with the private entry of F.H.B. Samuelson and F. R. Kindell in the 1930 Belgian Twenty-Four Hour Race at Spa. The lone British entry in any class, their Midget took fifth place in the 1,100 cc. class. The Midget M 12/12 types almost always raced complete with cycle mudguards but with gauze windshields folded. Montgomery drove his own M-Type to a successful completion in the 1930 Monte Carlo Rally and then won the 1,100 cc. class in Mont des Mules Hillclimb. Midgets also found their way to South Africa, Singapore and Czechoslovakia, where they won more races and awards in hill climbs and trials.

The Double Twelve Hour Race victory—the Waterloo of the 18/100 Six Mark III, as already seen—proved the worth of the modifications and they became part of the standard specification of the Type M Midget. In fact, the successes of the M-Type Midget inspired the development of the remarkable C-Type Montlhéry Midget, which went on to thrash the supercharged Austin Sevens and raise the MG banner higher as was seen in Chapter 3.

For the 1930 Motor Show, light metal panels replaced the fabric on the bodies and a "Sportsman's Coupe"—a two-seater with cycle fenders, sliding windows and a luggage boot—was introduced. There was also a "Double Twelve" replica on special order for £245. When production ended in July 1932, M-Type output totalled 3,235 cars. From mid-1931, the price of the metal-sheathed two-seater dropped to £185, while the closed Sportsman's Coupe was £235. By the end of 1931, MG types were rapidly overlapping each other and several production lines were busy at the same time. A new record breaker, the EX.127, would end the year with more MG victories.

Variously described as a four-seater tourer development of the Type M and as a "sports version of the Type C Montlhéry racing MG," the Type D Midget was, in fact, a distinctive and considerably different vehicle that owed much to both of its two illustrious forerunners. When introduced in October of 1931 in time for the Motor Show, in response to a need for a family sports car, the wheelbase was 84 inches and the gearbox contained three speeds with ratios identical to those in the M-Type. The open tourer was priced at £210; the closed model cost £250. After the first one hundred cars, a 4-speed transmission was made available as an extra cost option and the wheelbase was increased to 86 inches.

Though smaller than the contemporary 6-cylinder F.1 Magna, the styling was very similar and definitely sporting. The channel-steel frame was slung beneath the rear axle on fairly flat leaf springs, which were pivoted on shackles at the front and trunnion-mounted at the rear ends. The suspension was a legacy of the C-Type Montlhéry, an advance over the M-Type. Knock-off rather than bolted-on 19-inch wire wheels, heavier and smartly pointed fenders, exterior handles on the two cut-down doors, front bucket seats and a rear bench suitable for the kids made a very desirable but not very fast vehicle. The metal sheathing on the hardwood-framed body was moderately rounded in the rear where the spare wheel was carried.

Much like the original power unit of the EX.120, which displaced 847 cc., the D-Type's engine was rugged but with few refinements—inlet and exhaust valve ports were still on the same side, for example. Output was identical to that of the 12/12 Type M engine: 27 bhp at 4,500 rpm with a single SU carburetor, coil ignition and compression ratio of 5.4 to 1. Tests revealed that, due to weight, acceleration suffered and maximum speed left much to be desired by enthusiasts.

Roadability and handling, however, were excellent with the improved suspension, rack and pinion steering, a man-sized 16½ inch wheel and a low center of gravity despite a relatively heavy body. Ready-for-the-road weight was 1,484 pounds for the open tourer. With the optional saloon body, the curb weight was approximately 1,600 pounds. Overlooked by most enthusiasts, the D-Type was probably the most underpowered of the *marque*. Nevertheless, the MG works quoted 14.7 mph per 1,000 rpm, so that, with coaxing, one could hope for perhaps 65 mph at the best—on the slow side for an MG. The fuel tank beneath

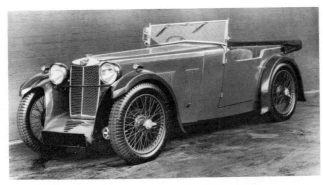

A sometimes overlooked model, the D-Type Midget touring sports car. (British Motor Corporation)

the sheet metal carried 4 Imperial gallons plus 2 in reserve and the wet oil sump held 4 quarts.

Only 250 examples of the Type D had been built when its eight months of production ceased, making this sports tourer one of the rarest of the Midgets. With more power, the Type D could have brought motoring sports to more single-car families. That day, however, was not far away.

When that jewel known as the J-Type began coming off the assembly line in July of 1932, the blood began stirring in sports car enthusiasts. The August 8, 1932, issue of The Autocar cautiously thought that "There is every reason to suppose that the new MG Midget will be a great success."

To the present day, this Midget model enjoys a following far out of proportion to the 2,494 actually manufactured according to factory figures. (Some accounts have stated that more than 5,000 J-Types were made. The author was mislead by such erroneous figures in his earlier book, The MG Story [1967], and he takes this opportunity to set the record straight.) Production of the J-Type ended in January 1934. The most numerous J.2 two-seater weighed 1,428 pounds, not much less than the D-Type, but it was propelled by the much-improved 847 cc. engine with opposed inlet and exhaust ports. It was still advisable to treat the two-main-bearing crankshaft engine with respect, however, to avoid disaster. Fast drivers kept an eye on the oil pressure gauge, too, because the sump carried only 4 quarts of oil and there was no reserve (with the exception of the nine racing J.4 models, which had a float-fed, 2-gallon reserve for competition). Maintain-

ing the engine with care assured the diligent J.2 owner very nearly 80 mph. The Autocar claimed an honest top speed of 80.35 mph. A short, vertical, remote gear change lever fell to hand readily and speeds in first through third gears were approximately 19, 38 and 62 mph, respectively.

Top gear was extremely flexible and, because of the long stroke, allowed smooth motoring on level roads as slow as 10 mph with the ignition retarded. Dual 1-inch SU semi-downdraft carburetors were standard on J.2 and J.1 models. Compression ratio was an improved 6.2 to 1 in the popular J.2, as it was in the less numerous J.1 four-seater tourers and the rare salonettes. The J-Type was the first Midget to feature 4-speed gearboxes (non-synchromesh) on all models. Single plate, dry clutches were used except on the J.4, which had two-plate clutches. Ignition was by coil. Much improved, the output was 36 bhp at 5,500 rpm. The Autocar, rather optimistically, credited this engine with a safe sustained 5,800 rpm capability. The driver sat low with legs nearly straight forward, and feet almost touching the fuel pump.

Though wood framed, as were all MG bodies through the Y-Type, the coachwork was kept as light as possible with deeply notched doors and non-adjustable seats. These had a one-piece backrest in the J.2 two-seater. The instrument panel was double-cowled and had two large instrument groupings of octagonal outline. The combined speedometer and

A. Restored in racing motif, this M-Type belongs to Harold Gray. The oil cooler at bottom of radiator, between dumb irons, is not standard, but is a wise addition because this Midget is frequently driven. Metal sheathing indicates a later M-Type.

B. Restoration is less authentic than he would have preferred. Instrumentation is more complete than obtained in the first M-Types of 1928–1930, and there were two seats.

C. Underslung rear suspension (leaf springs beneath the axle).

D. Ignition side of M-Type Midget's 847 cc. engine.

E. Expedience dictated efficient taillights and the law demands turn signals. The fuel tank is an adapted gasoline can until an authentic tank is obtained.

F. Single SU carburetor and exhaust manifold share the same side in the first Midget's engine. (Joseph H. Wherry photos)

A. The business-like instruments in Bill Holt's J.2 are more legible in this photograph than are many instruments in modern cars. Note engine controls forward of gear change lever. Octagons everywhere!

B. Octagons in the map pocket in door, and "The M.G. Car Company Ltd." name on the sill. The Holt J.2 MG Reg. JJ6063.

C. The aspiration side of Holt's J.2 Midget engine. Note the spare "sparking" plugs, upper left. (Joseph H. Wherry photos)

Lack of external door handles on Jarl de Boer's J.2 Midget indicates an early model. (Joseph H. Wherry photo)

The owner-restorer of this J.2 is Bill Holt of British Columbia. External door-latch handles indicate a later model in the production run. (Joseph H. Wherry photo)

D. The exhaust of the engine in Holt's J.2 Midget. Note aluminum housing over gear change remote mechanism.

E. Chassis for a J.2 Midget, being restored by Peter Welch, shows non-independent front suspension.

F. Bill Holt and his J.2 Midget have won many awards: Pebble Beach (L), the MGCC (R), and more. Note finned brake drums of 50 years ago. (Joseph H. Wherry photos)

tachometer were directly in front of the driver. Flat folding windscreens were fitted to all of the open J-Types. Of special note was the styling of the J.1 tourer, which closely resembled the D-Type it replaced.

The chassis was the classic channel steel and tubular cross pieces, underslung in back, and with MG's traditional half-elliptic leaf springs. Rear springs were shackle-mounted at the front ends, secured by bronze trunnions in the rearmost cross member and snubbered tightly with Hartford friction shocks. Large 19-inch wire wheels, center-locked on an 86-inch wheelbase, were standard, as were 8-inch-diameter finned brake drums on all J.1, J.2 and J.3 models. Brakes on the rare racing J.4 were 12-inch drums, while all models had a racing type, fly-off hand brake. Close-coupled, the length overall was just 124 inches.

The competition J.3 and J.4 engines were de-stroked to 746 cc. Of these models, only 31 were built; they were supercharged versions of the J.2 roadster. The J.3 engine had a 5.2 to 1 compression ratio and a fairly low-pressure 6A Powerplus supercharger. This was mounted between the dumb irons and shrouded beneath an apron. The works never specified the output. An excellent trials car, a J.3 was awarded a coveted Coupé des Glaciers in the 1933 Alpine International and secured several International Class H records at Montlhéry.

The more famous J.4 had a compression ratio of 5.5 to 1, a fully counterbalanced crankshaft and, with a more powerful blower, delivered an enviable 72.3 bhp at 6,000 rpm. With an unfortunate introduction in March 1933, however, the J.4 was overshadowed by the Type K.3 Magnette racer, which appeared almost simultaneously. The first of the J.4 victories was a class win in the hill climb event at the German Grand Prix in 1933, with Hugh Hamilton at the wheel. In the same year, a J.4 came in third in the Mannin Beg Race in the Isle of Man, and went on to place first overall in the 100 Mile Race at Southport.

In the 1933 Ulster Tourist Trials, a Royal Automobile Club event of considerable importance, Hamilton's J.4 finished less than a minute behind the more powerful K.3 Magnette with an average of slightly more than 73

mph for the entire race. The same Hugh Hamilton persuaded the Austrian racing driver, Robert A. Th. Mayer, to sell his 1.5-litre Bugatti, on which he had won many victories. Herr Mayer did so, switching to the MG J.4 and proceeding to triumph over various European 2-litre cars, according to an interesting yarn in the July 1980 *Safety Fast*.

In common with most sports cars of the 1930s—other makes as well as our subject car—there were styling variations within a single type. Some of the J.1 tourers and salonettes had swept fenders instead of the standard valanced cycle mudguards. However, most of them had lines much like those of the Type D Midget and the Type F six-cylinder Magna. Many J.2 roadsters had external door handles while others did not, and there were minor differences in the wedge-shaped fuel tanks. Fuel capacity was 9 Imperial gallons, plus 3 reserve gallons on all models except the J.1 touring types, which carried 4 (plus 2 in reserve). J.2 fuel consumption, even with fairly hard driving, usually was more than 30 miles per gallon. Types J.1 and J.2 had well-muffled road exhausts with tailpipes beneath the chassis. The competition J.3 and J.4 Types had the regulation Brooklands exhaust, which was well able to sensitize all authority within a wide radius. The J.3 Midget won its share of records, too. In February 1932, a works-prepared J.3 specially fitted with a high-pressure blower, with George Eyston at the wheel, shattered *all* of the International Class H records (which the EX.127 had not already taken) to give MG a clean sweep. Austin had been humbled!

By far the most sensational performance of the J.4 was placing sixth overall at Le Mans in 1934. The high point *might have been* the 1934 Tourist Trophy Race. Like the K.3 Magnette, however, the J.4 was ruled out by the ban on superchargers.

For a price of £200 for a J.2 roadster—a little under $1,000 at the time—one could scarcely go wrong. Open and closed four-seater J.1 models were priced slightly higher. The blown J.3 and J.4 competition types were nearly twice as costly, but one got more despite the lack of doors—useless objects on a racer. As for performance, the J.4 is said to

Concours points are scored with engines like the Jensen's PA Midget Airline Coupé.

Luxury in a small package, the MG PA Airline Coupé.

The sunshine roof on the PA Midget Airline Coupé, a standard item in 1934–35. Note "Trafficator." (Joseph H. Wherry photos)

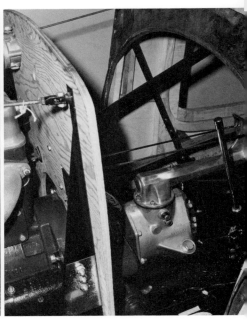

have been capable of close to 120 mph. Such performance, with 750 cubic centimetres winding a two main bearing crankshaft, was remarkable a half century ago.

While superbly roadable, the popular Types J.1 and J.2 were raucous and rough on tender torsos. Though they were fun to drive, improvements were needed. Abingdon phased out the Type J and commenced producing the new Type P in January of 1934. Persons outside the sports car fraternity would not have been impressed at first glance. The P-Type Midget *looked* like a small edition of the 6-cylinder Type L Magna, which had just gone out of production. Enthusiasts being what they are, many lamented the passing of the austere J.2, and were horrified at the new PA— the *first* Midget to have a running board. Effete, thought some zealots.

The PA was produced from January 1934 to July 1935, during which time nearly 2,000 were sold, a good sports car business in those years. The latter date, observed previously, is of immense importance in MG sports car history. The takeover of MG by Morris Motors, the ascendancy of an impersonal board of directors over enthusiast Kimber, the immediate ban on factory-sponsored racing, and the end of Type PA production all happened at once! Two months passed before another Midget

Above, L: This PA Midget two-seater's body metal components and coachwork are being restored by owner Don McLellan of British Columbia. Note the careful fitting of the hardwood framing in door and body. Framing kits are available from coachwork suppliers. C: Door frame, scuttle, and after-body restoration. R: Transmission housing and the octagonal-shaped tube containing the gear changing mechanism. Note bracket on housing supporting engine controls. At center right is the fly-off hand brake. (Joseph H. Wherry photos)

was in production. This was the PB, which was produced from September 1935 to May 1936. A total of 2,499 Types PA and PB were built as two-seater roadsters, four-seater tourers and the beautiful Airline Coupe. The latter, with coachwork by Carbodies of Coventry, was smart, comfortable, and rakish. The spare wheel was recessed in the rear deck, but only one hundred were built.

Cries of anguish fairly rent the air at meetings of the MG Car Club when the P-Type replaced the beloved Type J. The P-Types were truly "born to trouble," but they were splendid sports cars. Raced much in club events, they more than proved themselves in the rough trials and bashes until the war. Today, after more than four decades, many consider the PA and PB to be the most attractive of all the Midgets. Others prefer the P-Types because they were the last of the OHC Midgets. They also were the largest: 7 inches longer overall, at 131 inches, than the J.2. The PA also was slightly longer in wheelbase at 87⁵/₁₆ inches. In addition, the two-seater was some 225 pounds heavier at 1,652 pounds. On the other hand, the tread was not changed and, though the frame design followed prior practice, all members were heavier. The PA, compared to the J.2, was better engineered and stronger throughout. Precisely what had Kimber and his staff done with the PA to deserve verbal abuse from those who thought the J.2 was without possible equal? Actually, nothing but good things.

Starting with the engine, the pair of 1-inch-diameter SU carburetors and the bore and stroke were unchanged. The compression ratio, at 6.2 to 1, was the same as that of the J.2. Out of sight, however, was a long-needed and much stronger three main bearing crank-shaft, the *first* ever in a Midget. The oil sump held 5 quarts without apparent need of a reserve, and there was a new external oil filter. The cooling system held 11½ quarts, 1½ more than the J.2, and, like previous Midgets, there was no water pump. The traditional thermal syphon cooling system was intact. With the same displacement but so vastly improved, one would suppose (cried the critics) that the output would have been more than that of the J.2-Type, but the PA engine developed the same 36 bhp at 5,500 rpm.

How come? Sound engineering improvements were responsible for the changes. The crankshaft was heavier, stronger, and had one more main bearing. The block was also a bit heavier for the same reason, and the entire valve gear was strengthened. What the PA engine did not gain in output, it more than

An unrestored PA Midget owned by Bob Hicks. (Joseph H. Wherry photo)

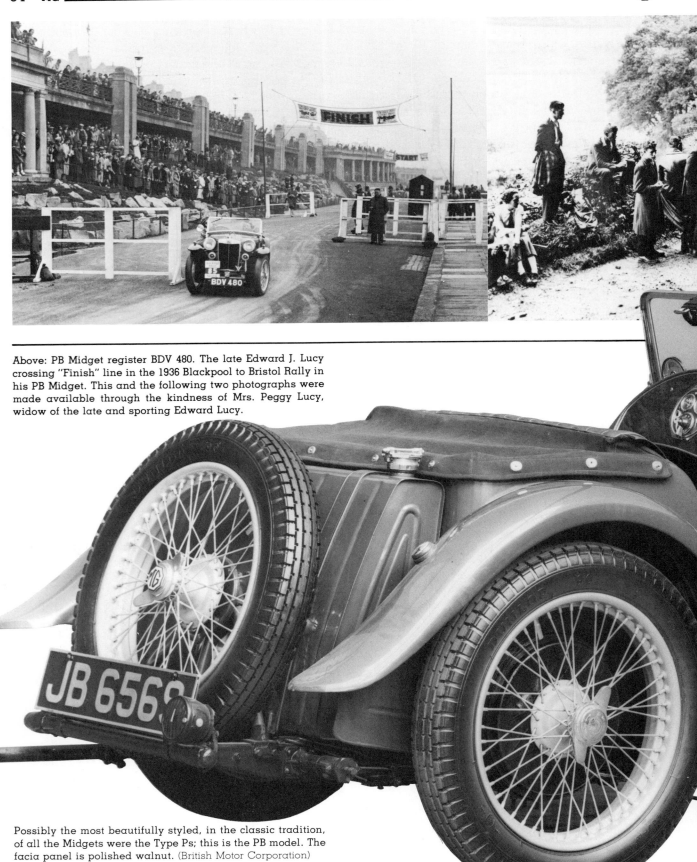

Above: PB Midget register BDV 480. The late Edward J. Lucy crossing "Finish" line in the 1936 Blackpool to Bristol Rally in his PB Midget. This and the following two photographs were made available through the kindness of Mrs. Peggy Lucy, widow of the late and sporting Edward Lucy.

Possibly the most beautifully styled, in the classic tradition, of all the Midgets were the Type Ps; this is the PB model. The facia panel is polished walnut. (British Motor Corporation)

Top right: the first use of a vertically slatted radiator grille on Midgets shows clearly in this unidentified 1936 action photo of PB BDV 480 being driven exuberantly by the late Edward J. Lucy. Note that front wheels have left *terra firma* and are being monitored by the passenger. (Top photos courtesy of the present owner, Frank A. Ward II)

Top center: probably the start of a bash or a hill climb somewhere in the United Kingdom in 1936. Driver of PB Midget BDV 480 is the late Edward J. Lucy; the passenger is not known.

gained in obvious durability. The power curve was superior to that of the J.2 engine because, despite the extra 225 pounds of total weight, the maximum speed of the PA was not much less than that of the average J.2. The PA's maximum was about 75 mph. For good MG measure, the PA was quieter, better handling and safer. The latter virtue was due to 12-inch brakes on all models.

After the big July 1935 shakeup, the new and improved PB Midget began to materialize. Upon its introduction two months later, the improvements were mechanically extensive — and just as invisible, on the surface, as had been the changes in the PA.

The bore was increased by 3 mm. for a displacement of 939 cc., and the cylinder head was shaved to increase the compression ratio to 6.8 to 1. The ignition timing remained at 20 degrees before top dead center, and the valve timing was identical to that of the PA. These modest changes increased the output to 43 bhp at the same 5,500 rpm. The frame, overall weight, and suspension were unchanged. Predictably, the new PB was an 80 mph sports car — with windshield folded — at no sacrifice in durability or safety. The "Safety Fast!" slogan still had meaning.

One had to look closely to discover differences between the PA and the later PB. The

The owner of this beautiful PA Midget two-seater (Chassis No. PA/289) is Mr. James Dovey of England and South Africa. This car was restored by the late Ivor Dovey. This roadster is well-known on two continents. Recently the original license, LOL 786, has been obtained by owner Dovey. (Courtesy: John Watts)

vertically slatted radiator grille, a smart finishing touch to the honeycomb of the cooling core, was introduced to the marque by the PB. For all practical purposes, the only change of consequence in the PB interior was the instrument layout: the PA dashboard was similar to that of the J.2, whereas the PB tachometer, very large and inside an octagonal rim, was in front of the driver. The smaller speedometer was relocated to the passenger's side in a matching instrument cluster.

The Midget was maturing: the interior was now reflecting the customers' demand for comfort — without compromising the handling qualities required of a true sports car. A successful mount in trials and hill climbs, the PA was raced, too, but only by private owners.

The PB, with its increased power, proved to be an even better trials car. No options were listed for the rear-axle gears, but competition drivers knew how to get around that minor irritant. Owners were discovering the susceptibility of either the PA or PB engine to judicious tuning before the last PB was assembled in May of 1936. Superchargers, usually low-

pressure units, found their way into the position forward of the radiator and performances increased proportionately. The "Cream Crackers," a cycle-fendered trials team with supercharged PB Midgets painted deliciously in the cream and brown official MG colors, won award after award during 1936 and 1937, in the most bone-bending of all motor sports. Many supercharged PB specials have topped 100 mph without undue strain.

The greatest single blessing bestowed by either the PA or PB should have been confidence. This was due to the obvious superiority of the three-main-bearing crankshaft over the long-used, two-main-bearing device in all of the previous Midgets. Refined, more powerful and with an engine more fit to sustain high speeds, the PA and PB were, in retrospect, certainly the best of their tribe of overhead-camshaft Midgets. They were also the last.

Three months after P-Type production was terminated, the unthinkable happened—another reason for more sackcloth and ashes because Abingdon had been forced by Morris Motors to let down the bars to modern design! The T-Type, with *pushrods*, arrived. Of that famous clan, more later.

A beautifully restored PA Midget, Chassis No. 0671. The owner is Slobodan Jelić of Split on the Dalmatian coast of Yugoslavia. "To achieve the original specification, I spent several years collecting the original parts and assembling them carefully," writes owner-restorer Jelić, the Secretary of the MG Car Club Dalmatia Centre. (Courtesy: Slobodan Jelić)

Magna and Magnette:
Light Sixes for All Seasons

Chapter V

This F.1 Magna, registered MG 1435, was restored by owner Ernie Kallvert of British Columbia. Note the Hartford friction shock absorber just inside the near wheel. (Joseph H. Wherry photo)

From the autumn of 1931 on through 1936, small and attractive six-cylinder cars were built by MG. Contemporary with the two-seater Midgets, which were beginning to open overseas markets, the four new Types would cater in part to a segment of the motoring public who preferred an under-1,500 cc. "Light Six" all-purpose vehicle. A "Light Six" should be both economical to buy and to operate. The large and costly 18/80 models could not fill the bill; moreover, the end of their production was within view.

Even more worthy of consideration, for a relatively small manufacturer of specialty cars such as MG, were the thousands of would-be enthusiasts who were family men of modest means. These people yearned for a sporting four-seater that could double as a family car and still serve as a mount in the popular reliability trials, hill climbs, rallies and various non-racing events.

Clearly something a bit larger than the M-Type Midget was required. Whether or not Cecil Kimber was hedging his bets is not known, but with the 1931 Motor Show in mind, two new models were prepared for introduction. Alongside the new D-Type Midget (which soon proved to be underpowered and too heavy at 1,484 pounds at the curb for four occupants, and hence was rather short-lived)

was a new MG Light Six. The new Light Six was the F-Type and it was soon given the name "Magna," which, loosely, meant greater. The Magna, somewhat true to its name, would prove to be reasonably popular and would be produced in greater numbers than any other MG Light Six.

The F-Type Magna chassis was developed alongside that of the D-Type Midget and, consequently, owed much to the C-Type Montlhéry racing Midget. Underslung, with the half-elliptic springs sliding in bronze trunnions at the rear and pivoted in front, the frame was built up of channel steel rails with tubular cross-members. Virtually a duplicate of the D-Type frame, it was lengthened to accommodate the longer 6-cylinder engine and the much better 4-speed E.N.V. transmission. The 94-inch wheelbase was 8 inches longer than that of the D-Type Midget, the 8-inch cable-operated brakes were retained, and the price of the open tourer was £250, about £40 more than that of the similar though shorter Midget. The F.1 Magna also was available as a closed two-door Salonette, with luggage boot, at £289.

The new 6-cylinder Magna engine was developed from that of the M-Type Midget by the convenient expedient of buying in complete Wolseley Hornet engines from the Morris

Motors organization, which had previously acquired Wolseley.* The Abingdon shops treated the engines to cosmetic camouflage, with the distinctive finned exhaust manifolds and the MG octagon in evidence. The displacement was 1,271 cc. and the rating, for registration tax purposes, was 12 horsepower. This was the source of the 12/70 name appended to the F-Type Magna. The cylinder head was a lengthened AA type with inlet and exhaust ports on the same side, but the compression ratio was raised slightly, to 5.7 to 1. The overhead camshaft, already expected of MGs by this time, operated the valves by means of fully adjustable rockers, and there were dual 1-inch horizontal SU carburetors and coil ignition. Valve timing was the mild, non-overlapping of the first M-Type Midgets. Brake horsepower, the officially stated output, was 37.2 at 4,100 rpm. Weighing a bit more than 1,700 pounds ready at the curb—at least 216 pounds heavier than the D-Type Midget, to which the first Magna is inevitably compared—the F.1 was certainly no world-beater in performance. This probably was just as well, considering the small 8-inch brakes, but *The Autocar* credited the F.1 with what seems to be a remarkable 72.6 mph in a timed speed

The F.1 Magna tourer, a close-coupled motor car, brought motoring sports to the one-car, small family man who insisted upon a "Light Six." (Joseph H. Wherry photo)

test over a measured quarter-mile. The overall test conditions are not known, but it is possible that the increased flexibility of the 4-speed gearbox provided a quicker impetus for the speed run.

Visual similarity to the D-Type Midget was even more evident and, at a distance, the F.1 Magna tourer—"wings" and all—is barely distinguishable from the shorter, 4-cylinder type. But the initial Magnas *were* attractive. The fine-grained, highly polished walnut facia contained a small glove case at the left

The 1,271 cc. Wolseley Hornet's engine stimulated F.1 Magna development. Photos of the Hornet are scarce. (British Motor Corporation)

*See Chapter IV.

side, and a full complement of instruments was centered. That a fair number of F.1 models were offered for export is evidenced by the left- and right-side cutouts in the facia for the steering column. The rounded rump of the tourer and salonette coachwork contained a 4 gallon (plus 2 reserve) fuel tank. No new F.1

Octagons everywhere: this one is on the exhaust manifold—on same side of engine as induction—on an F.1 Magna. (Joseph H. Wherry photo)

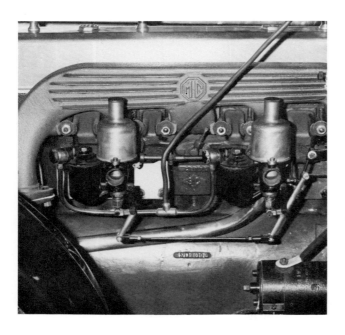

The fuel tank was concealed on F.1 Magna and later F.3. (Joseph H. Wherry photo)

Magnas are known to have been exported to America.

In September 1932, the F-Type was improved by upgrading the inadequate brake system with 12-inch drums. This necessitated—after established MG custom—a new designation, and the tourer and salonette became the F.3. To round out the F-Type line, a two-seater roadster, with cycle mudguards and a slab tank at the rear, became available as the F.2 with the fitting of the J.2 Midget body to the chassis. Throughout its 15 months of production, all F-Type models were fitted with 19-inch, knock-off wire wheels, fly-off handbrakes, and the standard 4.78 to 1 rear axle ratio. The latter provided 16.7 mph per 1,000 rpm, in top gear, which allowed a theoretical maximum speed of 68.47 mph. Taking the weight into consideration, the previously mentioned 72-plus mph attained in a road test is a credit to the amenability of the engine to fine tuning of the SU carburetors and valve timing.

The F-Type engine's Wolseley Hornet ancestry is not to be disdained; it is remembered that the engine of the remarkable M-Type Midget came into the Morris empire via

F-Type Magnas utilized the AA-type cylinder head with inlet and exhaust valves on same side of the block. Sharp eyes will check lubrication nipples, bottom right. (Joseph H. Wherry photo)

Ignition side of F.1 6-cylinder engine has a brass plate with complete engine specifications on the valve gear cover. (Joseph H. Wherry photo)

Wolseley. Comparatively few Hornets, however, were manufactured; in fact, they are scarcely remembered today and seldom illustrated. Not often employed in competition other than trials and club events, the F.3 tourer did itself justice in the hands of one driver, Dick Seaman, in the internationally prestigious Alpine Rally of 1932. Seaman went on to become a distinguished racing driver on the K.3 Magnette and other mounts.

When the 1932 London Motor Show opened in October, the main attraction on the MG stand was the first K-Type, a four-seater sports car named Magnette. Because of the name, one might conclude that Magnettes would be smaller than Magnas. That was Kimber's original plan, but it would not long be sustained. Creative and innovative people, like the engineering staff at the MG works, are rarely susceptible to the confinements of alphabetical order or names. No MG series, before or since the Magnette, owned such a perplexing set of specifications. MG enthusiasts have enjoyed many a debate over the K-Type for nigh on a half-century.

With the exception of the K.3—engineered and produced exclusively for racing*—there were three distinct variants or types mounted on two wheelbases using four somewhat different overhead camshaft engines of two pis-

ton displacements. (Through the years, some automotive historians have made a case for as many as six "distinct" K-Types. These historian *types* may be correct depending upon just *how* one decides to identify types, sort out production periods and a myriad of specifications.) The method the MG works employed to indicate seating capacities of the F.1 Magna types generally prevailed with the K-Type: four-seaters were K.1 types and the pair of two-seaters were K.2 types. This lasted until the advent of the KN-Type, a series of four-seaters that used the N-Type engines during the year or so while KN production overlapped that of the shorter and narrower N-Type, the reason for combining the Type designations.

The one consistency in K-Type specifications is that all K-Type four-seater open and closed cars sat on 108-inch wheelbases in contrast to the 94³/₁₆-inch wheelbases of the two-

*See Chapter III.

An F.2 Magna two-seater, with external slab fuel tank. Note hinged door. (British Motor Corporation)

F-Type Magna cockpit was right for sports car enthusiasts. Note octagons on side and top of gearbox housing, and the long push-pull engine controls beside the remotely operated gear change lever. The instrument panel is walnut. (Joseph H. Wherry photo)

seater roadsters and coupes. Both sizes shared a common front and rear wheel tread of 48 inches; thus suspension components, axles, steering and brake systems, and the like, were common items.

Types K.1, K.2 and KN were refinements of the F-Type Magna which, like the final Magna, was smaller in wheelbase and tread than any of the Magnettes. Obviously something went haywire in the naming department, but MG was by no means the only carmaker with such minor problems. Such industrial *faux pas* make history interesting.

All K-Type variants employed half-elliptic leaf springs. The rear ends of these were hung in the now-familiar bronze-bushed sliding trunnions in the tubular frame cross-members, while the front ends of the springs were pivoted. Likewise, all models used open propeller shafts terminating in spiral bevel differentials. Hartford friction shock absorbers were standard. The steering was improved and lightened in touch by a split track rod. Larger, 13-inch diameter cable-operated brakes were actually effective, for a much-needed change. (Ettore Bugatti once observed that he made his cars to *go*, not to stop.) Sporting fly-off handbrake levers were standard, as were 19-inch wire wheels with Rudge knock-off hubs. All K-Type models had 4-speed gearboxes. Wilson Preselectors were used with the KA and KD engines; traditional non-synchromesh "crash" boxes were teamed with the KB and the NA engines.

The fine coachwork of the K.1 four-door saloons merits attention: most were *pillarless*. No sill-to-roof body pillars separated the front and rear doors. Front doors were hinged at the front, the rear doors at the rear. When both front and rear doors were open, there was no entry obstruction other than the front seats on either side. Also absent were exterior latch handles on the rear doors, which could be opened only from the inside after the front doors were opened. Most popular of all the K-Types, the saloons appealed to family men partly because of the rear door security for small children. Sliding roof panels—"sunshine roofs"—came to the MG catalogue with the K.1.

The four diverse engines were scattered through the K-Type range and the reader is advised to consult the Specifications tables in the back of this volume because of the overlapping dates of production. Carbodies of Coventry supplied all of the standard bodies, which were designed by Kimber and his associates. Four-seaters outnumbered two-seaters and there were more closed than open bodies.

Engines for the approximately 405 K-Type Magnettes descended from the 1,271 cc. unit of the F.1 Magna. Kimber conceived the Magnette to fill the displacement slot between the 847 cc. J.2 Midgets and F.1 Magna. Therefore, the initial production engine—dubbed KA—was basically a Magna block destroked to 71 mm. to achieve a displacement of 1,087 cc.

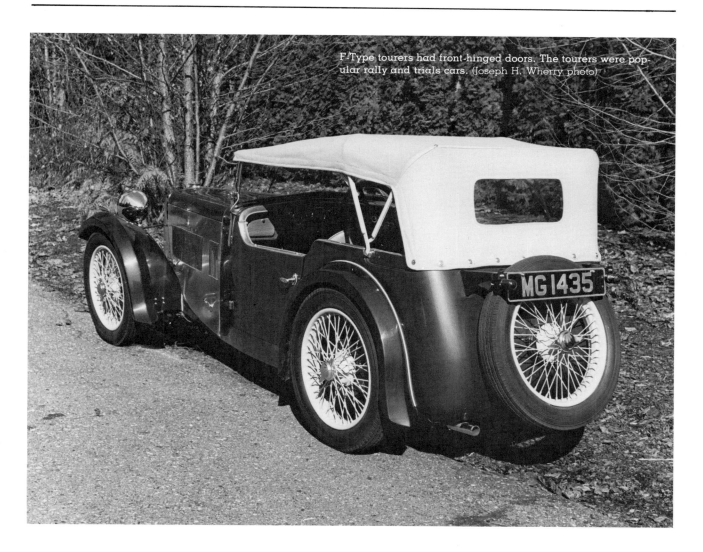

F-Type tourers had front-hinged doors. The tourers were popular rally and trials cars. (Joseph H. Wherry photo)

Shaving the head raised the compression ratio to 6.4 to 1, a standard specification on all K.1 and K.2 engines until production ceased at the end of 1933. Aiming at good performance, a new intake manifold mounting three SU carburetors was designed. Ignition was by magneto. Coupled to a close ratio Wilson Preselector transmission and a high ratio rear axle, the new K.1 Magnette was expected to turn in a rather exciting performance in view of the impressive increase in engine speed to 5,500 rpm.

The upshot, however, was disappointing: due to vibration, the complicated preselector gearbox clattered in neutral. To solve this unacceptable annoyance, the timing was altered and, though maximum allowable engine speed remained at 5,500 rpm, the output was barely 39 bhp. There were shortcomings in the design of the induction manifold and this was aggravated by the fascinating but touchy three carburetors, which caused some problems with synchronization. Overall performance—and particularly acceleration— suffered because torque was inadequate. Accordingly, the new KB engine, mated to the familiar non-synchromesh gearbox, with altered ratios, became available in the K.1 in February 1933 as an alternate to the KA unit. At the same time, in an effort to broaden the

The superb coach-built body of the K.1 Magnette four-door saloon had no central door pillar. (British Motor Corporation)

line to increase the Magnette's marketability, the K.2 two-seater on the shorter wheelbase was introduced with the KB engine.

With the same bore and stroke, the KB engine returned to the customary two 1⅛-inch SU carburetors and the non-synchromesh gearbox, which had altered ratios. Valve timing was normal, coils and distributors replaced the magnetos, maintenance and tuning were simplified, and the cylinder heads were of opposed port design. Curiously, the fashionable preselector gearbox was available as a special order option. Maximum output was nominally improved: 41 bhp at 5,500 rpm, and top speed edged a bit over an anemic 65 mph. This was not enough for a fairly expensive Light Six costing around £440 for the pretty, pillarless saloon. Only about 71 Type K.1 Magnettes were produced with KA or KB engines between October 1932 and July 1933. Sales of the K.2 two-seater were even worse—only a dismal 15 or so finding buyers. Enthusiasts expected performance from production MGs, and Kimber pressured his engineers.

An engine designated KC did exist, but information is scanty and documentation ob-

In many respects, the L.2 Magna was the 6-cylinder counterpart of the P-Type Midgets. (British Motor Corporation)

scure. We are left with the assumption that the KC engine was a developmental step, because it did not see series production, even on a small scale. To overcome the slump in sales, the new KD engine became available in July 1933, in both two- and four-seaters. The "new" engine for the Magnette had the same internal dimensions as the discontinued F.1 Magna engine. Judicious tuning and ignition system improvements, along with the standard Magnette compression ratio, raised the output to a more satisfying 48.5 bhp at 5,500 rpm in the four seat K.1 and 54.5 bhp at 5,500 rpm in the two seat K.2. The 1,271 cc. KD engine was always teamed with the Wilson Preselector, but an auxiliary clutch between the block and the gearbox effectively eliminated the vibration and noise that had cursed the KA engine. The K.1 and K.2 Magnettes enjoyed a new lease on life and remained in production until March 1934 and December 1933, respectively, but customers were still too few and only some 85 examples were built, all but five being the K.1 four-seater saloons and tourers. Sales of the K.1 dragged on until the end of 1934, months after production had ended. Fortunately, the Midgets and Magnas kept things humming in Abingdon.

When F-Type Magna production wound down in December 1932, the smart new

L-Type took its place. The L-Type was made in four-seater open and closed models, and open two-seaters (the L.1 and L.2, respectively). In production exactly one year, 576 were built, with the four-seaters outselling the two-seaters by more than five to one. Narrower than the Magnettes ("what's in a name?") with the same 42-inch tread as the F.1 Magna, the new L-Type had the same wheelbase as the K.2 Magnette. Close-coupled, all had just two doors. The closed L.1 Magnas were available with Carbodies coachwork in both a four-seater Salonette and a rakish Continental Coupé, with luggage boot of reasonable carrying capacity.

The familiar MG frame was little changed, with 12-inch brakes replacing the weak 8-inch drums of the F-Type Magna. The engine was the KB unit, displacing 1,087 cc., and the specifications were identical to those of the K.1 and K.2 Magnettes which were in production simultaneously. This was a no-nonsense sports car with a fairly close ratio, crash-type gearbox with a 3.58 to 1 ratio final drive, which provided 15.2 mph per 1,000 rpm in top gear. Theoretically, the flat-out maximum speed would be 83.6 mph. However, special considerations (such as a curb weight of approximately 1,765 pounds for the open two-seater) always reduce timed maximums for standard cars without minute tuning. Nevertheless, the motoring press of early 1934 generally agreed that a stock L.2 roadster, with flat-folded windscreen, should have no trouble attaining 75 mph or more. Acceleration was good, too: through the gears from stop to a true 50 mph was reached in no more than 19 seconds when properly driven.

Exceptionally attractive, the L-Type styling was much like that of the P-Type Midgets. The latter, by the way, were production contemporaries of this car, the liveliest across-the-counter Magna to date. (P-Type Midgets and L-Type Magnettes have been referred to as counterparts of each other through the years. L-Type and P-Type bodies were sometimes interchanged.) Slightly easier than the K-Type on the pocketbook of the one-car chap who had a family, the L-Type cost just £285 for the open two-seater L.2. The price increased to £345 for the closed Salonette, and the exotic Continental Coupé cost just £5 more. Fuel capacities ranged from 7 Imperial gallons plus 2 reserve in the Salonette to 9 and 3 reserve in the open L.2 roadster.

Responsive to precise competition preparation, the overhead-camshaft KB engine, unencumbered by heavy coachwork or over 100-inch wheelbase, finally brought sports car pleasures to "light six" enthusiasts at a moderate price. In the 1933 Brooklands Relay Race, a team of three slab-tanked L.2 roadsters ran under the banner of the MG Car Club. Minor but sensible and permissible modifications, such as porting and polishing, enabled the

A gathering of MG types in California: on left is business end of JB7261, an NB tourer; in middle is BYU271, the NA with Allingham coachwork owned by Rosemary Bayne-Powell. Allingham bodies were distinguished by rounded corners of bonnet sides, door cutout rounded at rear, raked louvres on bonnet, top louvres, etc. (Courtesy: Mr. and Mrs. S. Peter Thelander)

NA four-seat tourer with standard Carbodies coachwork. (British Motor Corporation)

MGCC team to win the event with an average speed of 88.6 mph.

The same trio of L-Type two-seaters ran in the 1933 International Alpine Trial, where they placed first in Class G and were awarded the coveted Manufacturers' Team Prize. Matched and balanced connecting rods and pistons, polished ports and careful synchronizing of carburetors and ignitions produced another amazing G Class performance in the 1933 Brooklands 500 Mile Race. There a superbly driven L-Type Magna two-seater ran a rapid second to a K.3 Magnette. The average speed was 92.24 mph. This was an excellent perfor-mance for an over-the-counter sports car that incorporated some vital parts of the J.2 Midget: the axles, which were responsible for the 42-inch tread—really somewhat narrow for a competition car in 1933. This surprising feat, however, encouraged the competition department to prepare one of the works L-Types for Montlhéry, where it covered 2,000 miles at an average of 80.49 mph and averaged 80.56 mph for 24 hours.

Four-seater L.1 Magnas were eagerly purchased and, for years thereafter, competed in

A famous NA Magnette in another part of the world is CE4842, a two-seater with Lionel Meyers aboard in South Africa soon after importing it from the U.K. (Courtesy: Dr. W. M. Pitt Fennell, M.B., Ch.B., F.R.C.S.)

The NA, with 2/4-seater occasional coachwork. Note first small
18-inch wheels on any MG. (British Motor Corporation)

Lionel Meyers and his NA Magnette stripped for action. In the
1936 South African Grand Prix, Meyers was the first competitor of his country to finish and fourth overall. (Courtesy: Dr.
W. M. Pitt Fennell)

many sports events to fulfill Kimber's dream of launching an MG assault on the "Light Six" sports car market. Today L-Type Magnas are as rare as they are desirable, and highly regarded by enthusiasts and collectors of vintage sports cars.

In March 1934, about two months after the cessation of L-Type Magna production, the N-Type appeared as a replacement for the 1,271 cc., KD-powered K.1 Magnette. The N-Type Magnette would be slightly longer in wheelbase than any of the "greater" Magnas but shorter than the "in-between" K.1 Magnettes. A bit more alphabet perplexity attended the birth of the N-Type: the P-Type Midget's introduction was in January of the same year. We may presume that conception of the N-Type preceded the P-Type in someone's mind. This was a minor problem, to be sure, but interesting.

Quite significant in the historical development of the *marque* MG, the N-Type Magnette was second in sales of the MG "Light Six" cars. The N-Type also has the distinction of being the last pre-war overhead camshaft MG, because production continued until November 1936—six months after the PB Midget was cut short. Moreover, as if the engineering department in Abingdon intended to make MG matters even more bewildering for future enthusiasts, the N-Type provided the *fourth* engine used in the K-Type that was oddly, though appropriately, designated KN.

Available with open two- and four-seater coachwork, plus an extremely attractive "occasional four" by H. W. Allingham, were the streamlined Airline Coupé by Carbodies and the practical Cresta, an open body by Cresta Motors of Worthing (on the southern coast near Brighton). Structurally, the N-Type chassis was like that of the K-Type. About June of 1935, the NB was introduced with front hinged doors; otherwise the NA and NB were identical. Close examination, however, revealed considerable changes of dimensional specification: the 96-inch wheelbase was only minutely longer than that of the related K.2 two-seater, while the tread was just 45 inches. This latter dimension placed the effective width of the N-Type squarely between the "intermediate"

K-Type Magnettes and the "greater" F- and L-Type Magnas.

Such differences should not be viewed as trivial nearly half a century later, however. This is the sort of interesting detail that lifts MG out of the monotony of orthodox conformity, which afflicted so many of its competitors during the prewar decade of its popular ascendancy over all other relatively low-priced sports cars. Of such stuff, faithful enthusiasm is born for a vehicle endowed with an enviable measure of personality. Not the least of the N-Type's distinctions was that it was *the first* mass-produced MG to introduce smaller 18-inch-diameter wheels. In addition, the vertically slatted radiator grille was pioneered by the NB. With the latter styling improvement, the NB Magnette, which was introduced in June 1935, preceded the PB Midget by about three months.

Other innovations were introduced by the N-Type. MG management recognized the public demand for quieter driving, so rubber blocks cushioned the bodies at the mounting points on the frame. Even rough-and-ready sports car enthusiasts seldom objected to a modicum of noise reduction, but if such refinement offended any, they were more than compensated by the livelier, higher-ratio Bishop cam steering. There was also a modification of the dual track rods, which reduced the lock to slightly more than one turn from left to right. The turning circle diameter was a mere 30 feet, a great improvement over 34 and 36 feet for the M-Type and P-Type Midgets, respectively, and the tightest for any of the other Magnettes and Magnas.

Prices started at £305 for the open two-seaters, which weighed about 1,960 pounds at the curb. Weights ready-to-drive for the other models were 2,040 pounds for the four-seaters and approximately 2,070 pounds for the Airline Coupés. Seemingly strange was the reversion, after the K-Types, to the slightly smaller 12-inch-diameter brakes.

The most improved component of the N-Type Magnette was the engine of this extended family of overhead camshaft MG "Light Six" types, a numerous and often confusing lot in any roll call of vintage cars. The KD engine

compression ratio was lowered slightly to 6.1:1, valve timing was modified, carburetion was by a pair of 1⅛-inch SUs, and engine speed was increased by 200 rpm. Maximum output became 56.6 bhp at 5,700 rpm. A margin of safety was provided by the 7-quart oil sump, and the gearbox was a no-nonsense crash type with a single plate, heavy duty clutch.

(Legends sometimes arise around facts which are considered to be bothersome. As

The Thelanders' NE, registered JB4607, which was driven in the 1934 Tourist Trophy Race by Bill Everitt. After World War II, this car was fitted with doors (to conform to new sports cars regulations) and a modified K.3 engine with preselector gearbox. (Courtesy: Mr. & Mrs. S. Peter Thelander)

mentioned early in this chapter, the 1,271 cc. OHC 6-cylinder engine gravitated into the MG firmament from the Wolseley Hornet via the Morris Motors organization. Some factions

The Thelanders' well-preserved NE Magnette was one of seven prepared for the 1934 Ulster Tourist Trophy Race.

The thermal syphon system of the Tourist Trophy NE Magnette. (Both courtesy: Mr. & Mrs. S. Peter Thelander)

within the "true believer" fraternity were—it is said—responsible for an engine modification that really never occurred, that the N-Type engine was stroked 1 mm. to 84 mm. This would have increased the piston displacement to 1,286 cc. Of course this never happened. This author admits to having fallen from grace because of this legend. The author has had plenty of company, through the years, including the compilers of the feature "MG Through The Ages" in the January 1975 issue of Sports Car published for the Sports Car Club of America by the author's old friend, David Ash. Such legends—or mysteries—provide endless grist for sports car enthusiasts, especially those of MG persuasion.)

Because of ample allowances for development, the NA engine was seized upon by the competition department as a plausible solution to the dilemma posed by the unforeseen exclusion of supercharged cars from the 1934 Ulster Tourist Trophy Race which was won in 1931, it will be remembered, by the C-Type MG Montlhéry. Again MG gained publicity and prestige when the K.3 Magnette won the six-hour 1933 event under the talented guidance of Tazio Nuvolari while Hamilton's J.4 Midget romped in a close second. (The 1933 TT was an exceptional race for Nuvolari too—never before or since did the great Italian race in a British car!) The MG works, naturally, had looked forward to a repeat performance by the K.3, so the ban on superchargers was a double blow because the abrupt announcement came less than six months before the 1934 Race.

No competition event, on the British sports car calendar was more important than the Tourist Trophy Race, which was held annually on the Ards circuit near Belfast. Charles, Jackson, Enever, Cousins and company subjected the 1,271 N-Type Magnette engine to every power-increasing development available. The compression ratio was increased to 9.8:1, and extremely painstaking machining of the head and block eliminated the need for a head gasket. A strengthened version of the close-ratio gearbox, used with the KB engine, was mated to a two-plate, heavy-duty clutch. Large, 1½-inch dual SU carburetors, increased valve overlap, a re-

serve oil supply, enlarged cooling capacity, and all reciprocating parts balanced and matched, were other modifications increasing engine speed by as much as 1,400 rpm. This produced a consistent 74.3 rpm at 6,500 rpm.

To decrease the weight and reduce wind resistance, lean, boat-tailed, two-seater aluminum bodies lacking even MG's traditional double-cowl scuttle were built. Double shock absorbers were used all around, the N-Type 12-inch brakes remained, and unusually wide and flared cycle-type mudguards were the final and very attractive touch. Despite occasional claims to the contrary, exactly seven NE Magnettes were built during the first half of 1934. Six of them were licensed and given the registration numbers JB4606, JB4607, JB4608, JB4748, JB4749 and JB4750. The first three cars were the private entries of Hamilton, Nuvolari and Norman Black, while the last three cars comprised the MG factory team and were scheduled to be driven by Captain George Eyston, Wal Handly and Charlie Dodson. NE Magnette JB4607, illustrated here (and powered since 1936 with a modified K.3 engine), has been owned for some time by Mr. and Mrs. Pete Thelander of California.

Driven in the 1934 Tourist Trophy Race by Bill Everitt instead of Nuvolari—a disagreement between the noted Italian and the MG Car Company caused the change—JB4607 was in third place at about half-time when a wheel collapsed and forced the bright red machine to retire from the field. The NE driven by Dodson, however, upheld the honor of MG and won the race by a scant 17 seconds. Dodson defeated several large and heavy "sporting lorries," including a Bentley, a pair of Lagondas, a leaner Aston-Martin and assorted other competition sports cars. Thus the NE won the important race for which it was specially constructed under the pressure of necessity.

A trio of NE Magnettes, one of them the winner of the 1934 Tourist Trophy, was equipped with K.2 bodies. Known as the "Three Musketeers," Welch and MG works employees Kindell and Nash, driving these, took the team prize in the Welsh Rally (which Nash won overall). The "Musketeers" also placed well in the 1935 London to Land's End

The victorious MG in the 1934 Ulster Tourist Trophy Race, old JB4750. In the late 1940s, new coachwork was fitted. (Photo by Robert L. Knudson, courtesy of Mrs. & Mrs. S. Peter Thelander)

Sorting out the Magnas and Magnettes is always a challenge. Though not identified, this old factory photo is believed to be that of a KN Magnette pillarless saloon, the oddly conceived K-Type with the 1,286 cc. engine of the N-Type. (The M. G. Car Company, Ltd.)

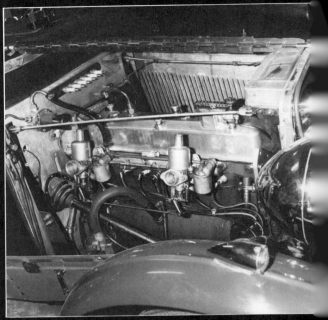

Trial, the event which had put MG on the motor sports map ten years earlier.

The advent of what became known as the NA engine enabled MG to give the K-Type a renewed lease on life late in 1934. So it was that an interesting K-Type Magnette saloon was introduced with the N-Type engine and gearbox. It seems that the MG purchasing department got carried away and, in a burst of over-optimism late in 1932, ordered more pillarless saloon bodies than K-Type production could accommodate. Now, nearly two years later, MG had around two hundred of these attractive bodies in storage, already mounted on the 108-inch-wheelbase K.1 chassis. Between October 1932 and March 1934, K-Type saloon sales had not lived up to expectations. Would the more powerful NA engine stimulate sales?

Deciding that there was little to lose, Kimber directed engineering to replace the 1,087 cc. KA and KB engines and gearboxes with the 56.6 bhp, 1,271 cc. NA power trains. Exhibited as the KN Magnette in the 1934 Motor Show, with additional body trim, dual-tone finish and badge bar, the outcome was most encouraging. The motoring press, always happy to have a new model to test, reported that the KN—never mind the confusion of the combined designation—had a maximum

speed of 75-plus mph, and could accelerate from zero to 60 mph in about 28 seconds. The improved performance was well accepted and, within one year, approximately two hundred KN Magnette pillarless saloons were sold—making KN the best-selling of all K-Types (and solving the problem of the surplus saloon bodies). The KN was popular, and a few were sold outside the United Kingdom; the October 1974 issue of *Safety Fast* reported the discovery of one in Sweden.

With the above sojourn back to the K-Type via the N-Type, the sorting out of the Magnas and Magnettes is virtually concluded. One little matter remains: there was another batch of surplus bodies (with two-seater open coachwork) that had been built for the K.2 chassis which was less than 2 inches shorter than the N-Type chassis. Regrettably, the short wheelbase K.2 two-seaters had a downright depressing sales record—only about 20 found buyers during the production period, which lasted from February 1933 to the end of that year.

Because of the modus operandi applied to the designation of the KN Magnettes, one might assume that the much-improved N-Type chassis would be fitted with the 40 surplus K.2 bodies, and that the Type designation would be NK. Right? Half right: the K.2 bodies were

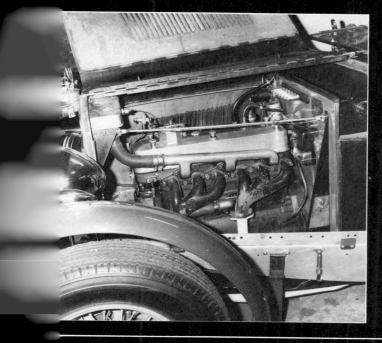

Owner/restorer Miles Fenton often races his potent ND Magnette in vintage races, despite the car's advanced age.

Top; L. to R. The cockpit of Fenton's ND. Note profuse application of MG octagons on the panel, grip for a riding mechanic, instruments, gear change gate and remote tube, and on bell housing.

The starboard side of the 70 bhp, 1,286 cc. engine. Note the spare sparking plugs on firewall, customary spares.

Port side of the spick-and-span engine room. Note the small panel, lower right, with lubrication fittings.

A Marshall 75 supercharger, with which Fenton's ND develops 95 bhp at 6,000 rpm. (Joseph H. Wherry photos)

Produced as a two-seater sports car on an N-Type chassis with K.2 coachwork, many ND Magnettes were raced. Few remain. (Joseph H. Wherry photo)

fitted successfully to the N-Type chassis, but alphabet and logic went out the window. The new N-Type variant became the ND (there was no NC), and research does not disclose the reason, if any.

The ND Magnette sold well and 12 are known to have survived in various states of health. One of them, still vigorous and vital, lives in British Columbia. Its owner/restorer lavishes tender care and provides regular exercise on the vintage racing circuits. The slab-tanked, two-seater body (one of the 40 K.2 bodies) is polished aluminum, with bonnet top and mudguards of British racing green. Assigned vintage racing Number 6 graces each door and the bare honeycomb of the radiator core. According to the owner/restorer, the chassis frame was shortened by 12 inches and one cross-member. This was standard works practice when NA/NB chassis were reconfigured to the ND specification to accommodate the K.2 bodies. This ND is a restored original—not a modern replica.

To campaign the venues in the American West—from the Westwood Circuit near Coquitlam, British Columbia, to Laguna Seca in California—the ancient ND has been "breathed upon" by the owner with the same care as obtained during the golden age of the MG competition department in Abingdon. Be-

ginning with the engine, the cylinder head was shaved to raise the compression ratio from the standard NA/NB 6.1:1 to 7.5:1. This moderate increase permits supercharging and, therefore, is considerably lower than the 9.8 to 1 of the closely related NE. (The latter had been specially engineered for high performance, primarily to win one race.) The camshaft and valve gear are standard but the cylinder head is ported and polished, the crankshaft is balanced, and the piston/connecting rod assemblies are balanced and matched.

Standard carburetion called for a pair of 1⅛-inch semi-downdraft SUs, but owner Miles Fenton usually runs with two 1¼-inch SU carburetors. In such "tune," Fenton states the output to be 70 bhp at 5,500 rpm, a reasonable figure. The competition 8/39 (4.875 ratio) rear-axle gears are the same as were used on the NE and the Q and R-Type Midgets. Because the speed of the standard NA was on the order of a true 83 mph (and more than one lapped Brooklands at speeds close to 90 mph in "well tuned" form), Fenton's more powerful ND Magnette's top speed, sans the blower, should be at least 90 mph, with an acceleration from zero to 60 mph in around 17—18 seconds. Fenton, though, quotes no precise figures.

With the Marshall 75 Rootes-type supercharger ramming air into a single 1½-inch SU carburetor, Fenton states that the maximum output is 95 bhp at 6,000 rpm. (The author is of the opinion that Fenton's figures are quite modest in the light of MG's official maximum engine speed rating of the standard unblown NE, said to have been 6,500 rpm.) At speed, with the supercharger operating, Miles says, "At 6 to 10 psi, the maximum speed is about 100 mph, maybe a little bit more." The "little bit more" sounds about right to the author. Miles and his rare ND Magnette have "stayed with" a *grand prix* Bugatti and have been faster than a 1.5-litre Aston Martin Le Mans and a 2-litre BMW 328.

Sorting out the diverse models and variants is a labor of love to automobile enthusiasts. To the devotee of the *marque* MG, however, this self-assigned task is an especially pleasant affliction. When we approach the Magna and Magnette, we are faced with a challenge worthy of the venerable occupant of Baker Street. Sherlock Holmes, alas, never knew these fascinating motor cars.

No doubt many search-and-rescue missions concerning the subject Types of this chapter are enhanced by the confusion engendered when their sorting is attempted. Indeed, the Magna and Magnette Types are most intriguing vintage cars. But so are the S, V and W Types—as we shall see.

Miles Fenton and his competition ND Magnette in "the corkscrew" during a vintage race at Laguna Seca. (Courtesy: Miles Fenton; photo by D. M. Woodhouse)

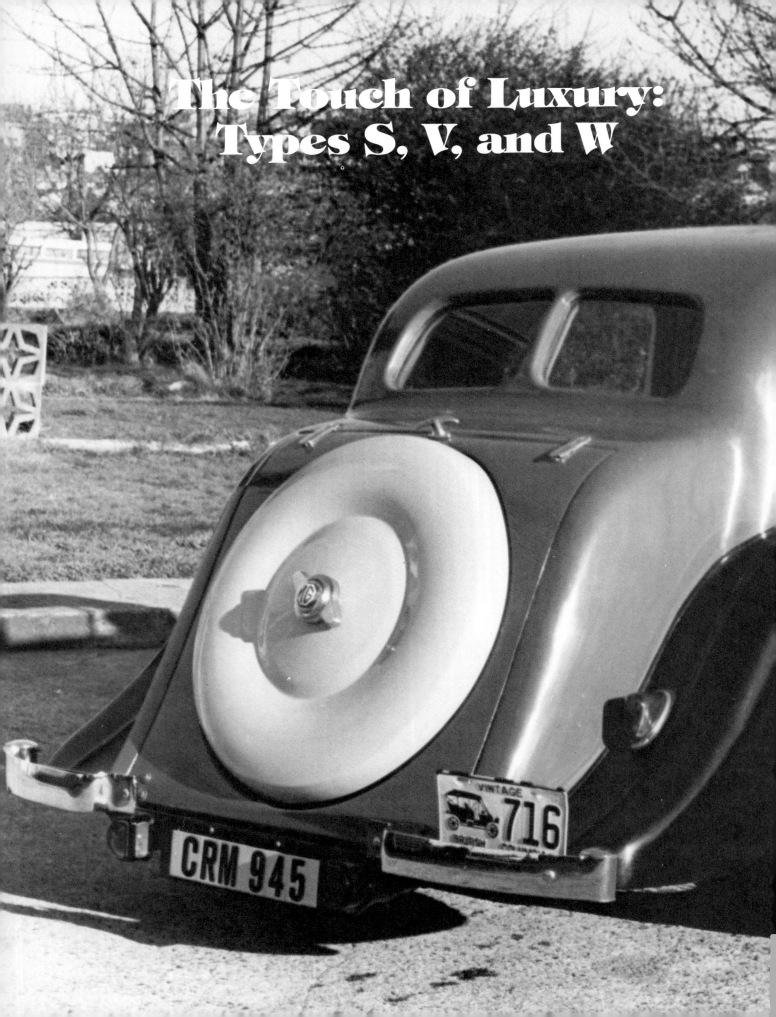

The Touch of Luxury:
Types S, V, and W

Chapter VI

MG SA 2-Litre sports touring cars were large and luxurious. Wheelbase is 123 inches. The saloon model. The owner/restorer is Victor Diggins of British Columbia. (Joseph H. Wherry photo)

When the corporate independence of The M. G. Car Company came to a precipitate end in the summer of 1935, Kimber and his ingeniously innovative staff—the entire Abingdon works, in reality—were stunned. Not only was factory-sponsored (read *financial*) racing brought to an abrupt end, but several far-sighted projects were consigned to oblivion—not even the back burner remained within reach. As mentioned previously, H. N. Charles quit and nearly every key assistant to Kimber, in the rise of MG as a *marque*, either resigned to go elsewhere or was discharged.

This disorganization, usually referred to as the "Nuffield takeover," came about because Lord Nuffield (Sir William Morris previously had been created a baronet by King George V) sold The M. G. Car Company, Ltd., to Morris Motors. MG had remained under his sole proprietorship since the W. R. Morris Motor Company issued stock and went public in 1926. The relationship between MG in Abingdon and the public Morris organization remained cordial, and MG continued to buy in components and parts as necessity required. When Lord Nuffield, who was Chairman of the Board at Morris Motors, cracked down on MG's racing activities in mid-1935, however, and sold The M. G. Car Company, Ltd., to Morris Mo-

tors, MG became a subsidiary. The word came down to Kimber's office that subsequent MG cars should cease to be as specialized as they had become after the introduction of the M-Type Midget. Sports car racing was anathema to the board over which Lord Nuffield presided—he seemed to have forgotten his own early fascination with, and participation in, motor sports.

In fairness, liability rates were high, and MG's concentration on sports cars to the exclusion of other types did seem to result in a decrease in sales after M-Type production ended in mid-1932. Kimber stayed on as manager and Syd Enever remained in the engineering office. The overhead camshaft P-Type Midgets and N-Type Magnettes remained in production, but clearly something had to be done or the *marque* created by Kimber would not survive. To keep things in perspective, one must remember that many components—particularly engines—had always been obtained from the related Morris companies. Notwithstanding the "tuning" and the even more extensive power-increasing modifications created by MG, there had been an air of independence. This would end and new MG models would, henceforth, be the result of financial and engineering liaison to a markedly increased extent. One of the first fruits of the latter dictum was that the days of the overhead-camshaft engines were numbered; they were complicated and required expert maintenance, which was considerably over the heads of the majority of owners.

So it was that when the new MG SA 2-Litre was introduced at the annual Motor Show in October 1935, hard-core enthusiasts were scandalized. Other segments of the motoring public, however, eagerly greeted the first big MG since the effective demise of the 18/80 Six models in 1931. Of course, the 18/80 Six Mark II Type A had struggled along with extremely low production until mid-1933, but MG's popular image had become that of a small sports car since the autumn of 1928.

MG had come full circle with the SA 2-Litre, which was a commercial success. The car filled a gap in the product line of what was becoming known as the "Nuffield Organisation," and enabled MG to gain a share of the market held by prestigious medium-level family sports saloons, tourers and coupés. These included Alvis, Humber, Riley, Sunbeam, SS (which later became Jaguar due to the unpalatability of the initials during World War II), and several other makes catering to buyers who demanded larger, more refined cars. Between introduction and August 1939, production numbers of the SA compared favorably with certain models of the named competitive *marques*.

The features of the new SA 2-Litre which offended MG purists began with the vast wheelbase of 123 inches. The frame was built up of box-section steel, rather than MG's traditional channel members, but the tubular cross members were familiar, as was the non-independent suspension by semi-elliptic leaf springs. The latter, however, were shackle-mounted rather than being secured by the traditional sliding trunnions. Luvax hydraulic shock absorbers were another logical touring car improvement. Large 12-inch brakes received approval by enthusiasts but they were hydraulically actuated Lockheeds, a system Kimber and his followers had always distrusted. Dual master cylinders took some of the ouch out of the grouch that such a concession to modernity produced, and happily the hand brake was the traditional fly-off type. An

hydraulic jacking system was standard equipment on the SA (and on the WA). When the prototype was first shown, bolt-on wheels caused another crisis of doubt among true believers, but their feelings were assuaged when proper centerlocking wires were used on production models.

Without doubt, the large engine stimulated the most anguish among the purists. MG was buying in and modifying the 2,062 cc. Wolseley Super Six engine. Gone was the overhead camshaft! In place of that delightful device were conventional pushrods operating the overhead valves—the first such engine on any MG chassis since *Old Number One*. The customary dual, semi-downdraft, 1¼-inch SU carburetors were there, but compounding the effeteness was a combined air cleaner/silencer, which masked and hushed the wide-open carburetor intakes. There also was a full-flow oil filter. The SA's more tractable power plant still had a long stroke of 102 mm. with a decently discreet cylinder bore of 69 mm. giving a displacement of 2,288 cc. The compression ratio was 6.5 to 1. The fuel tank capacity was 10 Imperial gallons and the oil sump contained 10 quarts. This 2.3-litre engine was officially designated as the "Two Litre." Because of the increased engineering and production liaison with the Nuffield parent organization in Cowley, whence came the engines, the cylinder bore became minutely larger (about March of 1937), thus increasing the piston displacement to 2,322 cc. But the catalogue name "MG SA 2-Litre" was retained, as was the stated maximum output of 78.5 bhp at 4,200 rpm.

Behind the 2.3-litre engine that carried the "2-Litre" name was a single-plate, cork-lined clutch in an oil bath and a tough, non-synchromesh, four-speed gearbox. The propeller shaft was open, had Hardy-Spicer universal joints, and the final drive was by spiral bevel gears; two alternate ratios were eventually offered. When the displacement was moderately increased (as mentioned), synchromesh was provided on the top two gear ratios. Of course, this compromise provoked more criticism among those sports car enthusiasts who insisted that this touring improvement was confirmation that MG was ruining its specialist

Opposite: An SA 2-Litre tourer, with coachwork by Charlesworth, owned by Peter Welch of British Columbia. An indigenous Indian totem pole is in the background.

Above, L. Leather upholstery is original in this SA tourer. Note wiper motor by Lucas at left base of folding windscreen.

Above, R. MG SA 2-Litre. A cylindrical air cleaner/silencer unti lies on top of dual SU carburetors. Exhaust is on same side of engine as intake. (Joseph H. Wherry photos)

car image. On the side of tradition, the faithful had a point, but the practical side was that the more than 5,500 S, V and W sports touring types enabled MG to survive as a distinctive *marque* during a particularly difficult period of economic stress.

As might be expected, the SA four-door saloon—said to have been a Kimber design—weighed some 3,300 pounds at the curb, while the elegant four-door Charlesworth tourer weighed about 30 pounds more. Lightest of the SA models, at about 3,050 pounds, was the beautiful drophead coupé by Tickford. Upon introduction, the SA saloon's price was just £375, £24 less than the best-selling Magnette saloon, the KN. Variations in the Charlesworth bodies existed, with deep cuts in the front doors and side-mounted spare wheels, which gave a very sporting appearance in some tourers. Other Charlesworth bodies featured a straight, unbroken horizontal line across the doors and a high belt-line molding, which was lacquered in colors

to match the skirted fenders. More formal-appearing, the latter styling characterizes the Charlesworth tourer (illustrated here), which has a single rear-mounted spare wheel. Tickford coachwork, on the other hand, offered little variation and door sills were straight (as pictured in this volume on the WA drophead). Some Tickfords mounted the spare wheel externally.

Readers who have never examined the hoods (convertible tops) that graced the quality coachwork associated with such firms as Tickford, Charlesworth and others, should avail themselves of the opportunity at old car shows. Although tourers and dropheads usually are shown with hoods folded, they are as warm and quiet as closed sedans when the hoods are raised because they have headliners. Charlesworth ceased coachbuilding activities sometime early in 1939; consequently, the drophead was not available during the last months of production before the war. Tickford, however, built bodies for MG and other car manufacturers right up to the outbreak of war and, from 1946 on, Tickford coachwork again graced fine British cars and was introduced into the USA on the Alvis and several other makes.

The WA, introduced in the October 1938 London Motor Show, could have been an answer to a car manufacturer in Coventry crypt-

ically known as S.S. Cars, Ltd. (remember Jaguar?), whose 2.5-Litre "Super Sports" saloons (actual displacement was 2,663.7 cc.) had complicated MG's sales efforts since early in 1936. Bored out to 73 mm., the engine displacement became 2,561 cc. Called the WA 2.6-Litre, the output was 95–100 bhp at 4,400 rpm. The extra power was needed because curb weights were upwards of 3,600 pounds. Other changes were 3¾ inches wider rear

Opposite, top: Saloon-bodied SA 2-Litre carries spare wheel in lid of luggage boot.

Opposite, bottom: All-leather interior of the four-seater SA saloon car.

Above, R. Ignition side of the engine in an SA 2-Litre saloon owned and restored by Victor Diggins of British Columbia. A cylindrical air-cleaner/filter cannister extends across the rocker cover. (Joseph H. Wherry photos)

tread and larger, 14-inch brake drums. The wheelbase and front tread remained the same as the SA, but the wider rear tread of the WA permitted increased rear-seat width. The saloon cost £442, the Charlesworth tourer £450, and the drophead Tickford coupé just under £470. When Charlesworth stopped coachbuilding, only nine tourers had been built.

The long stroke, low-speed engines of the SA 2-Litre and WA 2.6-Litre cars enabled them to amble along at 10–12 mph in top gear on level roadways. Smooth drivers could accelerate either of these large cars in top gear to cruising speed if traffic conditions did not necessitate changing to lower ratios. Both models had maximum speeds of slightly more than 85 mph.

Softer-riding than were any of the traditional MG sports cars, both the SA and the WA required more space to maneuver, with turning circles of 40 and 41 feet, respectively. Steering locks were 2½ turns and, once under way, this facilitated road manners despite overall lengths in excess of 16 feet. An SA was entered in the April 1937 Mille Miglia in Italy by Tommy Wisdom and his wife. They were well placed, with a high average speed, until an accident on a rain-slick mountain road put them out of the race. The SA is said to have enjoyed some success as a rally car in several club events.

As these were luxurious family cars, SA and WA coachwork featured the finest hardwoods on instrument panels and window surrounds; top quality leather upholstery was used in all models. A number of the four-door models, mostly the SA, served as military staff cars during the war.

Because of the similarity of the SA and WA, they have been discussed together. The other comparatively large MG of the period was the VA. Although announced in the proper MG Type alphabetical order in the autumn of 1936, the VA did not reach production until April 1937—or about four months after the last of the smaller Magnette four-seaters was phased out of production. There was a need for a mid-sized MG to fill the wide gap between the SA and the new TA Midget, which entered production in July 1936 and will be detailed in the next chapter. Astonishingly, the new VA pushrod-operated, overhead-valve engine's displacement was identical to that of "Old Number One"—1,548 cc. The VA engine, like that of the SA/WA models, was bought-in from Wolseley Motors, by that time well established as a division of the Nuffield Organisation and the source of MG engines since the inception of the Magnas and Magnettes. In many respects, the VA was a smaller version of the SA luxury models from the box-section construction of the chassis frame with

Owned by Malcolm Robertson, President of the MG Car Club in Canberra. The chassis, SA/1787, was imported to Australia by the late Dr. William Airy in 1937. Unique coupé coachwork is by Martin and King of Melbourne. (Courtesy: Malcolm Robertson)

shackled leaf springs, Luvax hydraulic shock absorbers, and the integral hydraulic-jacking system (illustrated here). The Lockheed hydraulic brakes were by 10-inch drums and, interestingly, the center-lock wire wheels had reverted to the old and popular 19-inch diameter.

Similarly, the 4-cylinder engine was two-thirds that of the 2,322 cc. SA engine with the same compression ratio and 69.5 and 102 mm. bore-and-stroke for a displacement of 1,548 cc. Larger 1⅜-inch SU carburetors were used with an improved air cleaner and silencing unit. Maximum output was 55 bhp at 4,400 rpm. With precise tuning made all the easier with the less fussy pushrod-operated overhead valves, the engine speed could be moderately increased to around 4,800 rpm. Initially, an oil bath cork-faced "wet" clutch was fitted but, within a few months, a more suitable dry clutch was standardized. Synchromesh on all but first gear was standard from the first models, and the ratios were close. The VA gearbox was shared with the TB Midget (see next chapter), both types being simultaneously in production.

In the author's opinion, the VA has had more than its share of undeserved criticism. Restorer/owners of this MG model defend their vehicles and hasten to point out that, had pro-

duction not been terminated by Hitler's war, the VA would have earned its rightful place as the worthy successor to the K.1 and KN Magnette four-seaters, which also sat on 108-inch-wheelbase chassis and rode on 19-inch wheels. Front and rear tread of the VA was 50 inches and the turning circle was 38 feet.

The basic VA was the open two-door four-seat tourer priced at £280 and weighing just under 2,470 pounds at the curb. The doors were deeply cut with styling nearly identical to some of the seldom-seen SA tourers with cut-down doors. The 2,690-pound saloon cost £325, while the 2,800-pound Tickford coupé cost just £10 more than the saloon. An indication of the attractiveness of the VA Tickford can be gained by examining the WA Tickford. By mid-1939, the prices had escalated some £10 to £25 for each model.

Telescoping steering column by Bluemel, with 2½ turns lock-to-lock, adjustable brake pedals and shock absorbers (the latter by a patented "Finger Tip Control"), and instrumentation as complete as the T-Types, which later introduced motor sports to America, were all standard equipment. A very complete selection of tools contained in a moulded tray inside the luggage-boot door on the closed models, fine leather upholstery over soft cushions, and good hip and leg space made the

VA a good value in the sports touring car market.

Performance and roadability received the fairly enthusiastic approval of the road test staff of *The Motor* in the July 1937 issue. With the windscreen folded, a timed speed of 81.82 mph was recorded. Acceleration from start to 50 mph through the gears was brisk, and required but 15.8 seconds. Not even the overhead-camshaft KN or NA/NB models did any better (nor did most stock TC Midgets without professional "tuning" a decade later).

The VA tourer found favor with several police departments. Bored out to 73 mm. and fitted with high-lift camshafts, counter-balanced crankshafts, and special connecting rods and pistons, the special TPBG engines had displacements of 1,707 cc. and developed 63 bhp at 5,000 rpm, certainly sufficient for more than 90 mph.

The SVW range came along at a time of corporate reorganization complicated by an economic slump, the Munich crisis and other international tensions. MG sales abroad were accounting for 15–20 percent of total production during those troubled times. Under more favorable circumstances, the VA almost certainly would have entered the overseas market along with the contemporary T-Types. (Such a sporting four-seater, just 172 inches long overall, would sell well today.) As it is, the SVW models are rarely seen. In many respects—and this is aside from the all-out MG sports cars—they were the finest of their *marque*. Their quality would not be seen again in any series of MG family cars. *Eheu, fŭgax!*

Calvin Tilden's MG WA 2.6-Litre Tickford coupé. The patented Tickford bodies were built by Salmons of Newport. (Joseph H. Wherry photos)

A. The manufacturer's chassis number is VA/2202 and the special 1,707 cc. Police Engine is indicated by the TPBG 2463 on the plate. Tourer tool boxes, seen at top, were beneath engine bonnets; engine crank is alongside box.

B. Usually overlooked among enthusiasts, the MG VA was a beautifully built and comfortable car. Note that the parking brake lever is located on passenger's side of transmission tunnel.

C. Built-in hydraulic jacking was standard equipment on the MG VA 1½-Litre touring sports cars. The jacking pedestal is the light-colored vertical object. (Joseph H. Wherry photos)

The MG VA 1½-Litre tourer. The owner is Bill Daugherty of Oregon. (Joseph H. Wherry photo)

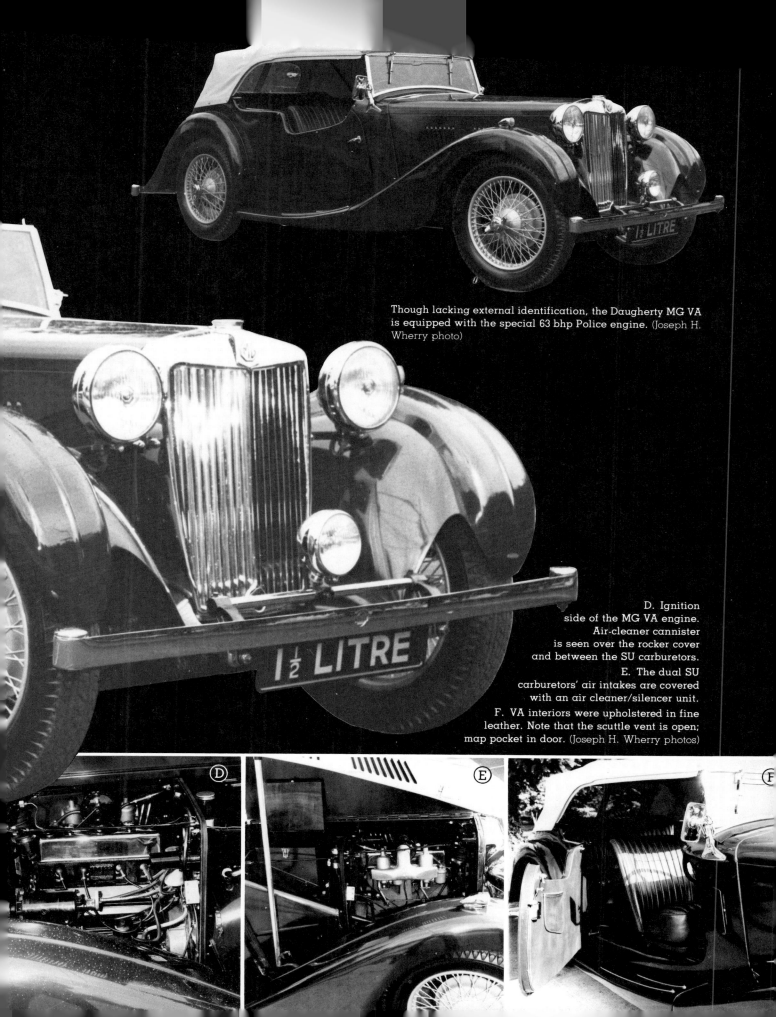

Though lacking external identification, the Daugherty MG VA is equipped with the special 63 bhp Police engine. (Joseph H. Wherry photo)

1½ LITRE

D. Ignition side of the MG VA engine. Air-cleaner cannister is seen over the rocker cover and between the SU carburetors.

E. The dual SU carburetors' air intakes are covered with an air cleaner/silencer unit.

F. VA interiors were upholstered in fine leather. Note that the scuttle vent is open; map pocket in door. (Joseph H. Wherry photos)

Ⓓ

Ⓔ

Ⓕ

Magic Midget, Humbug and Other Record Breakers

Chapter VII

The EX.127 *Magic Midget*, Captain George Eyston driving, gets a typical push-start at Montlhéry for a record run. (British Motor Corporation, Ltd.)

Thus far we have considered only one of the several "EX" numbered specials, which won numerous international records for MG. The Type M Midget-based EX.120 set many records with Captain George Eyston at the wheel and (as related in Chapter III) put its driver in the hospital at the conclusion of one such run in the spring of 1931.

George E. T. Eyston was a durable and interesting personality in his own right and a brief look at his career is enlightening. Born June 28, 1897, in Oxfordshire, he was attending Stonyhurst School when World War I erupted. Barely 17 years of age, young George left school and joined the colors. Eyston served with the Dorset Regiment, earned a commission, became aide-de-camp to General Wellesley and was wounded in the Battle of Arras in April 1917. (April seemed to be a key month for Eyston.) Emerging from the 1914–1918 war as a captain in the Royal Artillery, Eyston wore the Order of the British Empire and the Military Cross when he enrolled in Trinity College, Cambridge, where he earned his engineering degree.

Upon graduation, Eyston organized his own engineering firm and became involved in Power Plus Compressors, manufacturers of the superchargers bearing the same name. By 1923, Eyston was active in racing and drove

an Aston Martin in the Easter Meeting at Brooklands. Bugatti was another favored mount, but he also drove a Delage (in which he had another narrow squeak with fire during a record attempt). Before and interspersed with his MG adventures, other *marques* driven by Eyston were Alfa Romeo, Chrysler (in which he broke the Class C 24-Hours record), Riley, Hotchkiss and Panhard-Levassor. In the latter, an 8-litre monster, Eyston would set a new World Hour Record at 130.73 mph in April 1932. Always participating actively in an engineering role, and being an innovator as well, Eyston installed an 8.85-litre AEC diesel engine in a Chrysler Imperial chassis and drove a two-way flying kilometre on Brooklands at 104.86 mph. This was before there was an official international diesel class.

When the EX.120 was wrecked, Eyston's team brought the car's remains back to Abingdon, salvaged usable parts, and began to build a new car designed expressly for him — although he was still hospitalized. The new EX.127 body was slender and the cockpit would be a tight squeeze for Eyston. Off-center and near the left rear wheel, as in the EX.120, the location of the differential would enable the driver and engine to be reasonably centered. In fact, the entire power train (engine and supercharger drive, gearbox and propeller shaft) was offset 7 degrees longitudinally from the center line. With the seat of his pants a scant 6 inches from the roadway, the driver would sit beside the propeller shaft. Completed late in September 1931, the EX.127 was shipped to France.

Early in October, the crew readied the EX.127 at Montlhéry. There the consulting engineer, Ernest Eldridge, shorter and of greater girth than Eyston, had himself inserted into the EX.127. Years before Eldridge had lost the sight of one eye. Despite such a handicap for high-speed driving, Eldridge had been Eyston's assistant on many previous record runs. During May 28 to June 4 in 1930, Eyston and Eldridge drove a Riley Monaco to at least nine International Class G records at Montlhéry. Thus, intimately familiar with the famous circuit, Eldridge made several runs around the course. Then, exchanging signals with the crew, he opened up the Magic Midget and broke the Class H 5-kilometre record at 110.28 mph, a courageous feat. Finally fully recovered, Eyston arrived at Montlhéry in December and, defying the ice, took four records at 114 mph.

Next, the two-miles-in-a-minute goal spurred on the entire company and, in February of 1932, Kimber and the competition department personnel were on the smooth, wintry seashore near Pendine in Wales. A new three-piece windshield, steeply raked and with a curious horizontal open slit, had been fabricated after extensive consultations with aerodynamicists about the problem of obscured vision caused by seashore spray and mist at high speeds. And, to further decrease wind resistance, the full belly pan was given a new contour and all external bolts and rivets were streamlined.

At Pendine, the smooth sands were encouraging, but the tides were bothersome. Although the battery of stopwatches indicated that Eyston had topped 120 mph by a clear margin, the efforts lacked complete success when the official timing equipment malfunctioned and the average computed speed was 118.39 mph. This was a world Class H record for a 750 cc. car, but short of the magic two miles in one minute target. In a mood as dismal as the weather, the car was transported and the crew left the wintry Welsh coast.

Eyston and company returned to Montlhéry in December 1932 with the EX.127—by then dubbed "Magic Midget"—and soon gained the Flying Kilometre and Flying Mile records at 120.56 mph, and all the others up to 10 Kilometres. All of the targeted records were shattered. These victories were followed by Eyston on a specially groomed J.3 Midget, with which he broke the 24 Hour and 2,000 Kilometre records at more than 70 mph. Then, co-driving in alternating four-hour shifts with another accomplished competition driver, Bert Denly, Eyston put in another 24 hours on the EX.127. On this grueling stint, they averaged 86.67 mph and completed the conquest of International Class H records for MG. The events of December 1932 at Montlhéry would make a classic film of those incomparable men in their Midget speedsters. Christmas of 1932 was glorious and happy at the works. The press was generous with praise for MG and, as a result, overseas sales began to increase with the new year.

After a complete overhaul at Abingdon and construction of a new and even slimmer body too scant for Eyston, EX.127 was taken to Montlhéry where Denly drove the now famous "Magic Midget" to new Flying Mile and Flying Kilometre records at 128.6 mph. EX.127 was then purchased by Bobby Kohlrausch, a German driver of note, who broke the Flying Mile record with over 130 mph in Hungary in 1935. The EX.127 became an object of considerable technical interest to the Germans, and Kohlrausch had a bronze cylinder head made in Germany. The new head and other modifications raised the brake horsepower to 146 at 7,500 rpm with a new supercharger running at high pressure. In 1936, Kohlrausch raised the Flying Mile at Frankfurt to 140.6 mph, after which the EX.127 underwent more technical investigation by German engineers. The "Magic Midget" never returned to England.

Breaking records was becoming a pleasant MG habit, so when George Eyston ordered a car with which to assault Class G records—many of which he and Eldridge had taken on the Riley Monaco in 1930—Kimber provided generous assistance. A new K.3 en-

The EX.135 in 1934, when the official MG brown-and-cream stripes caused it to be dubbed *Humbug* during the period when it won 12 International Class G records. EX.135 was also called *Magic Magnette*. Note octagonal shape of nose scoop. (British Motor Corporation, Ltd.)

gine with a higher pressure Powerplus supercharger was installed in an underslung frame generally like that of the K.3. But with box-section rails rather than channels, the new EX.135 was actually a further development of the famed Magnette racer (see Chapter III). The power train was angularly offset 6 degrees and the driver's seat, as in the EX.127, was sandwiched between the propeller shaft and the frame side.

The fabrication of the EX.135 was as frought with humorous incidents as with technical problems. Designing the tiny record car around the owner was a literal necessity. Consequently, Eyston came to the works for frequent "fittings"—as is so aptly put by John Thornley in his *Maintaining The Breed*. (Thornley's account of the remarkable career of EX.135 is so extensive—and often hilarious—that interested readers are advised to consult this classic work.) Nicknamed "Humbug" because of its striped paint job in the official cream and brown MG colors, the EX.135 was also called "Magic Magnette," a sobriquet which the car paid off handsomely.

With Eyston driving, the EX.135 broke the Class G records for the Flying Mile and Flying Kilometre at 128.69 mph, the Ten Mile record at 128.5 mph, the One Hour record with 120.88 miles, and other Class G records for a total of

12 victories in 1934. Eyston also drove the EX.135 in the Mannin Beg Race in the Isle of Man, where he came in third overall and established a new Class G record, then won outright the British Empire Trophy Race, in which an MG team won the Team Prize. In 1935, when the Morris ban was dropped on MG works-sponsored competition, Eyston sold EX.135 to Donald Letts, a racing driver. Meanwhile, in Italy, an astonishing thing had happened: Raffaele Cecchini, who had purchased a K.3 Magnette, thrashed the best the continent could muster and won the Italian 1,100 cc. championship, the first time ever for a foreign car.

Late in 1937, Cecil Kimber got together with Lieutenant Colonel Goldie Gardner, a war veteran of the Royal Flying Corps who, like Eyston, had turned to motor racing. Gardner had established many records with a K.3 Magnette—the Flying Mile at more than 148 mph, for example. Together they decided that old EX.135 "Humbug", with a completely enclosed body, might attain 170 mph in Class G.

Gardner purchased the EX.135 and had it rebuilt at the works, where it was fitted with a streamlined body designed by Reid Railton. (Railton, incidentally, built fine cars under his own name from 1933 to 1949; they were based on modified Hudson chassis.) To decrease overall height, the driver laid on his back in a hammock-like seat. Further modified, the engine was fitted with a Centric supercharger.

Kimber, Gardner, his crew and the fully streamlined EX.135 then journeyed to a stretch of the German Autobahn near Frankfurt. There, on November 9, 1938, in two-way runs, flat out and experiencing problems with the blower, Gardner attained an average of 187.62 mph. This was a new Class G record and well over the goal of 170 mph. In the spring of 1939, Gardner, along with the EX.135 "Magic Magnette" and its crew, returned to the Autobahn,

this time near Dessau. With the engine now modified upward into Class F, Gardner broke the Flying Mile and Flying Kilometre records at 203.5 mph.

After World War II, Gardner had EX.135 rebuilt again and the engine extensively modified, so that the number of operating cylinders could be varied for the task at hand. (This "new" idea from Cadillac has a long history!) For record runs in Class H in 1946, the EX.135 would run on all six cylinders. In 1947 the car ran on four cylinders and in 1949 on three cylinders in Class I. In 1950, all but two cylinders were blocked off and records fell to this fabulous MG in the 500 cc. Class J.

The EX.135 *Magic Magnette*, with a new streamlined body and extensive engine modifications, continued its career on the Utah salt flats with Lieutenant Colonel "Goldie" Gardner after World War II. (British Motor Corporation, Ltd.)

Such efforts were designated as British Motor Corporation Development Projects in 1951. (BMC was a post-war corporate evolutionary change affecting MG.) In that year a supercharged Type-TD engine was installed, and Gardner and the veteran EX.135 went to the Bonneville Salt Flats in Utah, where more records fell in Class F. Still other records were captured in Classes F and E when the car was powered with a 2-litre Jaguar engine. In 1953, 64-year-old Lieutenant Colonel A.T.G. "Goldie" Gardner and the 18-year-old MG EX.135 retired after they had swept five of the ten International Classes with the greatest speeds ever attained.

The EX.181 MG record car was driven to six International records and 254.9 mph on the Bonneville salt flats by Phil Hill. (British Motor Corporation, Ltd.)

The records set by the EX.135 in Utah in 1951 and 1952 are of special interest to Americans:

August 20, 1951, Class F (with MG TD engine)	50 kilometres	127.8 mph
	50 miles	130.6 mph
	100 kilometres	132.0 mph
	100 miles	135.1 mph
	200 kilometres	136.6 mph
	1 Hour	137.4 mph
August 18, 1952, Class E (with 2-litre Jaguar engine)	50 kilometres	143.2 mph
	50 miles	147.4 mph
	100 kilometres	148.7 mph
August 20, 1952, Class F (with MG TD engine)	5 miles	189.5 mph
	10 kilometres	182.8 mph

In the autumn of 1951, the EX.135 was exhibited in the Autorama in Los Angeles. (Joseph H. Wherry photo)

A year after Goldie Gardner retired, George Eyston was again piloting an MG record car, the EX.179. The lines were similar to those of the EX.135 and the suspension included many Type-TF components and one or two Type-VA parts. Coil springs were used in the front, semi-elliptics aft, all snubbed down tightly and controlled by friction shock absorbers. Several special engines were based upon the then-new TF powerplant. Fuels were even more exotic than those used by previous MG record cars.

A sprint engine developed 97.5 bhp at 6,500 rpm, while the less highly tuned endurance engine developed at 81 bhp at 5,500 rpm. Compression ratios ran as high as 11.8 to 1, in those relatively simple overhead-valve pushrod engines; they were not supercharged.

Eyston's co-driver for long-distance records was Ken Miles, who was known to all MG enthusiasts as a top sports car competitor. When the 12-hour ordeal was finished, the EX.179 had guaranteed massive publicity for MG by taking seven International Class F records, plus some 25 American records, with speeds consistently around 120 mph. The sprint engine was then installed, and with Miles in the cockpit, the EX.179 was push-started. The mean of the resulting 10-mile, two-way runs was a shattering 153.69 mph, for yet another Class F record.

Fitted with a new twin-overhead-camshaft engine, and supercharged, the EX.179 captured no fewer than 16 Class F records in 1956, and in 1957, with a prototype engine, the descendant of the EX.135 took nine major Class G records running both with and without the blower.

This series of successes did not conclude MG's record-breaking career. In 1957, the works équipe was back on the Utah sands with the EX.181, a rear-engined car powered with another prototype of the MGA twin-overhead-camshaft engine—this one fitted with a huge Shorrock supercharger. Stirling Moss drove the EX.181 and captured five records in Class F with speeds timed as high as 245.6 mph, on August 27. Two years later, in 1959, Phil Hill piloted the EX.181, with the engine bored out, over the Bonneville sands to shatter six more records in class E with a maximum recorded speed of 254.9 mph.

MG had come a long way since that contrary 18/100 Six Mark III blew up in 1930, and the EX.120 captured those first International Class records at Montlhéry. The new records would serve MG very well—indeed, into the 1980s.

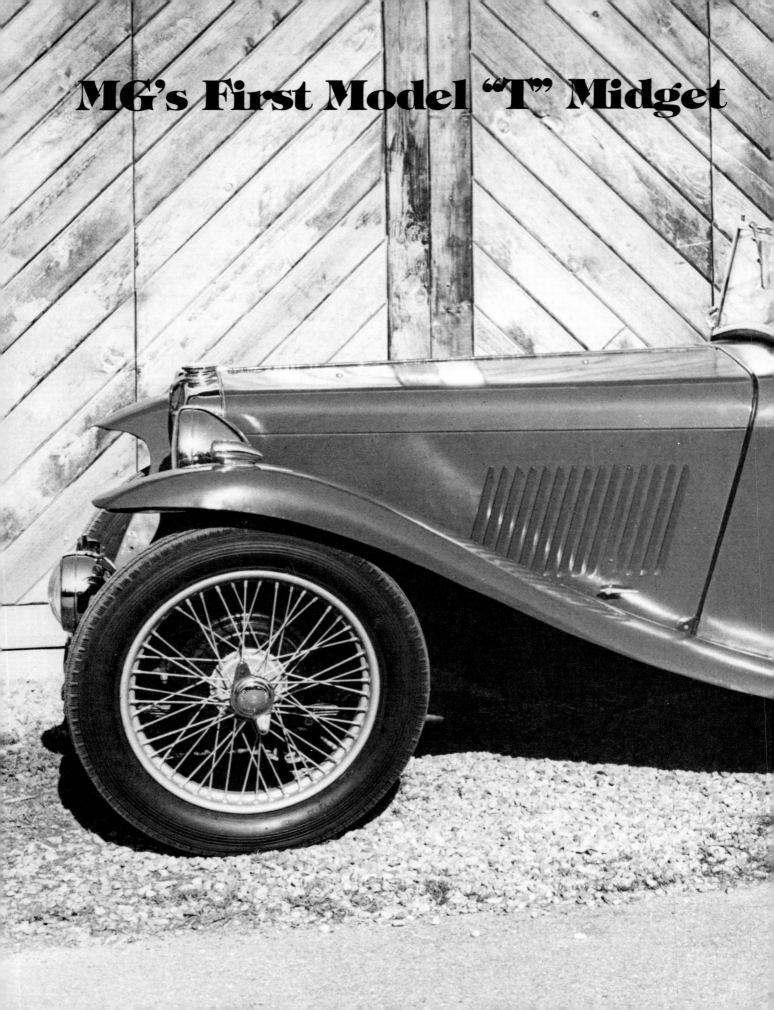

MG's First Model "T" Midget

Chapter VIII

Owner Colin Fitzgerald in his one-of-a-kind MG, the prototype TA Midget TA/0251. Note that the prototype does not have semaphore turn indicators, and that door has a slight curve in cut-out, but that outboard mounting of wire spokes is standard production. (Joseph H. Wherry photo)

For about three months during mid-1936, no Midgets were produced in Abingdon. This peculiar hiatus, following the end of PB Midget production in May, was occasioned by the sale of The M. G. Car Company, Ltd., to the Nuffield Organisation. The consequent loss of the autonomy prevailing as long as MG was owned solely by Lord Nuffield (the former W. R. Morris) resulted in increased coordination of engineering developments and products, which led to the MGSA, VA and WA models, already detailed.

MG enthusiasts have always been an articulate lot and especially so in the case of the Midgets. Changes have never been taken lightly and suggestions to the Abingdon works were considered quite seriously in the old days, at least. The works telephone number, Abingdon 251, was widely known and, despite the new and unaccustomed inability to act quickly, Kimber managed to prepare a prototype and to announce that there would be a replacement for the PB Midget, which, upon its own introduction, had received criticism from the irate hard core of enthusiasts. The June 1936 issue of *The Autocar* carried a brief description of the new "MG Midget Series T Two-Seater."

Examined from the front, the prototype TA/0251 looked very much like its predecessor

PB-Type. From the rear, however, the prototype TA Midget appeared altogether different. The expressions of agony—actually as traditional as the features the purists claimed were indispensable—have not been preserved in detail, but the lack of a slab-shaped fuel tank must have caused great consternation among the faithful who had a preview.

The prototype CJO618 (illustrated on these pages) bears the key TA/0251 chassis number and has survived to become the prized possession of a Canadian enthusiast. Rarest of all existing T-Type Midgets, the proto TA has full sheet metal across the rear of the coachwork concealing the fuel tank, and a P-Type instrument cluster. Prototypically, a few other differences are noticeable, the most evident being the lack of central ridges on the rear mudguards, which terminated in points at the rearmost flares on all production T-Type Midgets through the final TF in 1955. Production TAs did, however, have slab fuel tanks and the styling was traditionally Midget.

Looking back more than 40 years from the 1980s, the hue and cry that greeted the new production TA Midgets in July 1936 seems a bit overdone. After all, Midgets had always had overhead-camshaft engines of well under 1-litre displacement, and they were close-coupled with wheelbases of less than 88 inches—except for the exclusive few Q- and R-Type racers. The critics, therefore, felt justified with their list of engineering inequities.

Clearly the new TA seemed to be an L-Type Magna development rather than a Midget. The weight was the same as the L-Type's, the 94-inch wheelbase was almost the same, and the 45-inch tread was wider. The latter improvement permitted a wider, more spacious body. On cursory look, the frame appeared to be traditionally MG: the rear ends of the springs still slid in bronze trunnions, and the 19-inch, center-lock wire wheels were retained in all of their glory. Luvax hydraulic shock absorbers, though, had replaced the Hartford friction snubbers; 9-inch Lockheed hydraulic brakes had come to MG's sports cars, and box-section frame rails were used in place of the traditional channel sections. Higher ratio steering reduced the lock to a quicker and more sporting 1½ turns, but some critics feared that softer suspension and longer wheelbase might lead to four-seater tourers. Fortunately, this was not to be, because the previous Magna and Magnette four-seater Light Sixes had not sold all that well. That lesson had been learned by MG management even before Cowley tightened the leash on Abingdon's engineering department.

As if to allay purist suspicion, the new TA Midget soon proved to be one of only four MG types to surpass an annual prewar production rate of more than 1,000 cars. Interestingly, TA/TB Midgets edged out the M-Type to become the best-selling of all pre-war MGs. To Americans, such low production seems illogical. In pre-war Britain, however, many specialist *marques* persisted with no greater production than MG and enjoyed vigorous followings: Morgan, HRG, the chain-driven Frazer Nash (not related to the American make, Nash), Aston Martin, and even Triumph (which was taken over by Leyland in 1961, seven years before MG itself was swallowed). By the time MG was 10 years old, continental cars such as the French Amilcar and the Salmson were overshadowed on the British market by the M-, J- and P-Type MG Midgets. Clearly, Kimber's management had been fairly enlightened despite the criticism he was receiving in the board room in Cowley. To keep MG alive, Kimber was forced to make the best of things and cater to a wider, if allegedly less interesting, market.

Not only was the new TA Midget larger and, at about 1,765 pounds curb weight, some 114 pounds heavier than the replaced PB, but the larger 1,292 cc. engine delivered 52.4 bhp at 5,000 rpm—more powerful even if the overhead valves *were* pushrod-operated. Actually, the TA Midget engine was the 63.5 × 102 mm. Wolseley Ten unit and the pair of 1-inch-diameter SU carburetors were effectively muzzled by an air cleaner/silencer. Coil ignition was by Lucas, and the full-flow oil filter was the first on any standard production MG sports car. The first TAs had a quiet exhaust, a concession to an anti-noise campaign. Customer demand, however, necessitated some minimizing of the muffler restriction, and some of the "burble" was restored.

Initially TAs had crash-type gearboxes with single-plate, cork-faced clutches. After the first few hundred cars, the ratios were changed and synchromesh was employed on all but first gear. Early models had 12-gallon (Imp.) fuel tanks plus 3 in reserve; later this was reduced to 10½ plus 3. Other capacities were 7 quarts in the cooling system and 5½ quarts in the crankcase.

Widely read by enthusiasts, *The Light Car* editorialized on the deserved and rapid popularity of the TA despite scoffers, and the September 18, 1936, issue of *The Autocar* included a two-page road test. "A 'different' Midget, admittedly" said *The Autocar*, "but one with some distinctly practical features embodied, and giving plenty of performance in an interesting way." This important weekly reported quite decent performance in some three hundred test miles, during which the testers achieved 27—29 miles per Imperial gallon, and a maximum timed speed of 79.65 mph over a quarter-mile with windscreen folded. The importance of the latter is emphasized by a maximum of 73.77 mph with the windscreen raised. Maximum gear speeds were 23 mph in first, 39 mph in second and 61 mph in third gear. The gear change lever—short, firm and operating through remote rods as in previous

From this angle, the first of all T-Type MGs looks like the famous post-war TC. Bonnet hinge is a piano type, like the PA/PB and previous MGs.

TA Midget prototype's rear mudguard crowns are smooth, lacking the central ridge of later T-Types; nor do they terminate in points. (Joseph H. Wherry photos)

MG models—provided improved control. Acceleration times from start to 50 and 60 mph were 15.4 and 23.1 seconds, respectively. All of *The Autocar* performance figures were "the means of several runs in opposite directions" with speedometer errors corrected.

Pound sterling—or dollar—the value of the TA was beyond doubt: £222 for the two-seater roadster compared to £280 for the counterpart N-Type Magnette, which remained in production until November 1936. Also available were the Tickford drophead for just under £270 and the Airline Coupé by Carbodies of Coventry for £295. Just one Airline body was fitted, but the Tickford Coupé was popular; neither would be offered after World War II. The additional 3 inches of body width was another improvement over the PA/PB.

TA owners continued the tradition of com-

peting in the "mud-plugging" trials and hill climbs; these activities ushered in the time of the relatively inexpensive "specials," which were seldom used for daily driving. Highly tuned and modified, the specials were rarely driven to events; rather, they were lashed onto trailers and towed. Abingdon built numerous modified TA roadsters; three of these were supercharged with Marshalls for the "Cream Crackers," and developed approximately 80 bhp. Several of the VA-Type special TPBG 1,707 cc. engines were installed in competition team cars—including several for the "Cream Crackers" that repeated their pre-

The prototype MG TA Midget, unrestored but operating, owned by Colin Fitzgerald of British Columbia. Note badge for New England T Register of MGCC on badge bar. (Joseph H. Wherry photo)

vious Team Championship victory. As with the larger VA tourers (Chapter VI), several police agencies purchased TA two-seaters equipped with the 1.7-litre TPBG engine. No official performance figures have been found for the Police TAs, but it is logical to assume flat-out performance to be around 100 mph.

Quietly and without fanfare, TA production ended in late April 1939. The TB Midget took its place with virtually no changes other than a new 1,250 cc. engine, which had a shorter stroke and larger cylinder bore. Parliament had increased the tax based upon the formula horsepower. Because the new XPAG engine's dimensions were 66.5 mm. bore and 90 mm. stroke, the TB was rated at 11 horsepower rather than 10 hp—as was the TA, whose bore was 63.5 mm. The larger cylinder

bore and the coming tax increase meant that buyers of the new TB Midget would pay more.

Visible differences between the 1,292 cc. TA and the 1,250 cc. TB were so slight as to pass without notice to all but the most observant. *Most* TAs had two chromed studs near the top on each side of the slab fuel tank, the TB's tank ends had only one stud. Close examination of the 19-inch, center-lock wire wheels will disclose another difference: TA wire spokes terminated toward the outer edges of the rims, whereas TB spokes were secured near the center of the wheel rims. A key word

Manufacturer's chassis plate shows (upper right corner) "Car No. TA/0251" designating this one-of-its-kind as the prototype of all TA, TB, TC, TD and TF Midgets. (Joseph H. Wherry photo)

L: Tool box on firewall is smaller than those in production TAs. Belt-driven dynamo is visible behind headlight in foreground.

R: Instrument layout of the prototype TA Midget is that of PB. Production models were much like the familiar TC. If appearance seems less than pristine, note that this 1936 MG has *not* been restored. (Joseph H. Wherry photos)

in pointing out the slight visible differences is *most;* these differences were common but not always consistent. For example, *most* TA roadsters had semaphore turn-signal indicators located in the cowl sides—while TB roadsters had none. As if to complicate identification, the Tickford drophead coupé bodies mounted on both TA and TB chassis had the turn semaphores. Beneath the bonnet were the important changes in the TB Midget—the true prototypical forerunner of the TC Midget, which introduced sports car fun to America.

The new XPAG engine, though of reduced displacement, was more sophisticated with counterbalanced crankshaft and larger 1¼-inch SU carburetors. Again, MG had come full circle: the XPAG was a modified Morris M.10 engine. Valve timing was modified and the tappet clearances were increased. Compression ratio was boosted to 7.3 to 1 and the belt-driven generator—introduced on the TA—was retained. Crankcase oil capacity was reduced to 4½ quarts. Maximum output was slightly increased to 54.4 bhp at 5,200 rpm and the better, closer ratio VA-Type gearbox (driving through a dry clutch) was mated to a lower 5.125 rear axle gears. Speed per 1,000 rpm was reduced slightly—to 15.8 mph in top gear—but total weight was about 30 pounds less. Performance was slightly improved, but

the outbreak of war cut production short and only 379 TB Midgets were produced, mostly open two-seaters more easily maintained and remarkably adaptable to radical modifications, the new XPAG engine would be the nucleus of MG into the mid-1950s.

When Kimber abruptly suspended production in September 1939, approximately 22,454 MGs had been built since the *marque* was conceived in Oxford some 16 years earlier. A way of life was ending, and nowhere was this more evident than in the MG works in Abingdon-on-Thames. Producing the implements of war for the defense of the realm became the order of the day. Even the days of Kimber's tenure were numbered, and MG catalogues never again listed a choice of coachbuilt bodies on sports car chassis bearing the octagon.

Rather than dwelling on the dismal wartime activities in Abingdon and then proceeding to the TC Midget, a brief consideration of the coachbuilders' skills is warranted due to currently increasing interest in collecting and restoring vintage cars.

Coachbuilders of the old school presided over their exclusive little worlds with all of the eccentric non-conformity of the great masters of the fine arts. In fact, when talented craftsmen succeeded in mastering the dozen or more specialties required in coachbuilding, they were entitled to call themselves "master coachbuilders," and to ply their trade with the prestige of artisans.

The present high cost of professional restoration of vintage car bodies becomes understandable with a brief consideration of the distinct crafts involved. In a nutshell, the

were attractive because of their lightness and quietness. However, they required much care and within a few years they deteriorated to worthlessness.

Well-formed aluminum or other light metal panel sheathing over the mitred, tongued-and-grooved, pegged, clamped and glued ash and similar hardwood body frames was another matter in the years before pressed steel bodies became virtually universal. Thus panel-beating became a valued skill (applied equally to the "wings" or fenders) and a fairly large industry was built around coachmaking—which required smithing, brass and nickel workers, platers, fitters, joiners who created the body interiors, wood finishers and varnishers, painters (Morgan sports cars were beautifully brush-painted by hand well into the 1960s), electricians, and upholstery work-

By comparing this view of a production TA Midget with side view of prototype TA/0251, one can observe differences in door tops: production TA has a straight door top, while prototype's door top is slightly curved. (British Motor Corporation)

sharply defined crafts, widely practiced until circa 1940, began with designing and pattern-making for the hardwood frame of the body, and progressed to wood-shaping, assembling and making the body frame. Descended from the coachbuilders of the Renaissance, who catered to the needs of the wealthy for luxurious enclosed bodies for horse-drawn vehicles, several of the firms specializing in car bodies had their origins in the early years of the nineteenth century. With the availability of aluminum and the other lightweight alloys as a result of World War I, metal panel beating skills became essential. For six or seven years after about 1924, leather- and fabric-covered coachwork—as was initially utilized on the M-Type Midget—enjoyed some popularity. The invention of the French coach-builder Weymann, the fabric or leather bodies

ers skilled with the finest textiles and leathers. Polishing was an honored trade in itself and, until around 1920, heraldic artists were in demand in the finest coachworks, such as those of Barker and Hooper, which had their beginnings in England in 1710 and 1805, respectively.

An enthusiast embarking upon the authentic restoration of a valued vintage machine of quality, such as an SA MG or a TA with Tickford drophead coupé coachwork, must either be a skilled craftsman or retain a professional. (In Chapter IV, coachwork in progress on a PA Midget is illustrated.)

MG restorers are fortunate in that patterns have been preserved and parts for the hardwood-framing and metal panels are available in kits with blueprints, a virtual necessity if one intends to accomplish an authentic restoration. MG aficionados are faced with this time-consuming and usually expensive routine with cars up to, and including, the TF 1500 Midgets in 1955.

When production ended on the mix of TB, SA, VA and WA models in September 1939, all parts, left-over sub-assemblies, tooling and jigs were stored in anticipation of contributing to the national defense. Without any assistance from the Nuffield boardroom—according to F. Wilson McComb, who worked a decade later for MG—Kimber characteristically exercised his initiative and sought military contracts. Soon the Abingdon works was manufacturing artillery shell racks, overhauling armored equipment (including Matilda tanks of "Waltzing Matilda" fame), and assembling trucks made in the USA.

One particularly difficult project which had stumped many larger firms—that of building fuselage nose sections for the RAF's Armstrong-Whitworth *Albemarle* reconnaissance bombers—was being successfully implemented. Apparently, succeeding where others had faltered, and doing so without cooperation, encouragement or forbiddance by the corporate parent in Cowley, brought condemnation upon Kimber. (The creative, innovative person is much feared in bureaucratic organizations.) A new managing director had taken charge of the Nuffield Organisation *after* Kimber had gotten his factory busy with military contracts, and this was seized upon as a convenient excuse to oust MG's creator. Conse-

quently, sometime in November 1941, Sir Miles Thomas told Kimber "that he had better look out for another outlet for his energies because he did not fit into the wartime pattern of the Nuffield Organisation," as he related later in his book, *Out On A Wing*.

Frangas non flectus!

Temporarily shocked, *broken* but *not bent*, Kimber left The M. G. Car Company, which he had created with the same enthusiastic initiative he had employed to create the *marque*. During 1942, Kimber was employed by the Messrs. Charlesworth, whose coachbuilding works he reorganized for essential military production. In 1943, Kimber joined the Specialoid Piston Company, Ltd., where his organizational and production talents were outstanding. His untimely death came in a railroad accident on February 4, 1945, in his 57th year.

Production of sports cars was resumed after the war and MG's "Model T," the T-Type, went on in the form of the TC Midget to do for sports-minded motorists what Henry Ford's "Model T" had done for people of modest means back when W. R. Morris was dreaming about building cars in his Morris Garages in Oxford.

This TB Midget with Tickford drophead coachwork was rescued from a scrap yard in 1964. Owner is Mr. Dave Dean, who restored chassis No. TB/0435 to road condition and used the TB Tickford as daily transport. Note that wire spokes' outer ends are secured in center of rim, one of the few differences with TA. (Courtesy: John Watts)

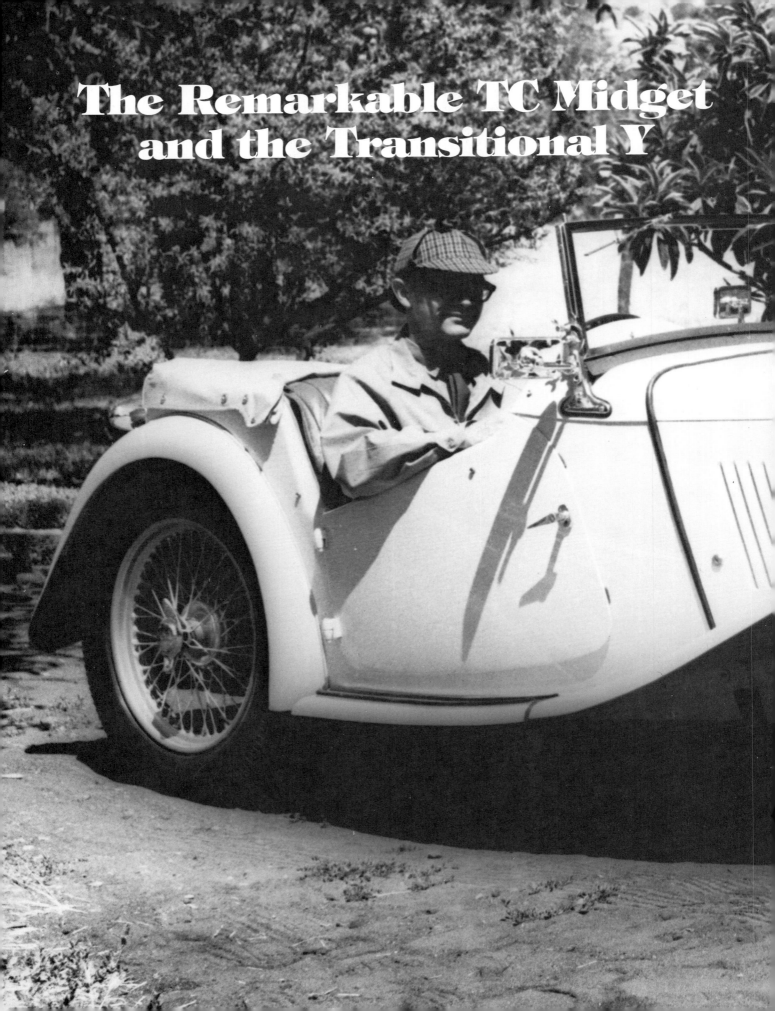

The Remarkable TC Midget
and the Transitional Y

Chapter IX

Only the vertical bars in front are non-standard for protection. TC of owner/restorer Gert Orla Jensen. (Joseph H. Wherry photo)

The end of six years of war in mid-August, 1945, was not accompanied by any immediate or grandiose plans to flood the world with sports cars. Clearing the Abingdon works of the tooling and equipment that had kept the factory busy with war-related contracts, rescuing surviving automotive production equipment and parts from storage, assessing a renewed program in the light of material shortages and restrictions, and close liaison with the Nuffield overlords in Cowley occupied the Abingdon management staff well into September.

The need for new cars of all kinds, however, and the urgency to begin meeting the public demand, led to a decision for the MG works to produce one model based upon the last prewar model—with as few changes as possible. (This Abingdon-Cowley decision was really not unique in the automotive industry in the United Kingdom or elsewhere. Virtually all industrial effort everywhere was to pick up at the point where production for civilian needs had been suspended with the outbreak of war.) Rising prices, a government program of austerity, and the traditional Motor Show month of October all combined to facilitate the introduction of the TC Midget.

A sharp eye was required to distinguish the new Midget on the MG stand in the Oc-tober 1945 London Motor Show from the briefly produced 1939 TB. Most noticeably, the body was 4 inches wider to allow more hip and shoulder space. This welcome change narrowed the running board, on which there were two step strips rather than the three of the TB. Overall width, however, was still 56 inches. The 139.5-inch length was identical to the TB and there were no bumpers to disfigure the crisp lines. There was a badge bar, and even the single chromed stud on each end of the slab-shaped fuel tank tallied with the TB. Cut-down doors, clamshell fenders and 19-inch, knock-off wire wheels were all familiar. Out of sight underneath the frame—still under-slung in the rear—there was another change, however. Predictably, the switch from trun-nions to shackles on the rear ends of the semi-elliptic leaf springs upset some purists. (Objecting to any changes was a sacred MG enthusiast tradition.) Brakes were 9-inch-diameter Lockheed hydraulics.

Inside, the two-seater TC was also like the TB. Right-hand drive, left-hand gear change lever and fly-off hand brake lever were the same—no one had dared to think of exporting such an ascetically basic roadster, the only body style available. Instrumentation, with the speedometer located in front of the passenger, was unchanged. Even the rectangular rearview mirror—which should be positioned vertically—and the folding windscreen were in their traditional locations. They were placed in front of the dual-cowl humps, which faired into an engine bonnet long enough to cover a big, straight-8-cylinder power plant. (To the uninitiated, it seldom occurred that it was necessary to provide space for foot controls and the occupants' pedal extremities in such a close-coupled sports car.) The curb weight of 1,730 pounds was almost identical to that of the TB.

The splendid XPAG engine, introduced in the TB, was unchanged except for a minimal decrease in compression ratio from 7.3:1 to 7.25:1. The dual 1¼-inch SU carburetors were the same as were ignition components, and maximum output was still 54.4 bhp at 5,200 rpm. Gear ratios, with synchromesh on the top three gears and the final drive, also were unchanged.

Principal features of the XPAG engine merit brief consideration in the light of its continuing use—with only minor modifications—until mid-1954. The main characteristic was the strength of all component parts. This began with the heavy, counterbalanced crankshaft, which resided in a beautifully cast, 5-quart oil sump with a screened pick-up on the left side beneath the three-bearing, chain-driven camshaft. Located externally at the left front of the block, the oil pump was driven by one of a pair of worm gears at the middle of the camshaft; the other worm gear drove the Lucas distributor.

Pushrods operated the overhead valves, which were angled enough to provide mildly wedge-shaped combustion chambers over the flat-topped, full-skirted pistons. There were double valve springs, case-hardened tappet faces, orthodox rockers and timing sufficiently feisty to enable lead-footed drivers to run the willing engine as fast as 5,900 rpm—the factory-quoted engine speed where valve lash began and things could start coming apart. At 5,900 rpm, piston speed was 3,484 feet per minute, whereas at the normal maximum recommended engine speed of 5,200 rpm, piston travel was 3,071 fpm. In comparison, the piston speed (at 5,500 rpm) of the beloved J.2 and PA/PB Midgets of 1932–1936 was 2,995 fpm.

Improved metals and alloys developed during the war were to be responsible, in the main, for the greatly increased durability of pistons, rings, valves, connecting rods and all of the engine parts subjected to sustained high speeds. Stage "tuning" would boost outputs remarkably, as will be seen, and XPAG engine speeds would exceed 6,300 rpm (with piston speeds in excess of 3,700 fpm) before the end of the T-Types.

Driving a TC was a pleasure and still is, but keeping a few of the Midget's idiosyncrasies in mind has always been advisable. The flexibility of the box-section frame, traditional in prewar British and continental sports cars, can be downright alarming to those unfamiliar with the species. If the driver cannot persuade the passenger to direct his/her undivided attention to the speedometer, or the scenery, chances are that the passenger's optics will be riveted upon door joints and other flexing body parts when the road gets rough, the turns become abrupt, and the gears are being used to advantage. The body craftsmen—the coachbuilders—purposely made the body to flex with the frame. The latter had to do so in the days of solid axles and firmly snubbered leaf springs. The durability of the metal-sheathed, usually ash-framed bodies is a tribute to the practitioners of coachbuilding, an art that is fading from the scene in these days of designing by government regulations.

The TC stuck to the most twisting roads with tenacity. Low center of gravity and firm suspension limited the angle of roll, and if steering was not always neutral, understeer was only slight. Quick steering, by a rather unsophisticated and slightly rough worm-gear system, gave just 1½ turns lock-to-lock. The turning circle was 37 feet in diameter. As for performance, British motoring journals were handicapped by the poor quality of what little gasoline was available immediately after the war, and maximum speeds reported varied from 74 to just under 78 mph. The best acceleration to 60 mph was reported as being 21 seconds. When the TC reached the United States, the better fuel produced top speeds of 80–82 mph, and acceleration from scratch to 60 mph in 19.5 to 20 seconds was common for well-maintained, strictly stock Midgets. Pitted

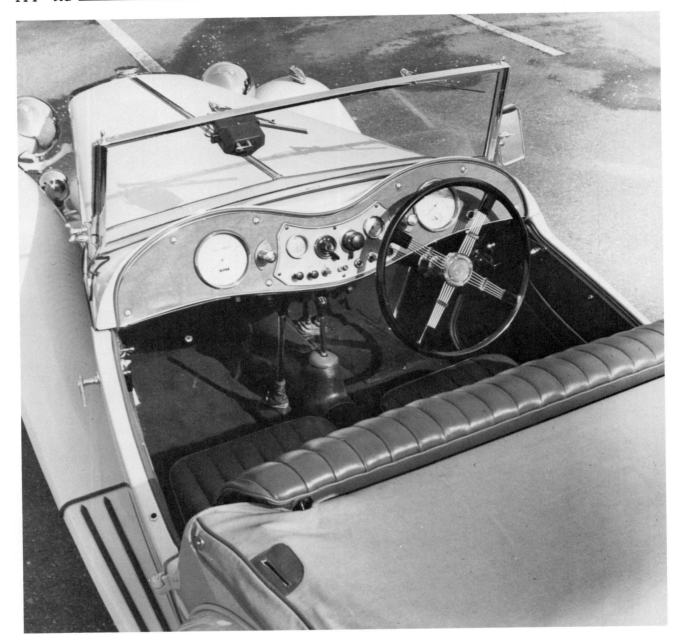

against almost any post-war American car, the TC Midget's performance was not overly impressive, but the big domestic iron was unable to match the handling or fuel economy of around 25 miles per 4-quart gallon.

Some 1,580 TC Midgets were built by the end of 1946 and the home market price was £412, to which was added a purchase tax of £116, a whopping 28 percent, for a total of £528. One of the TC Midgets was purchased by Lieutenant Philip Mountbatten, now Duke of Edinburgh. In 1946, the Pound Sterling was the equivalent of $4.03, but despite the de-

Note the speedometer's clever location directly in front of the passenger; this diverts his attention from the flexing of body sections on rough roads. Peter Welch's TC. (Joseph H. Wherry photo)

mand and need for new cars in the United Kingdom, there were relatively few who could afford them. For the more than $2,100 an MG cost the British in their money, Americans could buy *two* low-priced family cars (no matter if they handled little better than trucks). However, some of the American servicemen stationed in the U.K. immediately after the war had observed the antics of small sports cars in a few sporting events. That pleasant malady for which there is no known cure, sports car enthusiasm or motor sports, infected a few. Thus, sometime early in 1946, a TC appeared in the USA. Things here have never been the same since.

Much has been printed about the 6,000-plus TC Midgets imported into the USA over a period of four years, until production ended late in 1949. Those reports are erroneous, although the effect of the 20 percent of produc-

tion that *were* imported was out of all proportion to their actual numbers. Wilson McComb, a post-war MG publicity staffer for a decade, accurately states that the total production of TC Midgets was exactly 10,000 cars. Of that number, 3,408 were sold to eager Britons and exactly 2,001 were exported to the USA through normal trade channels—about 600 of them in 1946 and 1947. According to old MG Car Com-

The immortal TC Midget. Owner/restorer Gert Orla Jensen. (Joseph H. Wherry photo)

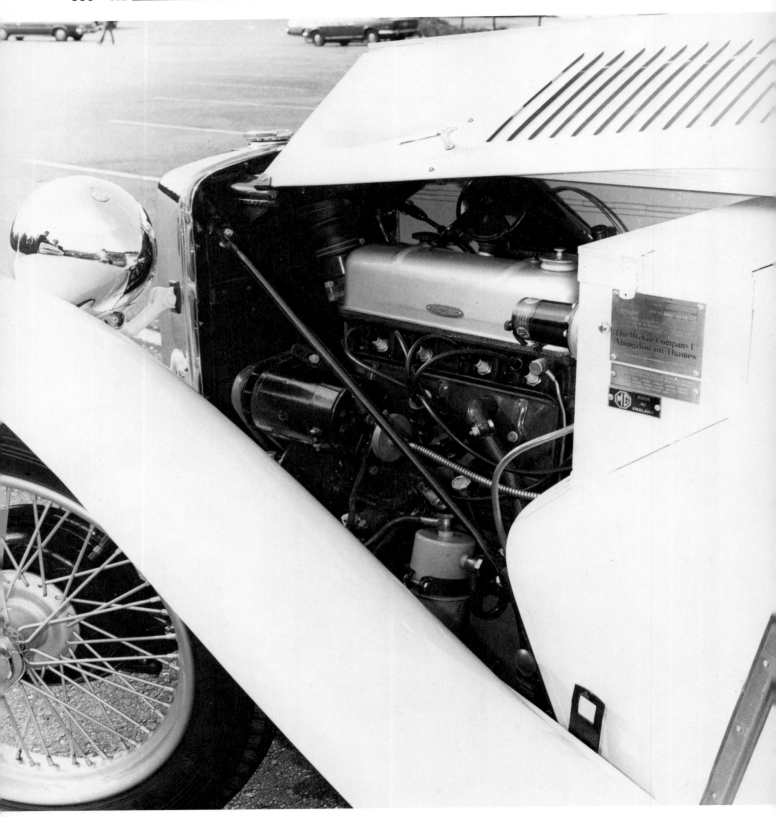

Ignition side of XPAG engine in TC shows sparking plugs,
dynamo/generator, oil filter, manufacturer's plate on side of
tool case on top of scuttle, etc. (Joseph H. Wherry photo)

Aspiration side of XPAG engine in Welch's TC. Note cylindrical air cleaner and horizontal air way, which covers the intakes of the dual SU carburetors. (Joseph H. Wherry photo)

TC Midget with original equipment tools, Owner's Manual and brochure displayed on a hooked octagonal rug; SA in background. Owner, Peter Welch. (Joseph H. Wherry photo)

pany figures, an additional 1,439 TCs were shipped to the USA in 1948 and 1949. The remaining 4,591 were exported all over the free world, with most of them going to Canada, Australia, New Zealand, South Africa (now The Republic of South Africa), and other Commonwealth nations. Inevitably, a few hundred TC Midgets were purchased in the U.K. and brought home by American military people. Quite possibly as many as 3,000 TCs were in America by 1950, and others have been imported during the past decade as the little roadster has become a prime car for collectors.

The idea of driving for fun hit the fan of latent enthusiasm when the TC appeared in dealer showrooms on the East and West coasts. Soon chapters of the MG Car Club were formed, gave impetus to the Sports Car Club of America (quietly formed in 1944 without any MG owners, by the way), and by 1950 the term "sports car" was an household term.

A color MG portfolio

PHOTOGRAPHY BY JOSEPH H. WHERRY

F.1 Magna MG (Owner—Ernie Kallweit)

MG PA Midget Airline Coupe (Owner—Gert Orla Jensen)

MG SA Charlesworth 2-Ltr. Drophead
(Owner—Peter Welch)

MG SA 2-Ltr. Saloon (Owner — Vic Diggins)

MG VA 1.25-Ltr. (Owner — Bill Daugherty)

MG WA 2.6-Ltr. Tickford Drophead Coupé
(Owner — Calvin Tilden)

MG TC Midget (Owner—Peter Welch)

MG Y-Type 1.25-Ltr. Tourer (Owner—Harold Dick)

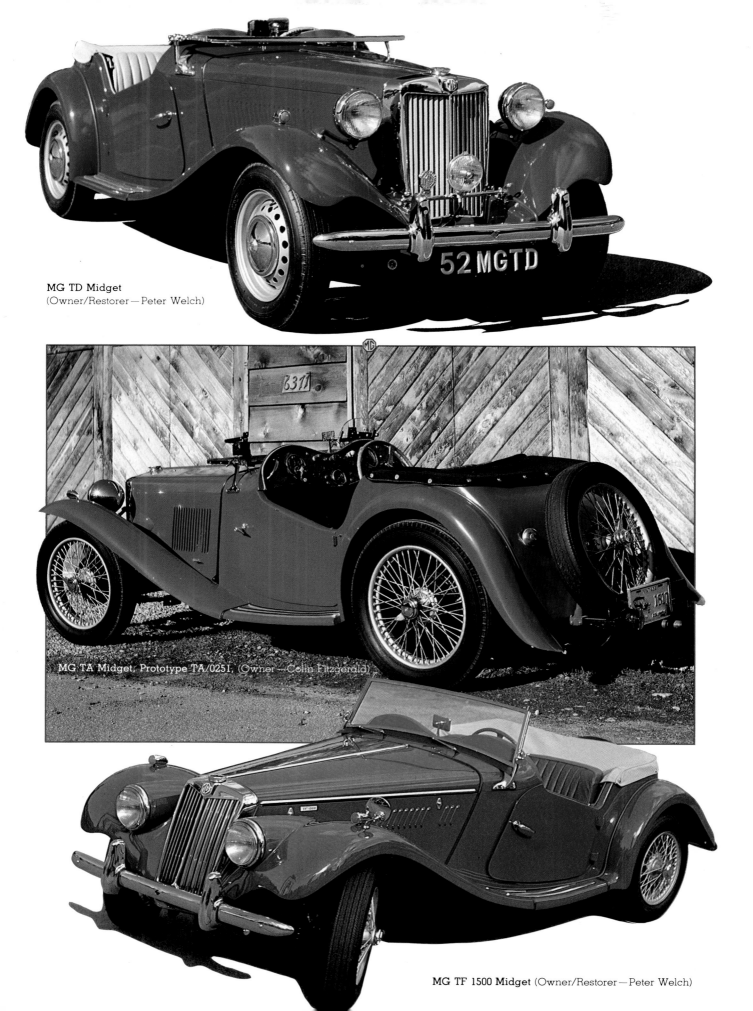

MG TD Midget
(Owner/Restorer — Peter Welch)

MG TA Midget, Prototype TA/025I, (Owner — Colin Fitzgerald)

MG TF 1500 Midget (Owner/Restorer — Peter Welch)

MGA 1600 Mark II De Luxe (Owner/Restorer—Glen Tarlton)

MGA 1600 Mark II De Luxe (red and white), MGA Twin Cam
(blue); (Owners—Mike Walsh, Glen Tarlton, Ron Thompson)

MGB (1979 model) (Owners – Harry and Bill Wappler)

MGC GT Six (1969 model) (Owners—Steve Hendricks and Laura Chandler)

MGB Limited (1980 final model) (Owners—Steve Hendricks
and Laura Chandler)

The Collier Corporation—under Barron Collier, Sr., and his son, Barron, Jr.—had imported some MGs before the war and their Motor Sport, Inc., office in New York City would deliver a TC Midget for $1,995 in 1946. Delivered in California, the price was about $100 more, but there was no efficient dealer network. In 1947, Kjell Qvale organized British Motor Car Distributors, Ltd., in San Francisco and established franchises in major West Coast cities outside of Southern California, where International Motors was the MG distributor.

Around September of 1948, J. S. Inskip of New York City obtained import rights to MG for the entire 48 states. Within three years, there was at least one MG franchise operation in every state. This was the work of an importer of fine chinaware named Jocelyn Hambro, who established Hambro Trading Company of America, Inc., in Louisiana in order to take advantage of more favorable port costs in the Gulf Coast states. Importing a half-dozen TCs as a test, Hambro packed them off to Dallas—where they were snapped up pronto. The resulting negotiations with the Nuffield people in Cowley were productive—Britain was in sore need of dollars and exports were the solution—and Hambro became the exclusive importer for the USA. The country was

Owner/restorer Don McLellan's bare TC chassis discloses more engine, leaf-spring/beam-axle front suspension, wheel hub (brake drum and shoe are not installed). (Joseph H. Wherry photo)

divided into five distributorship zones: S. H. Lynch, Inc., in Dallas; British Motor Car Company in San Francisco; International Motors in Los Angeles; J. S. Inskip in New York City, and Waco Motors in Miami. This situation held until shortly after February 1952, when Nuffield and Austin merged to form British Motor Corporation. Continued economic troubles in the United Kingdom led to BMC's merger with British Leyland in 1968, which brought further expansion—and centralized control—of MG distributorships. This, however, is business talk and not much fun, but the initial sales organization deserves consideration.

Without doubt, the MG TC broke the ice and paved the way for waves of imported cars. The handwriting was on the wall, but Detroit was wedded to the myth that "biggest is best" and was unable to read the evidence that a stark, simple, 4-cylinder two-seater roadster was the sort of car that countless people were anxious to own.

The debut of the MG TC Midget in a large road race in America was in October 1948, in upstate New York. The event was the idea of

Cameron Argetsinger, an SCCA member and new owner of a TC, which he'd purchased from Inskip. Sponsored jointly by the village of Watkins Glen and the SCCA, two races run before more than five thousand spectators comprised the event. A four-lap Junior Prix around the 6.6-mile course, which included the village streets, decided starting positions for the main event, the First Watkins Glen Grand Prix. TCs won third through 12th places in the GP, in which there were a variety of sports cars including a 3-litre, 8-cylinder Alfa Romeo 8C 2900 and at least one Bugatti.

By the time of the 1950 Watkins Glen Grand Prix, more than 25,000 spectators were on hand to watch over 100 drivers. Stage tuning and superchargers were common. The Queen Catherine Cup Race of 52.8 miles was won by a driven-to-the-race 1948 TC with the cylinder block sleeved down to 1,096 cc. displacement. This would have placed owner/driver Roland Keith of Peacedale, Rhode Island, in the 750–1,100 cc. Class G, but the installation of a 6-pound boost Arnholt blower and the increase of the compression ratio to 7.6 to 1 with special sodium-cooled valves kept him in 1,100–1,500 cc. Class F, with the unblown 1,250 cc. TC Midgets. The supercharger, special head and valves were the only mechanical modifications on the TC, which had seen more than twenty thousand miles in daily driving. Thus modified, Keith's engine wound out considerably more than 5,900 rpm when valve lash will occur in a stock 1,250 cc. TC engine. The blown TC topped 105 mph at least once during the race, and Keith won the Queen Catherine over a gaggle of stock TCs and other quick machines, including an HRG (a 1.5-litre, low-production British sports car of enviable reputation, and outright winner of the 1.5-litre class in the 1949 Belgian Grand Prix). Thus qualified for the Grand Prix, Keith and his blown TC won Class F.

Sports car fever swept across America— and this includes Canada—and MG Car Club *centres* sprang up in every region. The Abingdon works, with the benign blessing of Cowley, was again assisting Goldie Gardner in his record runs (see Chapter VII) and, on the side, MG issued a "tuning" manual. This enabled competition-minded MG owners to increase the output, through *stages*, to a maximum of around 90 brake horsepower.

Requests began arriving in Abingdon in May 1949 for an improved, less frugal, "more comfortable" Midget. Independent front suspension (IFS) was high on the request list ("Not

as stiff as that beam axle and corners just as well"), and there was resistance in some quarters to those spartan clamshell mudguards. The fact that patrol officers in a number of police departments alongside major highways outside of London, along with many of the "upper class," still found their "stage-tuned" TC Midgets to be more than adequate was not influential in keeping such a "real car" in production. Progress cannot be denied and, as the ten-thousandth TC left the production line

MGCC officials marshaling TC Midgets for a two-mile-long parade of MGs from Cintsa to East London, Republic of South Africa, for a Golden Jubilee Mayoral Salute. (Courtesy: Norman Ewing)

near the end of 1949, there appeared a new Midget—the TD.

That the ancestry of the TD was mixed, that, in truth, it was not really all Midget in the strictest sense, may come as a surprise to some readers. But downright discomforting to

With hood folded and stowed in the boot and three-quarter tonneau cover in place, Gert Orla Jensen could be set to race his beautifully restored TC Midget. (Joseph H. Wherry photo)

Peter Welch and Colin Fitzgerald wrestle the hood. (Joseph H. Wherry photo)

An optional hub, to mount dual spares, was available. Peter Welch's TC. (Joseph H. Wherry photo)

The TC Midget, made from late 1945 through 1949, and cast in the image of the TA/TB. (Joseph H. Wherry photo)

the traditional hard core of true believers was the origin of the IFS and, indeed, all but the last half-foot of the frame. These developments bring us to consider an MG type which is only now gaining well-deserved recognition—the humble Y-Type, which was designed just before the war to fill the price and size niche between the VA and the TA/TB. Of course, the true believers howled and wailed with the advent of the Y-Type, which had the sort of modern features the hard core considered heresy.

Still underslung in the rear, the box-section, 99-inch wheelbase chassis had independent front suspension by means of unequal wishbones and coil springs. Obviously, the inspiration was the racing R-Type of 1935. In the rear were shackle-mounted leaf springs as on the TC. No other *marque* in the Nuffield range—the ubiquitous Morris, or the rescued Riley and Wolseley—had IFS or coil springs. The Smiths Jackall hydraulic-jacking system

was standard, and the first application of rack-and-pinion steering on any MG was another surprise. A Bluemel adjustable steering wheel added to the comfort. Steering lock was 2¾ turns, and the turning-circle diameter of 35 feet assured maneuverability.

Announced in April 1947 as the MG 1¼-Litre, and assigned the alphabetical Y, the new saloon car seated four in a comfortable, leather-upholstered interior. The price was £575, plus another £97 for Purchase Tax. Front seats were separate buckets and the rear bench seat had fixed armrests on either side, plus a folding armrest in the middle. Each rear-seat occupant also had the traditional convenience strap. Body styling, with separate fenders and running board, was in keeping with traditional British family car styling. The overall width of 59 inches provided 46 inches of shoulder space in the rear seat. The height was 57 inches and overall length was 161³⁄₁₆ inches. Bumpers were standard, fore

The 1.25-Litre Y-Type saloon was a comfortable, four-seater family car and the first series production MG with independent front suspension.

A sliding roof panel and genuine leather upholstery. An MG YB saloon. (Joseph H. Wherry photos)

XPAG engines in Y-Types had rounded horizontal air cleaners. Note MG octagon on induction manifold over dual carburetor intakes on this Tourer. Tool box is located on top of scuttle firewall. Owners, Douglas and Marilyn Salmi. (Joseph H. Wherry photos)

and aft, but the most obvious styling change was the invisibility of the spare wheel and tire. These were stowed beneath the floor of the luggage boot, and were reached via the registration-number panel below the boot lid. A steel sliding sun panel in the roof was standard, as was a rear-window shade and a single fog lamp. The latter was mounted on one of the bottom front fender aprons, which simulated the paneling over front leaf-spring dumb irons which, with the IFS, were absent.

Instrumentation was quite sporting, set in half of the polished veneer facia panel in two dials with octagonal rims. The remaining half of the facia contained an exceptionally large storage bin with a hinged door. Above the top-hinged and flat windscreen (which could be opened) were sun visors. The rearview mirror, at the top center of the windscreen, was very small and was the magnifying type. Though rather small, the three foot pedals were well placed, while the medium-length gear change lever had a slightly willowy feel. The fly-off hand brake lever was between the individual front seats.

Built primarily for the home and Commonwealth market, most if not all Y-Type saloons had right-hand drive. The author drove a YB for a month-long road test in mid-1953, and found it to be a delightfully roadable car. Of

course the steering was slower than that of the TC (although much lighter), and the performance was somewhat less, but cornering was excellent and allowed all-day cruising at 60 mph. Ground clearance was 6 inches. The speedometer, as on American cars of that time, was a good 10 percent off on the optimistic side. Coachbuilt, with the customary hardwood framing beneath steel panels, the body was extremely tight and solid. It had but a single negative in the author's opinion: ventilation with all windows closed, during rain, was virtually nil.

Some 6,160 YA saloons were sold before it became necessary to upgrade the single-carburetor, 7.2-compression-ratio version of the XPAG engine that developed 45 bhp at 4,800 rpm. The 70—72 mph maximum speed, and the 29 and 18 seconds it took to reach a true 60 and 50 mph, respectively, from start, were a bit on the slow side for single-car families who wanted performance nearer that of the TC. The only engine modification undertaken was to increase the compression ratio to 7.4 to 1, raising the maximum output to 48 bhp at the same 4,800 rpm. A change to hypoid final drive was the only other power train modification, another contribution to the future TD Midget. Smaller 15-inch wheels, more efficient front brakes with two leading shoes, larger shock absorbers and an anti-roll bar in front improved the handling. The improved 1¼-Litre saloon was designated YB.

Keen owners went further because the XPAG engine, the same as that in the TC, except for carburetion, could be given the same stage tuning. Substituting a pair of SU carburetors with the stock TC manifolding increased performance by 8–10 percent. One British owner, Dick Jacobs, won his class in the annual Silverstone Production Touring Car Race with his "tuned" YB saloon for three consecutive years, from 1952 through 1954. De-

spite this and other successes in various touring car races and trials, the YA/YB failed to catch on in the USA and comparatively few were sold. To develop the four-seater sports car market in the USA, therefore, the works produced the Y Tourer. Sometimes erroneously called the YT—verbally and in print—the 1¼-Litre MGY Tourer might have scored fairly well had it appeared simultaneously with the TC early in 1946—or at least have been available at the time when the sports car gospel was wafting into the USA right after the war.

Initially greeted with much interest when placed in American showrooms alongside the

A snowfield on one of British Columbia's mountains forms the backdrop for an MG 1.25-Litre Y-Type Tourer. (Courtesy: owner/restorer Terry O'Brien)

The 1949 MG 1.25-Litre Y-Type Tourer in a Presidio concours d'elegance, San Francisco, 1969. An attractive, comfortable, economical and roadworthy four-seater with classic styling, the Y-Type MG is now receiving the regard denied it during production. The Salmi car. (Joseph H. Wherry photo)

An elegant 1.25-Litre Y-Type MG graced with drophead coachwork by Castagna of Milan. This unique car is owned by Roger Barlow. (Courtesy: Al Moss)

Y Tourer's instruments and facia were almost identical to those of TC Midget. The Salmis added a heater below the facia. (Joseph H. Wherry photo)

TC, with which it shared identical facia and instrument layout, the Y Tourer never quite managed to excite the sports car fraternity. In all, only about 875 were produced (though some sources say that exactly 877 were built). Intended solely for the American market, and with a single-carburetor XPAG engine, the Y Tourer might have succeeded but for two factors: very unexciting performance despite its advanced suspension system and superb roadability, and rather unattractive appearance caused by the unsporting disc wheels. The upshot was that the 73–75 mph Y Tourer was phased out of production early in 1950—the only MG to fail on the American market. The successful saloon, on the other hand, continued in production until late in 1953. Before the Y Tourer disappeared from the market, however, the TD Midget hit the showrooms and enthusiasts were surprised to find in it the independent front suspension of the open four-seater.

A poor seller in its day, the Y Tourer now is the object of demand by collectors. Several score still serve their owners as daily transport. This black Y-Type 1¼-Litre Tourer (illustrated) completed a casual three-thousand-mile tour throughout the Cascades and Rockies in 1980.

More than one Y Tourer owner has consulted coachbuilders about special body work in past years. The drophead coupé by Castagna of Milan shows lines similar to those applied to some Lancia models three decades ago.

Often called "MG's last thoroughbred four-seater," the Y-Type truly has come into its own as an interesting transition car.

The Harold Dick "Royal Tourer" Y-Type MG (note personalized license plate) is used regularly on long pleasure trips. (Joseph H. Wherry photo)

The Last Square-Rigged
Midgets: TD and TF

Chapter X

Elegantly restored in the motif of the "Cream Crackers" is this TD Midget. Owner/restorer, Ron Thompson. (Joseph H. Wherry photo)

By mid-1949, the days of the TC Midget were numbered. The dashing *box on four harps*—a romantic, tongue-in-cheek reference to square lines and old-fashioned, 19-inch-high wire wheels—had too many shortcomings to survive competitively in the marketplace. If the MG works in Abingdon was to continue building sports cars, something had to be done. The Nuffield board in Cowley would do something if Abingdon did not.

Time was short and there had to be a new MG sports car on the stand in the annual autumn Motor Show in London. Lacking a proper design shop—that had disappeared into the corporate scheme of things along with real engineering autonomy during the Nuffield takeover—Cecil Cousins pondered the bare chassis of a Y Tourer and discussed the problem with his staff. An MG veteran since the halcyon days of the 1920s, Cousins had been works manager for many years. Inspiration and perspiration, the time-honored formula for all MG successes to date, provided the way out of the dilemma.

Shortening the Y-Type chassis by 5 inches effectively reduced the wheelbase to the 94 inches of the TC Midget. Merlin could not have done better. A slightly altered TC body was fitted to the shortened chassis. The frame

rails had box-sectioned longerons, but first glance could have been misleading because the inside box facings were inset. The YB's smaller 15-inch wheels completed the prototype of a reasonably modern, slightly lower sports car with independent front suspension. Cousins and crew—without knowing so at the time—had created the most successful MG to date in no more than two weeks! Who needed a design department? When displayed to the Nuffield management, approval was forthcoming with the proviso that a few more changes would be made prior to preparing for production.

The new TD Midget finally was announced in January 1950, after the last TCs had left the assembly line. Distributors were waiting anxiously and the motor press was delighted. The old guard purists among the masses of enthusiasts, true to their calling, had been bewailing the demise of the TC before learning what Abingdon had wrought to replace the object of their affection.

A half-foot longer (at 145 inches overall) because of the bumpers—essential for the lucrative American market—and noticeably lower on the smaller 15-inch wheels, the new TD Midget won the blessings of the automotive press almost immediately. Those sports car people who wanted a softer ride and easier

The more generously curved fenders ("wings" or "mudguards") of the TD Midget. Owner/restorer (c.1967), Richard Negley. (Joseph H. Wherry photo)

steering were overjoyed with the IFS and the rack-and-pinion steering, which still gave less than 3 turns lock-to-lock. Rack and pinion steering, readily installed on either side, enabled the production department to equip export models with left-hand drive, one of the primary demands in America (where all of us "bloody colonists insist on driving on the wrong side of the road"). The scanty mudguards of previous Midgets, beloved by the diehards, had given way to more generously curved fenders while retaining the classic "clamshell" lines. Wider wheel tread and some 4 inches more shoulder space in the body convinced many of the most cantankerous, even among the hard-core traditionalists, that the new TD offered increased comfort and improved handling qualities.

The bench type seat was retained, as was the traditional leather upholstery. With the wider body came a wider scuttle and more space between the clutch, brake and accelerator pedals. Cramped foot space for the driver had been a sore point among big-footed Americans, Canadians and those "down under." More than one had hit the clutch and brake pedal at the same time when shifting down in a tough corner. So far, so good, but the TD feature that rankled traditionalists most was what had happened to the rear of the

frame: no longer was it underslung. The use of shackles rather than trunnions to position the rear springs was bad enough, although enthusiasts had learned to live with that oversight. Now, however, the frame was kicked up over the rear axle "just like on passenger cars," a radical change for any MG.

Then there were those "unsightly" disc wheels. Everyone had to admit, however, that the two leading shoes in the front hydraulic brake drums provided far better braking than the single front shoes in the same 9-inch diameter TC drums. The quick release virtues of the fly-off hand brake lever still graced the new TD, and the twin large dials containing the speedometer and tachometer were now grouped together directly in front of the driver. The steering wheel was the familiar wire-spoked type, with the center fittingly filled with the MG octagon. The double cowl over the facia—now leatherette-covered with a useful glovecase—and the windscreen, which could be folded flat, retained most of the traditional necessities. True, the standard rear-view mirror was centered between the dual cowls rather than being mounted outboard, but the

Restoration is well advanced on this TD chassis. Note two leading shoes in front brakes; the A-frames and coil springs of IFS; rack and pinion steering; the special polished aluminum Arnolt rocker cover on block. Owner/restorer, Colin Fitzgerald.

TD frame. Note inset inboard facings of box-section rails and kick-up over rear axle; shackle-mounted rear springs; independent front suspension and tubular roll bar at approximate position of firewall. (Joseph H. Wherry photos)

overall arrangement of all vital components would soon prove to be exactly what the overseas sales network wanted and needed. Invisible, but a godsend to those who raced, was a frame-mounted steel roll bar beneath the cowling.

Out in front—ignoring the bumper, of course—the TD was all Midget from the proper, nearly vertical grille and on back along the long louvered bonnet to the cutdown, rear-hinged doors. Beneath the bonnet, the familiar and tough 1,250 cc. XPAG engine had suffered no changes; it was identical in specification and output to the TC engine. The transmission, however, contained the same ratios as the YB saloon and Y Tourer, and the alternate wider third gear of the YA was available. In addition, the beneficial switch to hypoid differential allowed the entire drive line to be slightly lower than that of the superseded TC.

Behind the seat, the tonneau boot held a more generous supply of luggage for two people. The sheet metal over the traditional sea-

Another angle on the TD chassis being restored by Fitzgerald. The optional wire wheels will be fitted; note the knock-off hub.

One way to *skin a cat* that outweighs your TD Midget MG— a *Jaguar*, for instance—is to go all the way in stage tuning and add a Judson supercharger, as on this recent restoration/ modification for vintage racing by the Octagon Motor Group in Vancouver, B.C.

Many owners trimmed the TD's mudguards, used their Midgets every day, raced on weekends, and some forgot to sanitize the undersides when displaying their pride and joy in a show. Another look at the IFS of a TD in the 1953 International Motor Show in New York City. *"This TD was raced yesterday!"* (Joseph H. Wherry photos)

In Peter Welch's marina, the port side and . . .

soned hardwood frame was faithful to familiar lines and was squared off in the back where the slab-shaped fuel tank mounted the spare wheel. The changes—all for the better—did increase the curb weight to 2,005 pounds, while the 54.4 bhp at 5,200 rpm was the same. Surprisingly, the performance was not adversely affected by the weight and smaller wheels. This was due to the more favorable gearbox ratios and the Y-Type's cone synchromesh which, though delivering acceleration almost exactly that of the TC, enabled a properly maintained TD to reach 80—82 mph with relative ease and to cruise at 60 mph all day if required.

. . the starboard side of his immaculately restored TD engine.
(Joseph H. Wherry photos)

Car-starved and beset by large excise taxes, British enthusiasts who could afford the total cost of £569 in 1950, without pain, were scarce. America eagerly absorbed more than two-thirds of production while Common-wealth nations imported most of the rest; only a few hundred found UK buyers. Abingdon was pressed to keep pace with overseas demand for the TD, and the situation was aggravated by Nuffield requiring the MG works to produce Riley cars. The latter, fortunately, were built in only small numbers.

More than ten thousand MGs (including the relatively few Y-Types) would have been

The smaller diameter disc wheels of the TD offended some of the true believers; others found that they required less maintenance. Owner/restorer, Peter Welch. (Joseph H. Wherry photo)

built in 1950 alone, an unheard-of number in the "old days," had not valuable production space been devoted to the *blue diamond marque*. Such frustrations—coincidental with the corporate realignments, changes in top management in Cowley, and the various considerations and responsibilities to stockholders—may serve to explain another predicament facing the MG veterans when introducing the replacement for the TC: just *what* would be the new Midget's first letter designation? In immediate pre-war days, the two-seater that became the TD probably would have been designated as either the Y-Type— if that four-seater, though already designed as mentioned previously, did not enter production—or as the Z-Type.

In mid-summer of 1949, to call the TD by the last letter in the alphabet would have made sense, inasmuch as the IFS non-underslung frame marked a radical departure from previous MG production cars. It would also have continued the established designation custom of the golden age of the *Triple Ms*, the near-classic OHC Midget/Magna/Magnette types. That the XPAG engine and the TA/B/C body styling were used would not have been sufficient reason to retain the T-Type designation. The TC body was widened to fit the Y-Type chassis frame, thus becoming a *new* body despite utilizing the same styling. Remember that the replacement for the beautiful OHC P-Type Midgets was designated T-Type in 1936 only because of a new OHV engine, although the styling was *not* changed. Now, with an entirely new frame, front-suspension system and wider body, the unchanged Type designation did *not* reflect the major structural redesigning of the TC's successor, which was a much-changed vehicle. Of course, if the TD *had* been designated as the Z Midget, the alphabetical order would have had to be recycled with the multi-series of MG sedans, which were already in the Nuffield engineering process in 1950 and were "designed" by the badge-applying people, very rapidly, in mid-1953 (as will be seen in the next chapter).

Nevertheless, the TD Midget progressed from victory to victory and held its position as the world's best-selling sports car during the entire production run through 1953—even though another merger began to overcast the Octagon's firmament. In 1952, the Nuffield empire corporately merged with the Austin Motor Company and the former rivals became the British Motor Corporation (BMC). From this point on, Lord Nuffield retained little more than influence in the giant complex, which was the world's third-greatest automotive manufacturing enterprise. The Austin half of the combination, based in Longbridge and producing five distinct series, would soon play an intriguing part in the modus operandi of the Abingdon works. As already observed, the MG works began building Riley cars shortly after World War II. Over in Cowley, the Morris works was making the Wolseley range of 4- and 6-cylinder family cars and the Morris car—the small *Minor*, the 1.5-litre *Oxford* and *Cowley*, and the 2.6-litre, 6-cylinder *Isis*. By the mid-1950s, similarly sized, closed saloon models of the *five marques*—including MG—would share bodies and/or engines in an homogenizing effort to rationalize production to an extent that would make the five General Motors cars look quite distinctive by comparison.

Beyond doubt, the promotion of John W. Thornley to the position of General Manager of MG late in 1952 had much to do with the *octagon marque* surviving until the end of 1980. Thornley, who emerged from World War II service as a lieutenant colonel, had come on board MG in 1931 as an accountant. JWT was much more than a pencil pusher, however; he was a true believer, a sports car enthusiast *par excellence*, and a trials competitor in pre-war days. Thornley helped form the MG Car Club, in the year prior to joining MG, and was the club's first honorary secretary.

The instrumentation of the TD was an improvement, but the leatherette facia was a break with tradition. (Joseph H. Wherry photo)

R. J. McKinsey converses with his pit crew during a 1953 race meeting. The car: McKinsey's fast and capable modified TD Midget. (Joseph H. Wherry photo)

In spite of the identity problems being suffered by Thornley and his Abingdon people—perhaps even partly in spite to prove a point—MG owners everywhere, and particularly in the USA and Canada, raced and rallied and introduced gymkhanas to the sports car fraternity across America, with little regard to national borders. The cry for more power to enable them to humble the drivers of HRG, the Singer SM-1500 and several lesser-known *marques* such as the 90-mph Jowett Jupiter, had been acted upon by Abingdon even before Thornley took command.

JWT probably had more than a little to do with the enlightened decisions, however, that enabled the works to bring forth the TDC (TD Competition), which was officially designated the TD Mark II. The Mark II was a considerably improved job having larger 1½-inch SU carburetors with larger air cleaners, dual fuel pumps, a new and higher 8.0 to 1 compression ratio cylinder head with larger exhaust valves, a tougher clutch, and a host of other improvements. Andrex friction shock absorbers were added to supplement the Armstrong or Girling hydraulic snubbers, and the unsightly solid disc wheels gave way to better-looking discs with punched holes—which might have facilitated brake cooling. Even wire wheel conversions were authorized.

Abingdon distributed the information detailing the "what and how," which enabled thousands of TD (and TC) owners to raise their 54.4 bhp at 5,200 XPAG engines to the moderate but noticeably increased redline output of 57 bhp and later 60 bhp at 5,500 rpm (see Specifications).

Not a simple Saturday afternoon screwdriver-and-spanner chore, bringing a basic XPAG engine up to TDC/Mark II level is a rather extensive modification program that required considerable mechanical know-how and equipment in addition to the usual family workbench.

When the TD Mark II was wound down on the production line late in 1953, nearly thirty thousand of the Type TD had been built. Around twenty thousand of the total were exported to and sold in the USA—most of them as rapidly as they could be prepared by dealers, who began selling TDC "competition kits" in 1951.

Outselling all other sports cars was not enough to stave off the inevitable. In 1951, Enever and his design staff had constructed a streamlined body and mounted it on a TD

Mk. II chassis for Phil Hill, who intended to better his 1.5-litre class second place in the 1950 Le Mans 24-Hour Race. With only minimal tuning, Hill's streamlined TD was capable of 120 mph—due, mainly, to the streamlining. Unfortunately, engine problems that were never fully explained forced Hill and his quick MG out of the race. Based largely on the performance improvement, though, Thornley and his Abingdon colleagues sought approval of the new BMC board to produce an improved experimental model, with a low cockpit in a widely splayed frame, bearing the prototype designation of EX. 175. This was refused because of the corporate decision to have Austin produce Donald Healey's new sports car—powered by the 2.6-litre Austin A.90 engine—and so there was nothing left to do but soldier on, despite decreasing sales, with the

TDC/Mark II Midget. Abingdon was to be allowed to prepare an improved T-Type for the 1953 Earls Court Motor Show, rather than being turned loose to protect the overseas market they had pioneered. In consequence, MG had to content themselves with the 1,250 cc. XPAG engine rather than be allowed to adopt an existing 1.5-litre engine, which was sorely needed on the competition circuit.

The strictures under which the MG works labored did not discourage dyed-in-the-wool MG enthusiasts overseas, however, and scores of successful modifications, some home-grown, were applied to the XPAG engines, chassis and even the bodies. Many two-seaters were

The small metal marker on the near side of the nose (behind the headlamp) is the only visible indication that this TD is a Mark II. Owner/restorer, Dr. William Wilson. (Joseph H. Wherry photo)

"built" to top 100 mph with ease. The competition drivers on the SCCA circuit were not alone in making the MG a better car to suit their fancies.

Inskip Motors in New York City extended and strengthened the frame of a TD Mark II and rebuilt the body into an attractive four-seater. Displayed in the 1953 New York International Motor Show, this special TD Tourer was available on order for $2,925. There were few takers—the 2-litre Morgan Plus 4 cost no more, seated four, had superb roadability and could top 90 mph with ease. (The author photographed the Inskip TD Tourer and has always understood that two were built. Some have said that Inskip made four. Suffice it to say that it's worth nearly its weight in silver today, but in 1953, it began no trend. The Moss TD Pickup was more practical.)

More successful, more glamorous and more interesting was the program undertaken by S. H. Arnolt, Inc., the Chicago-based MG distributor for the Midwest. Around mid-1952, "Whacky" Arnolt arranged with Bertone, the famed Italian coachbuilding house, to design a series of aluminum-bodied, 4-seater (actually 2-plus-2) coupé and drophead "convertibles" on the TD chassis. Several were displayed in the April 1953 International Motor Sports Show in New York City, and somewhere around 90 examples were produced; they have been prime collectibles for more than a decade. The Arnolt MG's weight was over 2,200 pounds and performance suffered,

The four-seater Inskip TD Tourer during the 1953 New York International Motor Show. (In the background: an Austin A.125.) (Joseph H. Wherry photo)

Al Moss, a well-known MG enthusiast/dealer in Los Angeles, built this special MG TD Pickup and used it widely to service competitors in race meetings. (Courtesy: Al Moss)

S. H. "Whacky" Arnolt, the Midwest distributor, produced a series of superb TD Mark II specials with coachwork by Bertone. (Joseph H. Wherry photo)

The Thompson TD with hood raised.

Ron Thompson's very real TD Midget, one of ne
thousand reasons for the replicar business. (Joseph

The fiberglass apron is a recently developed protective device gaining favor among restorers. Thompson's TD.

but it was beautiful and could have been developed further.

The TD's finest hour in America took place in August 1951, on Utah's Bonneville Salt Flats, when a stock Mark II established 23 Class F records with a 12-hour run averaging 75.34 mph. This performance set records for distances from 25 to 1,000 kilometres. It took place under the supervision of officials from the American Automobile Association. Advertisements extolling the feat were still being used more than two years later.

The universal appeal of the T-Type Midgets, and the TD in particular, has not waned. Replica fiberglass bodies are available in both North and South America. Because an available chassis is required, many enthusiasts consider such "replicars" on VW and assorted homebuilt or kit-built chassis to be rolling heresies. In a larger sense, however, the popularity of such productions could be indicative of a growing admiration for the tough, squarish, practical and economical sports cars of three decades ago. An opposition viewpoint could be manifested by a letter, from an MGCC member, in the June 1980 issue of *Safety Fast!* This missive tells of "many of

these cars on the roads of Brazil" and goes on to say, "I think you will agree that it's all too obvious which car they have copied." People rarely spend hard-earned money to copy that for which they lack admiration.

Isn't it just as logical to assume that entrepreneurs have discovered a latent desire to own a feisty, rugged-appearing vintage sports car and that, for the average person, the most economically practical way to acquire a longed-for *marque* is to go the replica route? XPAG engines and authentic replica chassis could become realities in the near future.

The TD Midget delighted the majority of sports car enthusiasts after they overcame the initial shock. The combination of stiffer frame, independent front suspension and rack-and-pinion steering made for easier handling and greatly decreased a tendency for the inside front wheel to lift off the tarmac in a hard, fast corner. The TD had a softer, more comfortable ride, was less tiring on long trips, and converted thousands of ladies to the sports car gospel.

Unable to bring out a new two-seater by BMC decree, the cosmetically restyled TF on the MG stand in the 1953 Motor Show received

More people want a TF Midget today than during the unjustly maligned model's brief production period. A comfortable, well-appointed sports car. Owner/restorer, Peter Welch.

almost no plaudits. Motoring publications on both sides of the Atlantic were most uncomplimentary, and the majority of enthusiasts either howled with laughter or snorted in disgust. The separately adjustable bucket seats were about the best feature of the last of the T-Type Midgets. The XPAG engine did not quite measure up to the more powerful, dual fuel pump version of the later TD Mark II. The power plant of the "atrocity"—as some have termed the early TF—had reverted to the single pump, 57 bhp at 5,500 rpm unit of the early Mark II TD.

The resulting disillusionment of thousands of true believers in the *marque* of the Octagon was not the fault of the local management in Abingdon nor the in-works development staff. Cowley and Longbridge had called the shots. A facelift—which raked the grille and grafted the headlights into a rather appalling mating of bonnet and fenders—was matched, for lack of taste and efficiency, by the three dial group of instruments centered in the steeply canted facia between small open glovecases at either side. The center dial contained the oil pressure, coolant temperature and ammeter indicators. The 100-mph speedometer dial, on the left, included the total miles and trip odometer plus an electric clock, while the 6,500-rpm tachometer, red-lined at 5,500 rpm, and high-beam headlamp indicator shared the dial on the right. All three units were octagonal in shape.

Positive points for the TF were the quite commodious luggage boot behind the bucket seats, the same good foot space as in the TD, and the same improved chassis frame, running gear and all of the accoutrements of its predecessor. Disc wheels were standard—the later types with punched holes—but most TFs arrived in the New World with knock-off wires, which were listed as optional. At USA Ports-of-Entry, the TF's price was right and a bargain at the time, just over $2,000 including federal taxes. In Britain, still struggling with a government-imposed austerity program, the TF Midget cost £550, plus £230 in taxes.

Slightly longer than the TD at 147 inches overall, the TF's extra sheet metal and bucket seats on individual tracks increased the weight at the curb to 2,074 pounds. Heavier than the TD by nearly 70 pounds and lacking the TDC/Mark II dual fuel pumps penalized the TF slightly in acceleraton, through the gears. Top

A long delay in shipping TF Midgets to America cost Abingdon a widespread loss of media coverage.
(Joseph H. Wherry photos)

The aspiration side of the 1,466 XPEG engine in a TF 1500. Owner/restorer, Peter Welch. (Joseph H. Wherry photo)

speed, on the other hand, was quite good due to better airflow over the nose; 80 to 84 mph was attainable thanks to the XPAG engine's excellent valve gear, which took 6,000 rpm in bursts without fear of damage.

TF owners enjoyed the same sure "feel of the road" that made its immediate forerunner popular. The bonnet sloped downward a bit more toward the nose. This gave a slightly foreshortened view of the road in front of the bumper, but the purists found this view over the double cowling to be another irritant: the TF's radiator cap was a dummy. One had to lift the left top half of the bonnet to gain access to the filler of the 6-US quart (5 quarts Imperial) cooling system. Major tinkering on the engine required the removal of the lower side panels and, even then, access was restricted in comparison to the TC/TD Midgets.

Quality had not suffered and the body was still coachbuilt with a seasoned ash frame. The sturdiness and quietness of all of the post-war T-Type Midget and Y-Type bodies was a revelation to those unfortunates who had never driven anything other than Detroit iron; when a door was closed, the only sound was a "chunk" and slamming was unnecessary. Rock

solid on any road and even more impressive when down-shifting and powering through abrupt curves and chicanes, the TF was a first-class sports car. Once one became accustomed to the strange styling of expediency, and the controlled lean in corners, the MG love affair was renewed with increased fervor. Whether in city traffic and parking or in the countryside, the slightly more than 31-foot turning circle inherited from the TD was a boon unknown in America.

The TF hit the market at the time when the TD Mark II had all it could do to place consistently close to the top two or three places in class racing, nor could the stock TF do any better. That much better was possible was proven by Ken Miles, a well-known British racing driver, who wangled a 1.5-litre engine out of Abingdon. (The author believes the actual displacement was 1,466 cc. but some penciled notes, made back in 1953 during a meeting at Thompson Raceway or some other circuit, are smudged beyond legibility. If memory serves correctly, this engine was built around an XPAG block bored out to 72 mm., and was much like the record power plant used by Ken Miles and Captain George Eyston in some of their record runs in the EX. 179 on the Bonneville Salt Flats in 1954.) With proper preparation, the 1,466 cc. power plant was installed in a very special TF known as the Miles R.1. Further developments led Miles to "build" another special with more eyeball resemblance to a TF.

With the same hot-rodded 1.5-litre engine, Miles and his R.1 and "Shingle" R.2 MG specials devoured everything, in the up to 1,500 cc. class for modifieds, in nine out of ten SCCA races during 1953. He continued to terrify the opposition through 1954. More than a few times, Ken Miles placed well above his class by thrashing Porsche, HRG, an occasional Lea-Francis, Jowett Jupiter, Morgan Plus-4, Kurtis, Jaguar, OSCA and even a Ferrari or two. Such antics delighted MG enthusiasts, many of whom worked off their frustrations at the puzzling absence of a more potent stock MG by letting Abingdon know what should be done. Dealers let their wishes be known, too, and not a few of them succumbed to the lure of the lighter-weight, 2-litre Triumph TR-2. The

TR-2 had modern lines, passable roadability, could do 100 mph, and was making inroads into MG sales.

Success on the Bonneville Salt Flats gave Thornley and his key people some leverage with the Cowley/Longbridge overlords, and an improved two-seater entered production in July 1954. In appearance little had changed — just the addition of a small metal marker on each side of the bonnet near the nose. The marker said TF 1500. Underneath was an improved engine, the XPEG, displacing 1,466 cc. and sired by the Eyston/Miles record-breaking EX. 179. The timing was perfect because, the following month, the EX. 179 maintained an average of slightly more than 120 mph for 12 hours. Enthusiasts clamored for the first 1.5-litre Midget and dealers tore their hair because the arrival of the new model, in the USA, was delayed until late autumn. Again the fault was not Abingdon's: Nuffield Exports Limited in Cowley, Oxfordshire, was in complete control of MG's export negotiations and shipments. The TF 1500s finally arrived with a price tag calculated to dispel the gloom among the faithful: $1,995 including taxes at East Coast POEs. Eight years earlier, the TC Midget, the generator of the whole affair, had landed in America with the same price.

Improved foundry core technology enabled Abingdon to bring the new XPEG engine to mass production. Derived from the XPAG engine block, the larger cylinder bore was touchy, at first, because increasing the bore from 66.5 to 72 mm. required much closer tolerances with respect to the water jackets. This reminded the most vociferous diehard MG enthusiasts of the dreadful "business only" maneuvers perpetrated by the Nuffield side of BMC when the 1,250 cc. TF was introduced in the 1953 Motor Show. On the MG stand, beside the TF, was a Nuffield-designed saloon, named Magnette, labeled with an MG octagon and equipped with a 1.5-litre engine that made Midget drivers' mouths water. Both the motoring press and hard-core enthusiasts reasoned that "the TF should have had that engine."

A year later, with the 1954 holiday season about to begin, the TF 1500's engine was "too late" in the opinion of many enthusiasts and

The TF was the first MG to utilize a purely decorative filler cap atop the radiator grille. The real filler cap is beneath bonnet, on header tank. Note large tool box and convenient battery location. This beautifully restored example is Welch's TF 1500. (Joseph H. Wherry photo)

most segments of the motor sports press.

The TF 1500 was about 25 pounds heavier at the curb than the TF, but the performance was enough to assuage most of the disappointment caused by the long delay in arrival. Whereas the TF's maximum torque was 65 foot pounds at 3,000 rpm, the 1,466 cc. XPEG engine delivered 76 foot pounds at the same peaking speed. Top road speed was finally up to 90 mph with precise tuning, good gasoline, the windscreen folded flat across the cowl, the tires fairly hard, one aboard and tonneau cover lashed in place. Acceleration through the gears was moderately improved, but the sensitive pilot could feel the difference in the seat of the pants.

The love-hate-love emotional cycle in which MG enthusiasts were wont to indulge had never been more real than during the 15 months beginning with the introduction of the TF and concluding with cessation of TF 1500 production very early in 1955 after only 9,600 of both models had been built. Today, a quarter-century later, TF Midgets are highly

G. M. Gardner restored this TF 1500. The owner added the backup lamps but bumper guards were standard. (Joseph H. Wherry photo)

The TF's interior was more spacious, and the leather upholstery on the bucket seats was beautiful. Note passenger's handhold bracket beneath cowl at far right. (Joseph H. Wherry photo)

prized—and driven with pride and pleasure by anyone of any age who has been able to get the pink slip to either version.

From March 1955 to the London Motor Show in October, MG did not produce any sports cars! Only during World War II had such a peculiar state of affairs existed in Abingdon. Ironic, too, was the popularity of the 1,250 cc. XPAG engines. These continued to be available and were sold to the makers of Cooper, Kieft, Lister, Lotus and several obscure, low-production, competition sports cars. The four named *marques* were doing what MGs were supposed to do by tradition—winning races.

Abingdon's Last Sedans: Badge Engineering and Clones

Chapter XI

The ZA Magnette. (Joseph H. Wherry photo)

The saloon car that was introduced to the public alongside the 1,250 cc. TF in the 1953 London Motor Show—"labelled with an MG *octagon* and equipped with a 1.5-litre engine that made drivers' mouths water"—generated a renewal of the super-heated steam which sustained the stridency of the purist faction of sports car enthusiasm. The provocative latter-day Magnette was as neat an example of badge engineering as were the creations of Cecil Kimber in the good old days of the Bullnose Morris/MG 14/28 Super Sports. (In alien residency on the Atlantic Coast at the time, the author remembers being so irritated that he tried to ignore MGs and devoted his automotive writing time to several score other imported and domestic cars.)

Had Abingdon been able to argue the 1,489 cc. engine of the new Magnette saloon into the TF Midget, the true believers probably would have welcomed the Nuffield-designed, four-seater Z-Type into the fold of the Sacred Octagon with open arms, as a perfectly worthy companion to the two-seater. Enthusiasts who are devoted to an automotive *marque* mature emotionally as the object of their devotion develops. (Corvette devotees have managed to survive despite the fact that W. C. Durant founded Chevrolet around a big, 4.9-litre

6-cylinder tourer built by a Swiss racing driver named Louis Chevrolet and then purchased the firm that made the Little, a 4-cylinder car 1911–13, because the Little proved to be a sounder product with which to carve a slice of the more lucrative popular car market. "Badge engineering" began before MG.) So it has been with the MG fraternity, to the point that the 1953 through 1958 object of their disaffection is now on the verge of becoming a sought-after candidate for restoration.

(Only when compelled to road test the ZA Magnette, in order to have MG representation in a book during the absence of sports car production in Abingdon, did the author request the use of a press car. The experience was most pleasant and, although reluctant, the author had to admit that the Nuffield people had engineered a car worthy to wear the octagon. The January–February 1955 issue of *Motor Sport* magazine, edited by the late and well-liked William C. Callahan, also carried the author's test. Early in 1957, a week of road testing the more powerful ZB Magnette produced the same positive feelings. After all, the noted racing driver Ron Flockhart, winner of the 1957 Le Mans Twenty-Four Hour Race in a Jaguar, was the owner of a ZB Magnette.)

Because the ZA/ZB Magnette's new and deserved respectability justifies the coverage, the following condensed test results and driving impressions may be of value to the many MG enthusiasts who are restoring the once controversial machine. (The author wishes that he had a ZA or ZB in his garage right now.) The information is from the original reports:

Changed outwardly only in the color schemes available (stylish new two-tones and bright colors of all things), the Magnette ZB retains the same basic engine. The rated brake horsepower is increased from 60 to 4,600 to 68 at 5,500 rpm, due mainly to an increased compression ratio of 8.3 to 1.

The Magnette ZA saloon appeared on the American market early in 1954, and our request for a test example was duly registered with Inskip Motors, New York City area distributors. George Jessup facilitated availability of the car on a cool, soggy day so the Magnette probably felt at home in the London-like weather. Regular fuel was used for the tests. The road, blacktop, was thoroughly wet and rain glistened on the dark green ZA. After determining that the speedometer was only 3 mph too optimistic at 60 on the dial, six runs were made in opposing directions and the times were recorded with a calibrated stopwatch. The ZA Magnette's performance was:

From standstill to 30 mph: 7.2 seconds
             to 45 mph: 13.3 seconds
             to 60 mph: 22.8 seconds
Maximum speed on two-way runs: 81 mph.
Fuel consumption during acceleration, braking, and handling tests was 23 mpg.

To the enthusiast who loves sports cars, the Magnette has much to offer in its response to the slightest touch of the wheel. The person addicted to three or four times the engine displacement and several times the rated output, however, will not be impressed by the above figures. (In 1954, the five-passenger domestic sedan that could corner like a sports car and stop without slewing about in just 137 feet from a true speed of 60 miles an hour, was not available at any price.)

Bringing the Magnette performance figures up to date, our recent extended tests of the new ZB (called the "Series II" in Europe)

raises the top speed to 84 mph. With the increased compression and improved transmission with more favorable ratios, the well-tuned 1957 Magnette ZB fulfilled our expectations:

Zero to 30 mph: 6.3 seconds
Zero to 45 mph: 11.8 seconds
Zero to 60 mph: 20.5 seconds
Maximum speed over two-way runs: 84 mph.
Fuel mileage during acceleration and speed runs: 25.7 mpg.

Climb in and let's take a ride. You'll discover that the guttier new model is little changed in appearance or in its attachment to the road, be the corner oblique, reverse-cambered, or otherwise. Around town the Magnette, whether of 1954, 1957 or in-between vintage, is a pleasure to drive. The 68 bhp ZB can be safely started off, on the level, in second gear but with less acceleration. Driven thusly, the gear-change pattern of the floor stick will be familiar to those Americans who have never driven an imported car (if their driving experience extends back prior to the steering-column shift-levers). On hills of even gentle gradient, though, it's essential to start in the upper left first-gear position. Clutch action is smooth, but early ZA Magnette clutches require precise adjustment to avoid grab.

The three foot pedals are hinged from the firewall. Brake action is smooth and abrupt panic stops result in minimal nose dive. Clutch and brake pedals are a bit close together if you wear shoes much larger than size nine, and women sometimes complain that their right leg tires because of the top-hinged accelerator pedal rather than a conventional organ-type.

The independent front coil springs react a bit softly, especially as regards roll when cornering hard, but this is more evident to bystanders than to the occupants of the car. The rear wheels will hang on in tight cornering and the steering lock of just 2¾ turns, and moderate understeer, makes correction easy when throttle and gears are coordinated. Magnette lives up to MG's *Safety Fast!* motto.

Dips and abrupt rises fail to make this car bottom unless taken at speeds that are obviously too high. Road shock through the steering system is moderate—just enough to advise the driver of road conditions.

Motoring enthusiasts, sports car types, generally detest power steering because it tends to prevent awareness of chuck holes and other road surface irregularities. With power steering rapidly becoming virtually universal on American cars, those who enjoy steering for themselves are spearheading the movement toward the smaller, more maneuverable imported sedans for family touring. One finds it refreshing to visit the showrooms where imports are displayed; there is an agreeable absence of the familiar pressure to "load" the new car with expensive gadgets.

The Nuffield-designed bodies of the Z-Type MG Magnettes were shared with the Morris Oxford Series II and the Wolseley 15/50. (Joseph H. Wherry photo)

Rain and a London-like overcast proved Magnette's roadability during a week of tests. (Joseph H. Wherry photo)

The interior of the Z-Type Magnette was impressive: seating width was 50 inches front, 47 rear; leg room was 39.5 inches front, 41.5 rear. Chair-height seats of 15 inches, and head room of 38 inches front, and 36 rear, compares favorably with US compacts, which are longer and heavier. Upholstery was leather.

Spare wheel/tire and tools are stowed at side of commodious luggage boot in Z-Type Magnette. SU electric fuel pump is at spare's left. (Joseph H. Wherry photos)

Excellent fore and aft weight distribution allows comfortable and safe cruising at speeds of 50 mph on smooth graveled roads. Wind noise is markedly less than in most American cars, but drafts do annoy passengers when the windows are opened for warm weather ventilation. One might wish for better interior air flow. The heaters are adequate for winters in moderate climates, but are lacking in northern latitudes. The windshield defrosters, similarly, are not adequate in severely inclement weather.

Non-enthusiasts generally find the Magnette's price to be on the high side. Conversely, those who appreciate the quality of genuine leather upholstery and luxuries such as walnut veneer facia, large instruments that are readable and rheostat-controlled for brightness, and sporting characteristics in the family car, do not find the price out of line. Of course, the Magnette does not provide the status of a large engine or massive horsepower. Neither does it have a compression ratio that is dissatisfied with the lower-cost regular grade fuel. Driven correctly and properly maintained, neither the ZA nor ZB Magnette should require major repairs, even de-carbonizing, in less than forty thousand miles. It will suffer, however, from carbon deposits with continuous rounds of stop-and-

go driving at low speeds—as will any motor vehicle.

On a recent trip to the West Coast, the author saw a number of Magnettes on the road. Several owners insisted that it is their only car, and that it was selected because family and budget required the combination of sporting and family vehicle. To the majority of owners, the Magnette is a sports touring car eminently suited to everyday driving and the occasional fun of a rally.

The designers did their finest work in the area immediately forward of the driver. Details are well wrought. The electric windshield wipers swing in unison and effectively eliminate the center blind spot. The rearview mirror, larger than on most imports, is easily adjusted and contains a polarized reticle for night driving. An electric clock, dual sun shades, and extremely com-

Ignition side of a ZA Magnette engine. Note radiator cap on header tank; the external bonnet cap was cosmetic.

The aspiration side of a 1,489 cc. BMC B-Type engine in an MG ZA Magnette. (Joseph H. Wherry photos)

fortable bucket-type front seats are standard items.

The availability of such a family car with quality appointments, the capability of day-long cruising at 60 miles per hour while you obtain 27–29 miles to the gallon, and have interior space comparable to that of many more expensive cars, is a worthwhile consideration. Acceleration and maximum speeds are admittedly not noteworthy, but the ability to maintain a high average is. Resale value, too, of the modern Magnette saloon has held up surprisingly well.

At extra cost, the new *Manumatic* transmission is available and eliminates use of the clutch pedal. Of course, the sports car fraternity is convinced that no automatic gearbox can match the handling of a manually shifted car with a positive clutch.

The very name, Magnette, stimulated adverse reaction among the faithful, who insisted that MGs had to be "thoroughbred" sports cars with a competition heritage. This contention was admissable in part. However, one must remember that the Magnette's October 1932 ancestor was the K.1 four-seat open tourer and saloon. But the zealots scored when they criticized a Magnette with only *four* cyl-

inders and a unitized body and frame inherited from the 1952 Wolseley 4/44, which used the 1,250 cc. XPAG MG engine of TB/C/D/F fame *(horrors!)*. Principal dimensions of the running gear and a whole parts bin full of components were also Wolseley out of Nuffield. Such a *raison d'être*, on the part of the upper échelon of the recently created BMC, was unforgivable to many votaries in the Triple-MMM fraternity. They conveniently (and understandably) overlooked the employment of similar methodology in the conception of the *marque* MG some 30 years earlier.

The ZA/ZB Magnette's attributes begin with the excellent 1,489 cc. engine, the development of which must be credited to Austin. The BMC "B" engine, which would power nearly 59,000 MGA two-seaters, boasted a strengthened block, big 3-inch main bearings, a very heavy forged steel crankshaft that was fully counterbalanced, full-skirted alloy pistons with three compression and one oil ring, and other advanced features.

This spacious, approximately 2,500 lb. curb weight family car was the *first* MG to have a unitized—or integral—body and frame structure. This characteristic assured rigidity, strength and fidelity to the *Safety Fast!* slogan.

To the delight of many (and the disgust of some), the ZA/ZB was extremely popular throughout four production years—until it was replaced by the inexcusably mongrelized Mark III in 1959. More important, the ZA/ZB Magnette was the *last* octagon-crested family sports saloon produced in Abingdon. The ZA/ZB Magnettes were the same except for the ZB's increased compression ratio of 8.3 to 1 and larger 1½-inch SUs, which increased the output to 68.4 bhp at 5,500 rpm. A restyling facelift gave the ZB new side trim with "Varitone" color schemes.

Distinguishing themselves in sports saloon meetings, a genré of organized racing in which the British excel, the Z-Type won its class in the Saloon Championship in 1958, the year of its greatest sales. In vintage saloon racing, the ZA/ZB Magnettes are presently

Z-Type's front interior attracted sports car enthusiasts with bucket seats, walnut facia and window sills, but not horn ring. Note large parcel case and electric clock between visors. (Joseph H. Wherry photo)

Independent front coil springs, rack and pinion steering, unitized structure, 10-inch drum brakes. The initial price was $2,695 at East Coast POE. The ZA Magnette early in 1955. (Joseph H. Wherry photo)

popular throughout the British Commonwealth and the Z-Type is found in daily use on every continent. Expert tuning of the 1,489 cc. ZB engine, which delivers a torque of 83 pounds/foot at approximately 3,500 rpm, increases performance moderately and enhances the stamina to sustain the latter.

The MG Car Club maintains a Magnette Register, which should not be confused with the MMM Register. (The latter Register is devoted to the vintage *overhead cam* Midget, Magna and Magnette sports cars of blessed memory.) For many years, the author has speculated regarding the origin of—or the inspiration for—the attractively curved radiator grille of the ZA/ZB Types. From the front, the grille was almost pure MG while, viewed from the side, the affinity with the splendid and respected Frazer Nash competition two-seaters was unmistakable. Durable and efficient automobiles despite their lack of coachbuilt bodies—another sore point with the diehards—approximately 36,600 ZA/ZB Magnettes were built before being phased out in the autumn of 1958 when, ironically, they were winning sports saloon races and continuing to enjoy good sales.

Very few of the more charitable among English-speaking MG aficionados are kindly

ZA/ZB Magnette shared a basic 1,489 cc. BMC B-Type engine with the Morris Oxford Series II, Morris Cowley 1500, Wolseley 15/50, Riley 1.5-Litre, and the Austin A-50 Cambridge (illustrated). (Joseph H. Wherry photo)

disposed toward the alien vehicles that replaced the ZA/ZB Magnettes. Designed, engineered and built from the ground up in premises quite removed from Abingdon, there was nothing, other than the MG octagon crest, to justify such cars being designated MG Magnette Mark III and Mark IV.

To the surprise of few outside the BMC vestry, neither of the contrived "MG" Mk. III/IV Magnettes sold well—fewer than thirty thousand in nearly 10 years of production. As of this writing, the author is not aware of any enthusiast interest in restoring and collecting the Marks III/IV. For the most part, ardent MG enthusiasts have forgotten these BMC clones. Automobile buffs are a peculiar lot, however, so a reason to ignore the questionable lineage of the Marks III/IV may evolve, thereby justifying this brief examination.

The Mark III Magnette had an all-new, BMC unitized-frame *cum* body making it 9 inches longer, at 178 inches overall, than its Z-Type predecessor. Virtually unchanged were the overall width and height of 63 and 58⅞

Nash Metropolitan, built by Austin, also used the BMC B-Type engine of ZA/ZB Magnette. This brisk-performing Anglo-American was listed as the Austin-Nash 1500 in the United Kingdom and Europe. (Joseph H. Wherry photo)

inches, respectively, but the Mark III *was* substantially a new car, a Cowley creation. However, the completely restyled unitized structure's wheelbase was nearly 3 inches shorter and was shared with the Morris Oxford and certain of the Wolseley, Riley and Austin sedans. These were demarcated by distinctive grilles, trim and pertinent interior fittings, the *marque* technique of the badge engineers.

The performance of the Magnette Mk. III was nearly identical to that of the ZB. At the curb, the weight was no more than the ZB, slightly less than 2,500 pounds. The suspension system was not changed but the steering had degenerated from the ZA/ZB rack-and-pinion to cam-and-lever. A family of four or five could be seated—one had to admit—in rather luxurious comfort on genuine leather. The front seats were individual semi-buckets. Walnut trim was used functionally and there was adequate luggage space.

In October 1961, the Mark IV Magnette replaced the Mark III. There was a new side styling strip and a de-tuned version of the 1,622

cc. engine used in the MGA 1600 Mark II sports car (see Chapter XII); the new power train extended the wheelbase minutely. Performance, however, was considerably improved over the Magnette Mark III, particularly in acceleration: zero to 60 mph was attainable in 17 seconds. The maximum speed of 84–85 mph was scarcely affected. Fuel consumption was in the 22 to 25 miles per gallon range. Though the Magnette ZA and ZB sold quite well in the USA and elsewhere, and are still well liked, the BMC-designed Marks III and IV—delivering at around $3,000 at Ports of Entry—never were impressive. Marks III/IV did not succeed in the USA nor did they sell well anywhere. Lacking the Abingdon touch, which could have legitimized designating them as ZC and ZD, their decade in the marketplace was indicative of the eccentricities permeating the BMC people in Cowley and Longbridge. Finally, after limping along in limited production through 1967, the Mark IV was dropped without lamentation from enthusiasts. Post-war Magnettes ended with the hybrid third and fourth types, Marks III/IV.

Different circumstances prevailed with the MG 1100. This car, through modifications, survived nearly a decade and was an eye-opener to many big car drivers and some engineers.

Also a product of the Nuffield/Austin merger and not built in Abingdon, the unfortunate little sedans were another result of the mongrelization of *marques*, design, engine-swapping and the consequential badge engineering.

Introduced in 1962 at $1,898 East Coast POE, the 1100 sports sedan was just 141 inches long overall, and had exterior appearance and interior space that belied its modest measurements. With BMC's unit-construction, the body was a full 60 inches wide, allowing for two adults or three children in the rear seat. Front bucket seats and a flat scuttle floor accommodated 6-footers in remarkable comfort. The small sedan was a family car in a spacious package, with 9½ cubic feet of luggage space in the rear and parcel shelves beneath the instrument panel and behind the rear seat.

Such generous space would have been impossible in a conventional layout. The BMC "A Series" engine was positioned transversely in front. Short shafts with universal joints drove the front wheels. The 1,098 cc. displacement engine was tuned like the same unit in the Mark I (GAN. 2) Midget, with the same dual 1¼-inch SU carburetors and 8.9 to 1 compression ratio. The modest rating was 55 bhp at 5,500 rpm. Curb weight was just 1,850 pounds. As obtains with front-wheel drive, the engine actually delivers more power to the driving wheels than with propeller shaft and rear-wheel layout. Less power is wasted.

Performance with two adults aboard was

ZB Magnette with "Varitone" colors and a wider rear window. (British Motor Corporation)

The Magnette Mark III. (British Motor Corporation)

The Magnette Mark IV. (British Motor Corporation)

quite good. Through the gears to 60 mph was attainable in a fraction over 18 seconds, and flat-out maximum speed was 80 to 82 mph. Exceptionally economical to drive at 60–65 mph over long distances, the 1100 delivered upwards of 27 mpg under average freeway conditions and 30 mpg at a steady 60 mph.

The unusually quiet and smooth ride was equaled by few cars at any price. The secret was the patented "Hydrolastic" four wheel independent suspension system, which employed wishbones in front and trailing arms to position the rear wheels. Conventional coil or leaf springs were not employed. Cylindrical rubber cones containing a patented, non-

The BMC-designed and built MG 1100 and 1300 four-seaters. Rear side windows were front-hinged. The 1100 model. (Joseph H. Wherry photo)

freezing, water-based liquid at each wheel took the place of shock absorbers and springs. Anti-roll bars firmly resisted undue healing over on sharp corners. The liquid-filled rubber cones, sealed against leakage, were interconnected between front and rear units. When one wheel abruptly rose or dropped, the displacing of the fluid was immediately compensated with corresponding leveling action at the other wheels.

The Hydrolastic suspension system was more efficient than the air suspension systems being promoted during 1957–1965. Maintenance was virtually non-existent when the car was new and if the driver responded to BMC's suggested pressure check of the suspension system after 12,000 miles. When road damage caused loss of fluid, rubber stops cushioned the suspension members enabling one to drive

safely at no more than 30 mph. The 1100 handled with the agility of a sports car and it was fun to drive except for the steep angle of the steering column, which placed the wheel at an uncomfortable, near-horizontal position. Quick at 3⅓ turns lock-to-lock, the rack-and-pinion steering was light and brought the car through a 35-foot turning circle with ease. On long trips, the "MG" 1100 was one of the least tiring small cars.

Comparatively generous 8-inch diameter disc brakes in front and 8-inch rear brakes with leading and trailing shoes provided powerful braking with minimal pressure. Stopping distances at any given speed were shorter than in most standard American passenger cars. Two- and four-door sedans were available. All side windows were curved glass, and the very slender windshield and door pillars, along with an unusually wide rear window, assured unexcelled visibility. MG's motto of *Safety Fast!* applied well to this "MG" designed and built by BMC.

The "MG" 1100, despite its irritating ancestry, was a good car and extraordinarily prophetic in view of Detroit's present stampede to counter the flood of imported cars with sensible, lightweight, front wheel drive, fuel-saving family cars. Efficient and superbly engineered, the "MG" 1100 was unable to maintain its initial success in the USA because there were precious few mechanics, outside of BMC dealerships, with front wheel drive experi-

One of the roomiest, toughest, and least appreciated (in America) of the small FWD cars, the MG 1100 was an astonishing success in the UK despite its lack of MG breeding. A spare wheel was secluded beneath floor, in boot. (Joseph H. Wherry photo)

ence. "Some mechanics," as the author pointed out in the August 1970 issue of *World Car Guide* in a road test report on the 1970 Austin America, "adamantly refused to have anything to do with the car which raised Cain with sales after the initial popularity wore off." Similar service problems deep-sixed the small front wheel drive DKW 3/6, the Goliath, and several others. Only Saab of Sweden succeeded in the 1960s with FWD economy cars.

In an effort to enable the little "MG" FWD sport sedan to cruise all day at 70—75 mph with up to 500 pounds of people aboard—thus catering to Detroit iron drivers who had been weaned on automatic gearboxes coupled to massive piston displacements—BMC replaced the 1,098 cc. engine with the 1,275 cc. unit. That BMC engine was shared with the MG Midget Mk. III, the Austin-Healey Sprite

and the above-mentioned Austin America—which would fare even more dismally *in America* than the "MG" 1300.

Entering production in mid-1967, early "MG" 1300s were equipped with a single SU carburetor, which was retained with the optionally available automatic transmission. So fitted, the maximum rating was 65 bhp at 6,000 rpm. The automatic gearbox, shared with the later Austin America, must be judged as excellent (for those unable to shift for themselves) in that it was a 4-speed unit. In the 1970 New

The excellent 1,098 cc. engine: starboard side forward, radiator at right, bonnet latch socket behind the *Sacred Octagon*. An MG in name only, the 1100 won its class in the 1962 Brands Hatch Saloon Race, the 1963 *Autosport* Championship Race, the 1964 1,000 Kilometre Nürburgring, and triumphed in many other events. The MG *octagon* was sufficient! (Joseph H. Wherry photo)

Only Saab of Sweden had much success in America before 1970 with small FWD cars. This is the Type 93 of 1956, which became Type 95 for the 1960s. (Joseph H. Wherry photo)

York International Auto Show, BMC was able to publicize the fact that only two other *marques* offered 4-speed automatic transmissions; those were Rolls-Royce and Mercedes-Benz.

Early in 1968, the 1300 model's 1,275 cc. engine was given a boost with dual SU carburetors and the rating became 70 bhp at 6,000 rpm. The 8.8 to 1 compression ratio was unchanged. A matter of interest—or perhaps fascination—was the advertised output of the identically powered 1,275 cc. Austin America: 58 bhp at 5,250 rpm. There was little difference between the methodology and fidelity to dynamometer verdicts in the publicity or advertising departments in Cowley and Longbridge, UK, and their counterparts in Detroit and Madison Avenue, USA. Horsepower ratings became status symbols.

As a consequence of its production date, the FWD "MG" 1300 was not available when the author was working on *The MG Story*, but a test example was obtained later for another assignment. The performance was virtually the same: from zero to a corrected 60 mph required 18.4 seconds through the gears, maximum speed was 82 mph (an average of a half-dozen runs in opposite directions on an airport runway), and 27 miles per gallon was obtained over some 300 miles of testing on diverse roads. The 1,275 cc. engine offered no substantial increase in performance, a finding verified throughout *the automotive* press at the time. An increase of approximately 35 pounds of weight was not sufficient to account for the absence of useful, improved performance.

After just over 26,000 "MG" 1300 models were produced—some 90,000 fewer than the 1100 "MG Sports Sedan," as BMC's brochures called the hybrid—production ceased in 1971. In many respects, the service problems were a pity. The 1100/1300 models departed from the scene about three years before Americans, behind steering wheels and in Detroit's engineering laboratories, became sensitized to the need for more efficient and economical personal transportation.

Badge-engineered or not, the little British front wheel drive cars were better products, and more prophetic, than many in and out of the industry care to admit.

MGA: First of the Marque in an Envelope

Chapter XII

IZM 362 MGA 1600 Mk.II De Luxe. Note distinctive horizontal
styling of tail lamps. (Joseph H. Wherry photo)

The unusual hiatus in series production of sports cars in Abingdon after the phasing out of the TF Midget in March 1955 (as mentioned at the end of Chapter X), came to a resounding conclusion after about five months.

The faithful were at once fascinated, bewildered and provoked by the appearance of the new MG.

Although the new creation sat on the same 94-inch wheelbase, as had every Midget since the advent of the TA nearly a decade earlier, the new MGA (the alphabetical order had to be recycled!) was not called "Midget" by the works. In the USA, even more than elsewhere, MG meant Midget and vice versa. Thus, there was a name problem.

The traditionalists, too, were offended. To this hard core, anything other than square-rigged styling was akin to heresy. Yet here was a new MG, simply named MGA, that was completely enveloped in a smooth, streamlined body without any characteristically distinctive protrusions.

"The bloody thing can be mistaken for a Siata or almost anything except a Morgan," one critic, within the author's hearing, observed at the press preview in New York City when the first batch arrived.

"Maybe so," a heretic who belonged to the SCCA retorted, "but a pair of prototypes did right well at Le Mans last June."

"I think it's great," an optimist said, "just what MG needs to finish off the Singer and HRG people."

And so the arguments went. The single point of agreement was that the new MGA was a complete break with the past.

The MGA came by its new look honestly. Actually the transition had its genesis when George Phillips captured second place in his class in the 1950 Le Mans. Predictably, the 1.5 Litre class winner was a well-tuned, modern Jowett Jupiter. Phillips' mount was a very special TC Midget with a streamlined body. So impressed was the works, with the improved performance of Phillips' streamlined TC, that management agreed to build an up-to-date special for the next year's event and Sid Enever and his design crew sharpened their pencils. Traditionalists notwithstanding, the old angular styling's wind resistance had to give way to the obvious benefits of streamlining, which, as Phillips' TC special had proven, spectacularly increased maximum speed. With only a couple of notable anachronistic exceptions, MG's contemporaries had already adopted modern, low-wind-resistance styling.

Coupé with winding glass windows was available in all MGA variants. (Courtesy: British Motor Corporation)

Enever's new design for Phillips was built upon a TD chassis with styling reminiscent of Gardner's EX.135. The public debut of the modernistic new streamliner was in the 1951 Le Mans Twenty-Four Hour Race. Despite a thoroughly satisfying performance—flat-out maximum approached 120 mph and was due mainly to reduced air resistance—engine failure forced Phillips to retire early. The TD engine of UMG400, as Phillips' car was registered, was simply not up to the radical tuning necessary for the sustained performance required in the 24-hour ordeal. Enthusiasts, nevertheless, were impressed with the car's performance before retirement, and the styling met with a favorable press with only one major negative comment: the narrow TD frame necessitated a rather high seating position for the driver. Clearly, a lower driver position would lower the center of gravity and decrease wind resistance even more.

Enever, therefore, began the design of a completely new frame with the longitudinal rails splayed outward to a width of approximately 45 inches. The frame, in fact, was much like that of the EX.179 record car (q.v.). Overall height was reduced thereby, and two occupants were comfortably accommodated in extremely low seats on either side of the gear-box and propeller shaft. Two such chassis were constructed and one was fitted with a body virtually like that on Phillips' 1951 Le Mans car. Wind screen, hood and side curtains, bumpers fore and aft, spare wheel and tools in the luggage boot, and all the other necessary highway accoutrements were provided. Everything was new except the T-Type engine which, being on the tall side, required a bonnet bulge. The new prototype sports car was accorded the experimental EX.175 designation.

Naturally the works management looked upon Enever's new creation as the potential solution to the slackening sales of the TD. Around the Commonwealth and in America, dealers were crying for a truly modern MG, one that could approach 100 mph and regain its old lock on the under 1.5 Litre competition class. In the old days the problem would have been solved, but because EX.175 was completed rather late in 1952, MG management ran into the stone wall erected by the new board. This body had been created by the merger of the Nuffield and Austin empires earlier the same year. The new British Motor Corporation poobahs had already committed themselves to manufacture the latest creation of Donald Healey. Powered by the 2.6-litre Austin A.90 engine and bodied with stream-lined aluminum elegance, Healey's two-seater already had been prominently featured in the 1952 Motor Show. Austin's Longbridge factory was selected to produce the newly christened Austin-Healey 100.

MG was left holding the bag. ("Wouldn't do to have two brand-new BMC sports cars, you know.") The superb new EX.175 was rejected in the boardroom and the face-lifted TF Midget was the only way Abingdon could remain in the sports car business. The fact that MG's worldwide sports car sales supremacy now depended upon the outmoded TF mattered not. Fortunately for such dismal times,

the Abingdon management office was occupied by that veteran MG enthusiast, John Thornley, who had become General Manager in 1952.

These technically encouraging developments did not immediately alleviate the struggle in Abingdon to produce a worthy successor to the T-Type Midgets. MG's identity problem, unhappily, did not rank high among corporate concerns, as the Austin representatives on the BMC board seemed to wield more clout than those from the old Nuffield Organization. Then, early in 1955 (about the time the last TF Midgets were coming off the line), John Thornley was able to obtain cor-

The office of the superbly restored MGA 1600 Mark II De Luxe owned by Mike Walsh. (Joseph H. Wherry photo)

Telephoto lens captures MGA 1500 roadster at speed on a Southern California freeway in 1958. Note optional wire wheels. (Joseph H. Wherry photo)

porate approval to organize a competition office, which would function in the interests of the entire BMC empire generally and for MG in particular.

Five months without a sports car branded with the MG octagon had never been a part of Thornley's plan, which was to have an all-new two-seater ready for introduction at the end of May, just before Le Mans. The second stage of Thornley's plan was pure old MG *joie de vie:* A factory-sponsored team of three of the new sports cars—the first such in 20 years—would run in the 1955 Le Mans race scheduled for June 11.

Entirely unforeseen, bodies for the first cars of the new production type were delayed, so the introduction program was hastily reorganized and the racing team cars were introduced about a week prior to Le Mans as EX.182 prototypes. This seeming misfortune probably muted the lamentations of the hard-core enthusiasts who, upon introduction of the team of factory-sponsored racers, admitted to a certain amount of pride that MG was again in the competition business after a long absence of factory participation.

When the day of the Le Mans classic dawned, the team of three new MGs, which had performed faultlessly during practice sessions, were resplendent in their streamlined aluminum bodies finished off in British Racing Green. Scarcely publicized, as their motive power were highly tuned versions of the BMC B-Series engine, basically the exceptionally successful 1,489 cc. units already familiar in the ZA and ZB Magnette saloon cars and the contemporary Morris Oxford, Wolseley 15/50 and the Austin A-50. Even the hard core had to admit that the much-maligned Magnette family types had distinguished themselves on the saloon car circuits, as has been observed. All factors considered, the large delegation of MG fanatics eagerly anticipated a proper show of MG performance in the 24 hours of Le Mans.

The race began with demonstrations of enthusiasm common to such events, but joy was not long to reign. A Mercedes-Benz went out of control, early in the race, and crashed through the barrier and into the crowd directly across from the pits. Many spectators were killed and more were injured. As the yellow flags fell, the MG driven by Dick Jacobs, of Magnette saloon racing fame, wiped out on the White House corner. Jacobs was seriously injured. The race was nearly called, but did continue amidst much gloom. This was motor racing's most serious accident.

At the conclusion, a bare third remained of the 60 cars that started. The pair of MGs accomplished the works' goal—to finish the race with decent averages. In fact, they finished impressively with fifth and sixth class places behind a well-developed team of three Porsches and a fast Osca. The MGs came through with 248 and 230 laps at 86.17 and 81.97 mph, respectively, for a happy "technical success," as John Thornley described the affair in his *Maintaining the Breed*.

Well proven, the EX.182 MGs served as prototypes for the long-awaited, all-new MG sports car that was introduced in September 1955 and which, despite the controversial styling, would be the best-selling MG to date. For Thornley, Enever *et al.* developing the new MGA had been more a battle of wits, with respect to policies mandated by the BMC overlords, than a shop full of engineering problems. The world had changed and sports car design kept pace. Square-rigged and classic-lined styling were passé. Streamlining added the necessary mph to enable modestly powered sports cars to attain the century mark the public was demanding.

The new MGA, a clean break with the past, looked almost exactly like the Le Mans cars. Full width, the rigid box-section frame was 45½ inches wide at cockpit and permitted low seating and the desirable low profile. With the all-steel enveloping body, the total concept was one of modern streamlined efficiency. The 1,489 cc. engine of the first production models had the same 8.3 to 1 compression ratio cylinder head as the ZB Magnette, which was introduced just a month after the MGA. Carburetion was also the same, a pair of 1½-inch semi-downdraft SUs. The rating of 68 bhp at 5,500 rpm also was the same. The gearbox had the same ratios but, of course, the 4.3 final drive ratio provided the overall ratios for high performance. The standard gearbox ratios would remain the same through nearly seven years of production, and the standard 4.3 rear-axle ratio would not change in standard specification until the last year of production. Maintenance, consequently, was unusually simple for a sports car

that would turn in a maximum of 95 mph in absolutely stock tune. In 1955–1956, that was splendid performance for an over-the-counter Class F production sports car that arrived at slightly less than $2,400 West Coast POE. Indeed, MGA was in a class by itself.

Independent coil spring front suspension was based upon that of the TF Midget, while the rear axle and brake system followed those of the Z Magnette. Rack and pinion steering was positive and light with just 2¾ turns lock-to-lock and practically no mileage wear, a virtue of this type of steering as owners have learned through the years. Separately adjustable bucket seats and a completely instrumented facia provided exceptional comfort and more spacious quarters than usually found in sports cars. Small parcels could be stowed behind the seats and large items—overnight cases and the like—were well accommodated with spare wheel and tire in the boot beneath the rear deck. Early options were wire wheels and an easily attached boot lid luggage rack. Still, the MGA was every inch a sports car, with a proper lack of external door latch handles (there was a grab handle for the passenger). Protection from the elements was via an easily erected hood and the side curtains contained a spring-loaded flap for extending one's hand at toll booths, signaling on rallyes, and the like.

If traditionalists had philosophical problems with the styling, the low seating, and the short gear-change lever, the typically throaty MG exhaust note was comforting as was the quick acceleration from rest to a true 60 mph in 15 seconds. Miles per hour per 1,000 rpm in top gear was 17. Maximum gear speeds were 26, 44 and 70 mph first through third, respectively, as reported by *The Autocar*. That respected motoring journal also credited the initial production MGA with a flat-out maximum of 98 mph with hood and side curtains fixed, a net gain of 3 mph over the factory's reasonable claim of 95 mph in open racing trim with tonneau cover in place over the passenger seat.

Enthusiasts soon discovered that the efficient streamlining, more than anything else, increased comfortable cruising speeds to about whatever conditions permitted. Fuel consumption was decreased, too, with around 24 mpg commonly attained at road speeds on the order of 70 mph. At speed, MGA tracked beautifully and surface irregularities were quickly dampened by the sort of firm suspension synonymous with first-class sports cars.

Introduction time followed the annual Ulster Tourist Trials in which a team of three prototypes was entered by the works, one with the pushrod engine and a pair with twin overhead camshaft units. The latter had valve problems and retired early, but the pushrod car performed superbly in every respect and finished fourth in class behind—shades of Le Mans—a gaggle of very swift Porsches. As fate would have it, tragedy struck again when seven cars were entangled in a single fiery accident that took the lives of two drivers. Though the MGAs were not involved in any

respect, this second appearance in factory-sponsored competition very nearly became the last. The BMC board, understandably, was horrified and suspended further racing sponsorship. An interesting aftermath to the tragic 1955 Ulster T. T. was the closing of the Dundrod course by the Royal Automobile Club.

In 1956, the first full year of production, more than 13,000 MGA 1500s left Abingdon. The bearings were strengthened and detailed "tuning" boosted the rated output to 72 bhp at the same 5,500 rpm. Model designation was not changed but the improved 1,489 cc. engine was identified as type 15GD. Synchro-

An MGA 1500 at work during a race meeting on a California course. Note small racing windscreen and roll bar. (Courtesy: Al Moss)

TCM 675, the MGA Twin Cam owned by Ron Thompson. (Joseph H. Wherry photo)

mesh detailing, propeller shaft improvements and a higher mount pad for the starter were incorporated, and the centerpiece of the MG stand at the 1956 Motor Show was the beautiful Coupé with glass windows.

In America, the MGA 1500 was an immediate success. A works-sponsored team of three cars won the team award in the 1956 Sebring Twelve Hours and placed first and second in class in the same event in 1957. For several years, MGA dominated Class F in Sports Car Club of America events. When the last of the 58,750 MGA 1500s rolled off the Abingdon assembly line in May 1959, the most potent of the type, the Twin Cam, was already a legend in its own right.

The MGA Twin Cam was announced in April 1958 and remained in limited production until April 1960. Produced for the serious competitions devotee, a mere 2,110 examples were built. All open two-seaters, they were a rare bargain at Port-of-Entry prices of $3,110 West Coast for the roadster and $3,329 for the coupé. In demand during its brief production run, the Twin Cam is even more eagerly sought today as a collector's car. Now the price is all the traffic will bear, at least six times their new price little more than two decades ago.

The enlarged bore increased the displacement to 1,588 cc. while the chain-driven twin overhead camshafts, high 9.9 to 1 compression ratio aluminum-alloy cylinder head with cross-flow induction by larger 1¾-inch SU carburetors required critical tuning for optimum operation. Timing was particularly sensitive and merited special attention. Admittedly the

The sacred octagon graced boot lid of all MGAs. Thompson's MGA Twin Cam. Note knock-off type hubcaps with bolt-on discs. (Joseph H. Wherry photo)

Intake side of Twin Cam engine shows ports located behind dual SU carburetors. Cast aluminum oil sump has cooling fins. (Courtesy: The Nuffield Organisation)

MGA Twin Cam was not for the average driver, but for the connoisseur. When meticulously maintained, the output of 108 bhp at 6,700 rpm assured a maximum of 115 mph and zero to 60 in 9 seconds with 100 octane fuel an absolute necessity. Stripped for racing with bumpers removed, small racing screen in place and tonneau cover fixed, a Twin Cam would do more than 115 mph with fine tuning and the sort of TLC mustered by the true enthusiast. Easily over-revved in incompetent hands, the Twin Cam suffered too much thereby, especially in the USA.

Chassis modifications also distinguished the MGA Twin Cam: Dunlop disc brakes were fitted all around and the special center-locking vented disc wheels were unusual. As a production machine, the Twin Cam's performance put it in league with larger, more powerful machinery. Numerous specials were fabricated, one of them being a partially sub-rosa 1,762 cc. coupé built up quietly in Abingdon for a group of members in the MGCC Northwestern Centre (United Kingdom). Entered in the 1959 Le Mans, the car sustained damage, resulting in overheating, when a dog disputed the right of way on the Mulsanne Straight. The next year, the same independent club entry averaged 91.1 mph for the 24 hours to win the 2-Litre class. The drivers were Colin Escott and Ted Lund; the latter drove the car home to Lancashire after the race.

In 1957, BMC shifted production of the Austin-Healey from Longbridge to Abingdon. This move further complicated matters for Thorn-ley, Enever, Reg Jackson and Gordon Phillips, who was in charge of service. Though unwelcome, the BMC management was increasingly aware of the greater efficiency of the smaller, much less mechanized MG works.

The MGA 1600 Mark I was introduced in May 1959 as a development of the MGA 1500; production was intermixed initially with the Twin Cam and used a pushrod version of the 1,588 cc. engine used in the Twin Cam. The 8.3 to 1 compression ratio was the same as in the original MGA 1500 and carburetion and valve timing was similarly moderate. The increased displacement boosted output to 80 bhp at 5,600 rpm. Disc brakes by Lockheed

The engine in Thompson's beautifully restored MGA Twin Cam roadster. (Joseph H. Wherry photo)

TCM 675 from the side. (Joseph H. Wherry photo)

were employed on the front wheels while gearbox and propeller shaft improvements closely followed the developments adopted on the Twin Cam. A genuine 100-mph sports car for the average, not overly technical-minded driver, the MGA 1600 Mk.I did not require more than careful, normal maintenance. Production lasted nearly two years, until April 1961, by which time 31,501 had been built.

A virtually new 1,622 cc. engine developing 93 bhp at 5,500 rpm powered the MGA 1600 Mark II. The 8.9 compression ratio required premium fuel. Introduced in June 1961, production lasted only 12 months. During this period 8,719 roadsters and coupés rolled forth from Abingdon. As obtained with its 1,588 cc. Mk.I predecessor, Lockheed discs were used in front with rear drum brakes, a system more compatible with the efficient hand brake required by most drivers. A higher 4.10 final drive ratio was employed, the first standard departure from the 4.3 rear axle of all previous MGA models. Improved low-speed torque and less exhaust rap at high road speeds were the obvious benefits of the larger engine.

Performance of the 1600 Mk.II was changed very little from the Mk.I, but sustained high cruising speeds were more easily attained. This was especially so in North America, where all Mark IIs were equipped with oil coolers. The 1600 Mk.II body was improved structurally although the appearance was changed very little. About the only styling alterations, throughout the entire six and one-half years of MGA production, were very minor detailing of the grille and tail light changes. Built-in seat belt brackets and beefing up of the drive line were the most noticeable changes, other than those beneath the bonnet.

Acceleration was only minimally better in comparison to the 1600 Mk.I, but maximum speed approached 105 mph with windscreen removed and tonneau cover secured. Bolted-on steel disc wheels were recommended by the works because of their greater strength. Fashion being what it was—and still is, for that matter—center-locking knock—off wire wheels were available optionally. Production ceased in June 1962.

One other MGA variant was turned out in very limited numbers late in 1960, after the Twin Cam was discontinued. The exact number is not known; *The Motor* described production as "... very few." Whether the few MGA 1600 Mark II De Luxes are figured into the official total MGA 1600 Mk. II models is not

known, but the author is of the opinion that they are. Possibly the slightly varying production numbers ascribed to the Twin Cam are due to this rare model. Most fortunately, the author was able to photograph not one but two of these most rare of post-World War II MGs during the preparation of this volume. Both roadsters, these are shown here. Not covered in the Specifications because of extreme rarity, the MGA 1600 Mark II De Luxe came about because of a small surplus of Twin Cam chassis, which were equipped with the 1,622 cc. engines of the 1600 Mk. II. The main difference in the specification of the seldom-seen De Luxe, therefore, is the four-wheel Dunlop disc brakes and center-locking disc wheels. There were a few 1600 Mk. II De Luxe coupés. Curiously, most lists of all MG types ignore the existence of this model.

MGA 1600 Mark II De Luxe. IZM 362's owner/restorer is Mike Walsh. (Joseph H. Wherry photo)

MGA 1600 Mk. II De Luxe engine of IZM 362 is topped with custom aluminum finned rocker cover. Carburetors are on opposite side from those on Twin Cam. (Joseph H. Wherry photo)

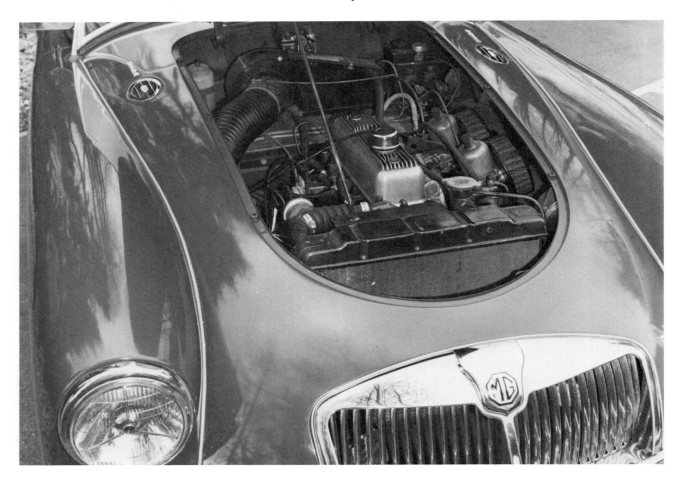

Standard rocker cover on engine IVN 511, the white MGA 1600 Mk.II De Luxe. Owner/restorer, Glen Tarlton. (Joseph H. Wherry photo)

A handsome red, white, and blue trio of MGAs: 1600 Mk.II De Luxe (left and right) and MGA Twin Cam (center). (Joseph H. Wherry photo)

The Last of the Midgets

Chapter XIII

The MG Midget Mk.II with 1,098 cc. engine and squared-off rear wheel arches. (Joseph H. Wherry photo)

Midgets had not been produced in Abingdon since the last of the TFs in March 1955. Such a vacuum produced nervousness in the ranks of the faithful. Clearly, the MGA had been accepted enthusiastically after a brief courting period, but there was an oft-expressed sentiment that the sports car world needed a new MG Midget. The Austin-Healey Sprite simply could not assuage the longing.

The solution was to engage in some more badge engineering—whether or not the old-line MG people in Abingdon liked such an exercise. For some time Abingdon had been building the Austin-Healey Sprite, an under 1,600 pounds two-seater powered by the BMC A.Series engine. Sprite's visage had been marked with bulging headlamps. During the spring of 1961, the design shop had restyled the Sprite with a small luggage boot and debugged the headlights with a more acceptable bonnet. Engineering improved the basic 948 cc. engine by modifying the transmission with closer ratios intended for the Mini Coopers. The result was a new and more conventional Sprite which became the basis for a new MG Midget, the Mark I, which was introduced in June 1961.

The face-lift got a good press while enthusiasts reacted predictably by choosing up sides. If the MGA had been a break with tradition, the new MG Midget compounded the act: not since the P-Type had there been a Midget with less than one litre piston displacement, and there never had been a Midget without a separate chassis frame. Instead, a unitized or integral frame and body structure was used. This arrangement was very rigid but loaded with joining components and seams, and welded into a single unit structure to which all suspension, power train and interior parts were secured. BMC trumpeted the new Midget as revolutionary and virtually rattle-free for life.

Initially powered by the three bearing BMC A.Series 948 cc. engine, the two-seater was small like a Midget should be. In fact, the 80-inch wheelbase was closer coupled than any Midget had ever been with the exception of the original Midget, the M-Type of 1928–1932. If this seemed to be a return to the ancient tradition, there was yet another note of nostalgia: the 948 cc. engine was shared, in basic form, with a contemporary Morris, the popular Minor. That was how "the whole thing" began. (The hard core could ignore the sharing of the same cylinder block with certain examples of the *marque* Austin.) Enthusiasts being what they are, it was no surprise that the new Midget was dubbed "Spridget."

First of the modern, streamlined MG Midgets, the 948 cc. Mark I roadster. (Courtesy: British Motor Corporation)

With 8.3 to 1 compression ratio and a pair of 1¼-inch SU semi-downdraft carburetors, the output was 46.4 bhp at 5,500 rpm. The four-speed transmission was synchronized on the top three ratios and the Hardy Spicer propeller shaft was open with Hypoid final drive. Within a few months of introduction, an alternate 9.1 to 1 compression ratio cylinder head was offered; this gave 50 bhp and a peak torque of 52.5 pounds feet at 4,000 rpm with no effect on engine speed. As economical to operate as to purchase, upwards of 28 miles per gallon was easily achieved. Performance was good, the top being between 85 and 89 mph depending upon the use of tonneau cover or hood and side screens. Optional gears were available for a wider 3.63 first gear ratio or a closer 2.93 depending upon the owner's preference. A weak point was the small 6¼-inch diameter clutch. This was rectified in October 1962 when the improved engine, bored and stroked to 1,098 cc. and with an 8.9 to 1 compression ratio head, became available.

Suspension in front was by wishbones and coil springs; in the rear were trailing arms, and quarter-elliptic, 15-leaf springs. Lever-type hydraulic shock absorbers were used front and rear. Inherited from the Austin-Healey Sprite, this system produced some bouncing on uneven surfaces and considerable understeer. Coupled with the light and sensitive 2¼ turns lock-to-lock rack-and-pinion steering, however, the net was precise and sporting handling with only slight movements of the steering wheel. Badge-engineered or not, the Mark I Midget was a fun car to drive under any conditions. (Many enthusiasts would like to see a small, light, sensitive and economical package cut from the same sporting cloth today.)

Length overall was just 136 inches, 20 inches shorter than the MGA, and curb weight was approximately 1,550 pounds. Interior simplicity matched the tight quarters; six-footers were not overly comfortable. Instrumentation was sufficient and included a tachometer. Very small children, if quiet types, could be accommodated on short runs on a tiny carpeted area behind the bucket seats. The latter were slightly adjustable. As had obtained with all MGs, the new Midget Mk.I was put to competition immediately with the expected success.

Totaling 25,681, Midget Mark I production ended just prior to October 1964, when the Mark II was introduced. First glance, at a distance, disclosed only the addition of swiveling side window vents. The latter were occasioned by wind-up windows in the doors. The Mark II was no longer a roadster in the classic tradition; the modern Midget had become a convertible with external door handles and locks. Also redesigned was the facia panel, with improved instrument grouping and toggle switches for controls.

Engine output was increased to 59 bhp at 5,750 by a slight boost in compression ratio to 9.0 to 1 and modestly altered valve timing, and the torque was 62 pounds foot at 3,250. The three main bearing, 1,098 cc. A. Series BMC engine was more widely shared in the rationalization of major components being pursued vigorously by management. The improved Morris Minor, the front-wheel-drive BMC triplets (the MG, Morris and Austin 1100

types), the attractive and quick Riley Kestrel and the aristocratically named Vanden Plas Princess 1100 were powered by the efficient unit, but of course not always with the same tune or output. Engine improvements inherited from the MG 1100 (q.v.) included a new exhaust manifold, a new cylinder head with larger intake valves and a stronger crankshaft with 2-inch main bearings. Finally, at long last, the Mk.II Midget was given an SU electric fuel pump.

Substitution of full semi-elliptic leaf springs for the quarter-elliptics in the rear of Mark I decreased the tendency toward rear-end

Midget production line in the Abingdon works. The unitized body cum frame is shown clearly. (Courtesy: British Leyland Motor Corporation, Ltd.)

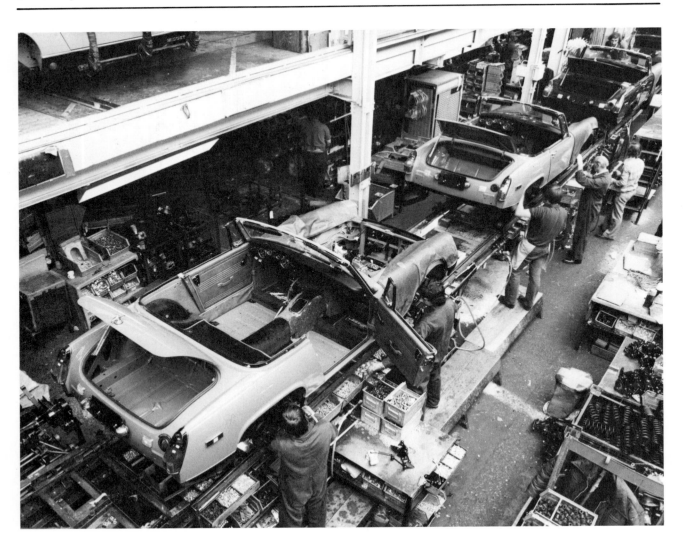

The 948 cc. Morris Minor of 1955 basic engine block powered the MG Midget Mk.I. (Joseph H. Wherry photo)

bounce. Lever type shocks were retained. The brake system also had undergone needed beefing-up with 8¼-inch Lockheed discs in front; in the rear, 7-inch drums and shoes were used. Rack and pinion steering remained and the three-spoke, 16-inch steering wheel was a welcome improvement. The lock, still quick, was very slightly slower at 2⅓ turns and wheel response was light. The tight turning circle, just a hair over 31 feet, and brief overall length of fractionally less than 138 inches enabled a Midget driver to insert the two-seater into the most restricted parking parallel to the curb. This close-quarters maneuver was all too often reciprocated by the drivers of huge American cars, and insurance rates on small sports cars rose in direct proportion. Sadly, the situation has not been reversed. The increasing ranks of drivers of small cars, including the author (a small car buff

since 1952), frequently feel as if they are driving a punching bag on wheels.

During the writing of *The MG Story* (1967), the author drove a Mark II Midget for an extended period. He noticed the improved cornering and smoother ride, which were facilitated by the improved rear suspension and a corresponding change in the front spring rates. Road holding was excellent despite the scant 1,566 pounds curb weight. The performance was exhilarating—the Midget still gave the impression of moving faster than the actual speed. With just under 1,000 miles on the odometer, the car was still a bit on the stiff side. Two-way flying miles, after speedometer calibration, produced a satisfying 93 mph in

The 1,098 cc. A.Series BMC engine in its natural habitat, the Midget Mk.II. (Joseph H. Wherry photo)

Comforts of the convertible Midget Mk.II were well-liked by the ladies. (Joseph H. Wherry photo)

A place of authority on road and track, the cockpit of MG Midget Mk. II. (Joseph H. Wherry photo)

Restyled grille, newly rounded rear wheel arches, side lamps and headrests distinguished the 1,275 cc. MG Midget Mk.III of 1973. (Courtesy: British Leyland Motor Corporation, Ltd.)

top gear. Transmission stiffness was moderate and gear speeds were 31, 50 and 69 mph, respectively, in first through third ratios. Acceleration times would have been much better had the car been run in to around 5,000 miles. From standing starts to true 30, 45 and 60 mph required a sufficient but stiff 4.2, 9.3 and 14.8 seconds.

City driving in the San Francisco Bay area (the test Mark II was supplied by Skjel Kvale's British Motors) produced 27 miles per gallon, a handy figure considering the small 7.2 gallon fuel tank. Fuel consumption decreased on open roads to more than 30 mpg even with spirited driving and manipulation of the gearbox in the sporting manner. This was somewhat better than reported by most British automotive journals, but one must remember that American premium fuel, in 1966, was of higher octane than that available in the United Kingdom.

Most MG Midget Mk.IIs were brought in with the optional center-locking Dunlop wire wheels. Delivery price, on the coasts, was around $2,150 without the optional radio or detachable hardtop. The standard bolt-on disc wheels were seldom seen on the road, but wise competition types favored the stronger discs, which were recommended by the works. In two years of production, 26,601 Mark II

Midgets rolled forth from Abingdon, some 900 more than the preceding Mark I, which was in production some 15 months longer. Around 75 percent were exported to America where, among other racing honors, the Midget Mk.II captured first in Class G in the 1965 Bridgehampton Double 500 Mile Race, a World Manufacturers' Championship meeting. The Midget also placed first in Class in the 1965 Sebring Twelve Hour, while another took first in Class G Production in the American Road Race of Champions at Daytona.

The MG Midget Mark III was presented to the public at the London Auto Show in October 1966. There were important changes beneath the bonnet, where the cylinder bore was increased and stroke decreased to 70.61 and 81.28 mm., respectively. Though stretching the BMC A. Series engine close to the limit of the venerable unit (introduced in 1951 with 803 cc.), the 1,275 cc. piston displacement (actually exactly 1,274.86 cc.) increased the output to 65 bhp at 6,000 rpm and the torque to 72 pounds foot at 3,000 rpm. The moderately reduced 8.8 to 1 compression ratio and the addition of an air injection pump, to conform to U.S. exhaust emission standards, fairly well limited any noticeable increase in performance. An optional oil cooler became popular because extended high-speed cruising resulted in pressure decreases of around 20 p.s.i. from the desired 70 p.s.i. This was particularly so in hot climates and in the USA, Canada and Australia, where long-distance touring is commonplace.

A "quick-lift," "installed" hood or "soft top" was an improvement over the previous cloth hood, and Rostyle wheels were Mark III features by 1969. At a price under $2,300 in the USA, the Midget Mark III continued to outsell all other sports cars. In 1971, the Austin Sprite was dropped from the BMC roster and, once again, Abingdon built only MGs. The MG works did, however, become the location of Leyland ST, the "special tuning" operation for

high-performance engineering of all British Leyland cars. In 1972, Midgets received a larger fuel tank and rounded rear-wheel arches. Detoxification was to bring more performance sacrifices and a slight increase in fuel consumption. When well-maintained, though, the 1,275 cc. Mark III still turned in a creditable performance of zero to 60 mph in 14 seconds and a full-bore maximum of 94 to 96 mph.

Throughout the history of the object of their affection, MG enthusiasts had been shocked and irritated many times. Corporate rationality seldom is compatible with a technical and/

Well-appointed interior of MG Midget 1500 Mk.IV. Dial control (far left on facia) adjusts heating system. Ms. Mustacich's car. (Joseph H. Wherry photo)

Last of the MG Midgets, the 1500 Mark IV. (Joseph H. Wherry photo)

or design philosophy conditioned by the emotions of true believers. The shocker that replaced the long-in-the-tooth MG Midget Mark III in October 1974 was almost too much for some of the hard core: The MG Midget Mark IV, the MG Midget 1500 in some quarters, had a Triumph engine behind a rubber nose!

As if draped in mourning front and rear, "deformable" black "soft" polyurethane bumpers almost obscured the established lines. Instead of a grille, there was a low, wide opening. Only by close investigation could one locate the Sacred Octagon, which was too small. Fortunately the lid of the 7-cubic-foot boot contained the *marque* symbol, but that device was easily overlooked because the location was only a few degrees off the horizontal. As if the fore-and-aft plastic adornments were insufficient to placate the safety bureaucrats, the already tight quarters suffered even greater restriction by a layer of mushy plastic plastered over and across the facia. Traditionally, Midget cockpits have always been cozy, but the layer of fluff over the facia was too much. Fortunately the facia panel was redesigned before too much damage was done, but no one ever did anything to restore a semblance of class to the grille.

The pushrod-operated, overhead-valve, 1,493 cc. engine was yet another of the curious consequences of the 1968 marriage of British Motor Holdings (a previously unmentioned conglomerate which combined British Motor Corporation, Jaguar Motors, the Daimler-Lanchester organization, etc.) with Leyland Motor Company to form British Leyland Motor Corporation, Ltd., better known as British Leyland or, more simply, BLM.

The single carburetor version of the 1,493 cc. Triumph Spitfire engine provided a shortcut to solving emissions problems with which the 1,275 cc. engine could not cope efficiently, provide improved performance, and continue in production. Widely known was the fact that BLM tolerated continued production of MG Midgets because of the unsatisfied demand in North America.

Other than the installation of the 66 bhp at 5,500 rpm Spitfire engine with clutch and gearbox, few changes were made during the Mark IV 1500 Midget's last four and one-half production years. The Feds mandated that the seating height be raised; this caused the overall height of the Mk.IV to be raised by a full inch. Precisely how raising the center of gravity could possibly increase safety is a question

Single carburetion 1,493 cc. engine in MG Midget 1500 Mk.IV. (Joseph H. Wherry photo)

Seven cubic feet of luggage boot. The MG Midget 1500 Mk.IV. (Joseph H. Wherry photo)

Some of the last of the long line of MG Midgets. Assembly line, Abingdon. (Courtesy: British Leyland Motor Corporation, Ltd.)

A pair of streamlined missiles, the MG Midget 1500 Mk.IV owned by Suzanne Mustacich and grounded Nike. (Joseph H. Wherry photo)

that has never been answered to the satisfaction of sports car enthusiasts—or automotive engineers, for that matter. The single styling change was a return to the semi-flattened rear wheel cutouts.

Upon introduction, the MG Mark IV 1500, tuned to United Kingdom specifications, topped out at approximately 101 mph. Acceleration through the gears to 60 mph was on the order of 12.5 seconds. Export models to the USA, however, were less swift. Experienced sports car drivers never ceased to complain about the noticeable decrease in roadability because of the heavier plastic nose and rear, and the higher center of gravity.

After some 72,000 Mark IV Midgets were manufactured—and sold as fast as Abingdon could comply with a demand that never diminished—the last of the long line of Midgets became the first of the *marque* MG to bite the dust. Production ended in the summer of 1979. The last of the Midgets are still lamented, rubber nose and all.

MGB and Rare MGC:
Roadsters and GTs

Chapter XIV

MGB GT, vintage 1966 (Mark I), with author's daughter at the wheel. (Joseph H. Wherry photo)

The most popular model of the world's best-selling sports car was introduced in the 1962 London Motor Show. The MGB would break all sporting vehicle sales records and continue in production, with few major changes, for 18 years. Sadly, the MGB probably would be *the last of the marque* to be built in Abingdon. Indeed, early MGBs would become collectors' cars before termination of production, an unique situation.

From the end of June 1962, when the last MGA left the assembly line, Abingdon had been preparing to produce the successor to the most successful MG sports car to date. Engineering and styling development had been under way for a good four years, however, starting with the customary sketches by the inimitable Syd Enever, whose ideas combined the roundness and low streamlining of the record-breaking EX. 181. An apprentice draftsman, Peter Neal, executed the initial art renderings based upon Syd's rough sketches.

Sometime in 1958, after much conferring with John Thornley, Enever directed the fabrication of a wooden model, which was followed by more renderings and detailed one-fourth scale drawings. Proceedings were more formal—nothing was off-the-cuff as in the old days—and there was the BMC board to please. Packing off the art work to Long-bridge, Enever soon had the approval of headquarters which, exercising authority, decided to have the Frua studios build a prototype. Abingdon was required to ship an MGA chassis to Italy and John Thornley and his colleagues had to cool their heels while the maestros performed their magic.

The resulting Frua prototype had two principal faults: the styling, though lovely to behold, looked too unlike a potential MG, and the interior space and appointments were deemed to be too restrictive. A new breed of sports car enthusiasts was loose in the world and economics dictated an integral frame and monocoque body to gain interior space and large-scale production. Consequently the ball was returned to Enever's corner to the delight of Mr. MG, John Thornley. After more sketches by Syd and finished drawings by Peter Neal and Don Hayter under the direction of John O'Neill, the chief of body design, another model was constructed by Harry Herring. Enever's original concept of a modern, low, streamlined sports car took shape early in the summer of 1959. Again Enever packed off to the Mecca in Longbridge to keep an appointment with Sir Leonard Lord, the chairman of BMC.

These latest Abingdon efforts, the ADO23 project, were approved and Thornley's people

Though still referred to as "roadsters" by the faithful, the MGB two-seaters were convertibles with wind-up windows. (Joseph H. Wherry photo)

were authorized to complete working scale drawings and construct a prototype roadster. Curiously, a closed GT coupé was being designed, under Enever's oversight, even as the prototype of the two-seater was taking form, but the Longbridge hierarchy inserted themselves into this project and Abingdon's preliminary GT sketches, along with a complete set of open two-seater drawings, were sent to Italy. This time Pinin Farina was commissioned to give his touch to the upcoming MGB. The *Gran Turismo* would not be available, however, until three years after the roadster. Abingdon, in fact, was not allowed to proceed with ADO23 right away, so the prototype MGB was not ready for testing until 1961. Even then, production preparations were delayed by BMC until MGA sales slumped alarmingly. Dealers in North America were relaying customer demands for increased luggage capacity and such comforts as windows and better heaters. The new breed of sports car aficionados were less willing to wrestle with side curtains and bundle against the chill of northern winters.

Abingdon's formula proved to be correct, because the new MGB Mark I two-seater drew kudos from every segment of the sports car world including the critical automotive press throughout the Commonwealth and in the United States. The announced price at the 1962 Motor Show was £950, including the whopping purchase tax, in the United Kingdom. Port-of-Entry price, in the USA, was just over $2,600. Meeting the practiced eye was a very modern but slightly smaller package than the superceded MGA. The MGB was shorter by 5 inches at 153¼ inches overall, lower by 1 inch but appearing even lower than its 49¾ inches height, and reduced by 3 inches in wheelbase. The 91-inch wheelbase was actually 3 inches less than that of the beloved T-Type Midgets, whose place had already been taken by the new tiny Midget.

The modern, wide and low radiator grille displayed the vertical ribs which had been traditional since the PB Midget. Inside were adjustable, leather-upholstered bucket seats with full instrumentation directly in front of the driver and a facia glove compartment on the passenger side. Wind-up windows and a generous, open luggage compartment behind the seats, a more easily erected hood (which stowed behind the seats) and an improved heating system provided the creature comforts in demand. There also was a generous 8–9 cubic feet of space for luggage beneath the

rear deck. The short gear-change lever and wall-to-wall carpeting met with approval. The major lament, on the part of the faithful, was a passenger car type handbrake lever. Dictated by Longbridge—no Abingdon aberration for certain—the absence of the handy fly-off handbrake lever would never be forgiven by the older generation (the new generation never knew any better).

There were compensations, though. The tried-and-true B. Series BMC engine had been enlarged to 1,798 cc. displacement by increasing the bore from 76.2 to 80.26 mm. This improvement over the related 1,622 cc. MGA increased the output only moderately, but the torque of 107 pounds-foot at a peak of 350 rpm was noticeably much better. The dual 1½-inch semi-downdraft SU carburetors and aluminum alloy pistons were familiar items. A higher rear axle ratio also improved high speed cruising. The compression ratio, at 8.8 to 1, was slightly less than that of the last MGA model, but there were other compensations: a larger, tougher clutch, a larger water pump, the engine basement was redesigned for improved lubrication, and there was a larger starting motor. The latter, with the improved water pump and 5½ quart cooling system, improved the lot of overseas owners who insisted on transcontinental touring at rather brisk

MGB prototypes raced frequently during early years of production. No. 39, a proto MGB, at Le Mans in 1965. (Courtesy: British Motor Corporation)

MGB Marks I and II were virtually identical in appearance until late 1968. This 1966 Mk.I two-seater is a modern contrast to a 200-year-old Spanish mission in Northern California. (Joseph H. Wherry photo)

speeds and daily service in weather of high and low extremes unknown in the United Kingdom.

Design of the monocoque unit was a primary concern with Enever. Double, longitudinal box-section sills beneath the doors provided the center section strength. The steel doors (aluminum on the MGA) were more rigid and added to the strength of the new body. All of the fixed welded parts of the body combined to assimilate all torsional forces. The first cornering and high-speed tests disclosed a not uncommon problem suffered by open roadsters—scuttle (passenger compartment floor and firewall) vibration. A welded, curved tubular section forward of the facia panel corrected that poser. Originally a welded part of the body structure, the main front cross-member transmitted excessive noise. Redesigning this member as a separate sub-frame with rubber mounts, and bolted to the structure, solved the problem. Front suspension was by coil springs and wishbones.

As obtains with all projected new designs, Enever considered independent rear suspension systems because of the slightly smoother ride. De Dion axles, trailing arms of several types, and various other refinements came under engineering evaluation, too, but the slight gain was not seen to balance out the increased cost of manufacture. The ride was softened a bit by removing one leaf from each rear semi-elliptic spring. Lever-type snubbers were retained. Suspicious recipients of demonstration drives, around introduction time, were pleasantly surprised at the improved ride of the new MGB, which weighed approximately 2,030 pounds, sopping wet, at the curb. Amazingly, the switch to smaller 14-inch wheels met scant resistance. Traffic maneuverability was excellent with a turning circle diameter of just 32 feet and slightly less than 3 turns, lock-to-lock, of the rack and pinion steering. Also, the MGB cornered well.

Performance was a bit improved over the MGA. With synchromesh on all but first gear, 60 mph was attained in 12 seconds in a well run-in car, and maximum speed was 103−105 mph. For the October 1963 Motor Show there were few changes, but the availability of optional hardtops and the excellent Laycock de Normanville overdrive, operable on third and fourth gears and actuated by a toggle switch, was met with the anticipated enthusiasm. Withheld for a time from the American market, the overdrive permitted 100 mph at just 4,485 rpm in top gear.

Production steadily increased, and by the end of 1964, nearly 70 percent of Abingdon's output was finding an overseas market that appeared to be insatiable.

For the 1964 Motor Show there were several improvements beneath the bonnet: a new, much stronger, fully counterbalanced crankshaft had five main bearings, there was a new electric tachometer, and the 5-quart oil sump was fitted with a cooler, another response to the growing export market.

The sensation at the October 1965 Motor Show was the addition of the long-rumored, longer in development *Gran Turismo*, the MGB GT. The Farina styling studios had successfully wedded the streamlined coupé body, with hatchback, to the Abingdon-designed two-seater. Behind the two bucket seats, a small bench provided occasional seating for children, making the GT a true family sports car. When folded flat, the luggage space beneath the hatchback was increased.

When the GT arrived in the USA late in 1965, the $3,095 Port-of-Entry price made the 107-mph car one of the most coveted on the market. With the new sealed propeller shaft, high-speed cruising was quieter, and the new 12-gallon fuel tank (98 octane required for maximum performance) extended the cruising range to 300 miles.

The author ran a quite stiff, under 4,000 miles MGB two-seater for two weeks during 1966 just about the time that the marque took first place in Class GT-9 in the Sebring Twelve Hour Race held in March. Mind you, this extended test of some 1,200 miles occurred when we still had the right to cruise at 70 mph on major highways. Overall fuel consumption checked out at exactly 26.6 miles-per-gallon average for freeways, back country and the mountains of Northern California during everyday driving, city traffic and acceleration tests. The test MGB weighed in, ready for the road, at 2,138 pounds.

When using overdrive, the fuel consumption came down to 28 to 30 miles per gallon. Mountain driving proved the MGB to be superbly roadable and the Lockheed braking system was excellent. The front discs were 10¾ inches diameter and the 10-inch rear drum types, combined, provided a total swept area of 239 square inches. Gear speeds achieved were 31, 48, 76 and 105 mph first through fourth gears, respectively. From start to true speeds of 30, 45 and 60 mph required 3.1, 5.9 and 11.1 seconds, respectively, and without overdrive in operation. Abingdon's claims of 17.9 mph per 1,000 rpm in fourth ratio and 22.3 mph per 1,000 rpm with overdrive were attained and checked accurately with several runs in opposite directions.

The lovely MGB GT epitomized a dream of John Thornley's for a low-priced, family *Gran Turismo*.

MGB GT had commodious luggage space. Here, the small, bench-type occasional seat is folded. (Joseph H. Wherry photos)

Several days spent in a difficult-to-obtain GT demonstrator, provided by Al Arth of British Motors in San Francisco, proved the worth of the streamlined coachwork. Consistent top speeds of 107 mph were clocked on a convenient, unused airstrip. Luxurious and sporting, the MGB GT truly was the "poor man's Aston Martin" that John Thornley had envisioned and, with few changes, the car remained in Mark I configuration until the summer of 1967 when the Mark II rolled forth.

Running changes characterized the four production years of the MGB Mark II in two-seater and GT form. Early on, the generator was replaced with a modern alternator. Most important was synchromesh on all four speeds, a concession (some said) to American drivers who were beginning to rediscover "stick shifts" and the necessity of good coordination. A better candidate as a "concession" to American drivers was the optional automatic gearbox. Minor changes embraced small items of door and interior trim. Backup lights became standard to conform to American legal requirements. The latter were practical, but in 1968 the horrible, Nader-inspired "Federal Dash" became the ultimate eyesore and made the interior resemble a padded cell.

Fortunately the "Federal Dash" eventually was discontinued and the civility of the useful

MGB two-seater, with hardtop, winning third place in GT category and first in Class G at Sebring, 1966. MGB went on to win Class G Championship of USA the same year. (Courtesy: British Motor Corporation)

facia glovecase returned to grace the interior of two-seater and GT. Less distasteful, though somewhat less attractive, was the blacking out of the grille, inside the outline, in 1969. A pleasant concession to good taste was the new leather rim grip on the steering wheel and optional reclining seat backs. In 1970, the ventilation system was considerably improved, as was the heater and defroster system. Steering column locks became standard the same year, as did an interior courtesy lamp and a self-locking device on the boot. The MGB and MGB GT Marks II remained in production until late in the summer of 1971. By that time, the first quarter-million of this most successful of all MGs had found eager owners.

The ugly "Federal Dash" turned the interior of MGB into a padded cell. Fortunately, this bureaucrat-inspired aberration did not survive. (Courtesy: British Leyland Motor Corporation, Ltd.)

Late in 1970, the quarter-millionth MGB was built. This GT Mk.II displays the blacked-out grille, which came along in 1969. (Courtesy: British Leyland Motor Corporation, Ltd.)

While the MGB Mk.II was exceeding all expectations and continuing to outsell all other sports cars, the limited production MGC shared production lines in Abingdon from October 1967 to September 1969. This was during the supplies crunch caused by the "safety" over-kill in federal regulations in the United States where Ralph Nader's every whim seemed to make every bureaucrat cringe in Washington, D.C. The efficient toggle switches were changed to rocker types—very inefficient—and costs zoomed upward to offset the expense of collapsible steering columns, strangled intake and exhaust systems, redesigned locks, new brakes, tires and a host of other devices to satisfy a couple of dozen specifications.

A strange time, it appeared, to launch a new MG model. On the other hand, MGB two-seater sales were sagging. On the happier side the 3-litre Austin-Healey, which Abingdon was required to produce for BMC, was similarly suffering. Actually the federal regulations were hurting the Healey even worse than the MGB, and Longbridge opted to discontinue production. Corporate politics were moving again: BMC and Jaguar Motors merged and a new name loomed in the automotive firmament, British Motor Holdings. The Abingdon works ceased to be called M. G. Car Company and was downgraded in name to simply M. G. Division. The upshot was that the new engine BMC had been pre-

Longer and higher, the 3-litre, 6-cylinder engine fills the space beneath bonnet in the Hendricks-Chandler MGC GT. (Joseph H. Wherry photo)

paring to replace the Austin-Healey unit was assigned to MG as the powerplant around which Abingdon would engineer a new 6-cylinder MG to replace the Healey. This was not an eagerly sought task.

Not since the luxury prewar SA and WA models had there been an over 2-litre MG or one with six cylinders. The new assignment soon produced a new crop of problems. Time was of the essence, so the logical base had to be the MGB. Because the Longbridge-designed 2,912 cc. engine was larger, the front frame member and the proven coil spring suspension system had to be eliminated in favor of torsion bars and wishbones. The longer 6-cylinder unit was a development of the MGB's 1,798 cc. engine with bore increased to 83.34 mm. Not only was the engine some 70 pounds heavier with a massive 7 main bearing crankshaft, but the hastily designed cylinder head and intake/exhaust systems resulted in increased overall height. Fitted with oil cooler, the crankcase held 8 quarts of oil. Large dual horizontal SU carburetors and alternator were standard.

Adapted from the MGB, the bonnet was quickly redesigned with a large hump to which was added a small bump for final clearance. To some enthusiasts, the bonnet was all wrong, but others were of the opinion that the new 3-litre MGC was in line with tradition by being distinctively different. Certainly the MGC could not be mistaken for its MGB stablemate; even the 15-inch wheels were larger because of the front suspension changes. The rear semi-elliptic springs were retained. Fully synchronized, the gear ratios were changed to conform to the higher 145 bhp at 5,250 rpm and the final drive ratio was considerably higher. Overdrive and automatic gearbox were optional.

Curb weight of the two-seater MGC was 2,425 pounds and the GT model tipped the scales at 2,575 pounds. As was expected, the flat-out speed was approximately 122 mph in standard tune, but the low end torque did not live up to expectations and acceleration through the gears was, disappointingly, little better than the lighter MGB. Steering was heavier, marked by increased understeer, and the turning circle was 34½ feet to the left and

The well-preserved interior of the Hendricks-Chandler MGC GT displays the original leather upholstery. At extreme left of facia the rocker switches are seen. Interior is virtual duplicate of MGB GT. (Joseph H. Wherry photo)

33¼ feet to the right. Inside, the MGC was a virtual duplicate of the MGB, and the outside dimensions were the same. Upon introduction, the two-seater cost £1,102 and the GT was £1,249, both prices including purchase tax. Price and handling deficiencies mitigated against popularity for the MGC, and negative road test reports in Autocar and Motor (both had shortened their titles) did not help matters. In just under two years of production, 8,999 MGCs were built. Few were exported to the USA. Today, however, their limited production has made the MGC a highly prized and eagerly sought vehicle.

The MGB Mark III was introduced in October 1971 as a slightly changed replacement for the Mark II. (The latter, as already observed, was produced for four full years.) The merger of British Motor Holdings and Leyland took place in May 1968. With the Triumph people thus dominant, Abingdon was unable to develop a new car and the MGB, already getting a bit long in the tooth, soldiered on to complete a decade in production. Thornley retired in mid-1969 after 38 years service and Enever's retirement followed in May 1971.

From this angle, one is hard put to identify this GT as an MGC. Only the "bump" on the bonnet hump can be seen. (Joseph H. Wherry photo)

This beautifully restored MGC GT is
owned and driven by Steve
Hendricks and Laura Chandler.
(Joseph H. Wherry photo)

Though listed as a 1969 production, this MGC GT mounts the
vertically ribbed, non-blackened grille interior. Such small
variations always add to interest when researching MG types.
Note "bump on the hump" on bonnet. (Joseph H. Wherry photo)

MGB winning another contest during a 1971 race meeting at Sebring. *Safety fast!* (Courtesy: British Leyland Motor Corporation, Ltd.)

MGB Mark III changes for 1973 were minute: slightly different badge and treatment around parking lamps. Headrests were standard by this time. (Courtesy: British Leyland Motor Corporation, Ltd.)

MGB Mark III was, alas, little changed. Nevertheless, at $3,075 and $3,435 at USA Ports-of-Entry for the open two-seater and GT respectively, the Abingdon marvel continued in high demand and thrived mightily. The slightly decreased output (due to federal regulations) failed to dampen the ardor of most enthusiasts, and the MGB was still the top-selling sports car worldwide. Visible alterations for the Mark III were confined to a new center console and armrests. On the GT there were nylon seat inserts. That good British leather was not long for the low-priced cars exported to America, where the natives were forgetting that leather and plastic are not from the same source.

As with the previous Mark II, there were running changes to celebrate the calendar cycle with Mark III. For 1972 the grille was modified slightly and—those Feds again—buyers got a seat belt warning system whether they wanted the buzzer or not. Most of them didn't, either, and they were quickly disconnected. The nameplate was also minutely changed. In 1973, the Port-of-Entry price of admission had escalated to $3,695 for the roadster and $4,070 for the GT. The latter price, twice that of the dashing post-war TC Midget, was still a bargain for a 100+ mph sports car.

Abingdon planned to export 50 of the remarkable MGB GT V8 models each month to the USA, but none arrived. Zero to 60 mph in 7 seconds. ID was by V8 badges in grille and on sides forward of doors. (Courtesy: British Leyland Motor Corporation, Ltd.)

About midway in the production run of the MGB Mark III, the most exclusive of all post-war, series-produced MGs was launched with a bit of low-level fanfare. The first V8-engined car to wear the Sacred Octagon was introduced in August 1973. Like several of the MG types in the old days, the MGB V8 (no one bothered to explain why this machine was not called MGD with due respect to the alphabet) was conceived in the private "tuning" shop of a specialist builder.

Ken Costello, a Kent specialist, began installing 3.5-litre Rover engines in MGBs during 1971. The powerplant was the aluminum alloy block V8 originally designed by the Buick Division of General Motors in Flint, Michigan. Although this engine was used in a compact Buick with scant success, the then-independent Rover Motor Company purchased the design and tooling. Rover then adapted the unit, with Solihull-engineered improvements, to the Rover 3500, a 1968 upgraded variant of the 4-cylinder Rover 2000.

A touring wild *mallard* (on pond above and beyond far head-lamp) was curious about Ms. Laura Martin's equally bright-colored 1978 MGB Mark IV two-seater. (Joseph H. Wherry photo)

MGB Mark IV owned by Bill Wappler, son of Harry Wappler, meteorologist of KIRO-TV, Seattle. (Joseph H. Wherry photo)

Interior of 1979 MGB Mark IV. The vertical rod, center of wind-screen, is a tensioning device for rearview mirror—common in all MGBs: (Joseph H. Wherry photo)

Generous luggage capacity of 9 cubic feet in MGB Mark IV. (Joseph H. Wherry photo)

On an MGB, even rubber nose and tail eventually look good. The Wappler MGB Mark IV, vintage 1979, with Bill aboard. Luggage rack was popular option. Zip-in rear window was introduced in 1976. (Joseph H. Wherry photo)

The MGB Mark IV owned by Bill Wappler. (Joseph H. Wherry photo)

Costello's special MGB V8 models were snapped up as fast as his small shop could turn them out (shades of Kimber's early days in The Morris Garages in Oxford!). Sir Donald Stokes of British Leyland got wind of them and decided that Abingdon should join the V8 bandwagon. The Rover V8 engine's light weight made it a natural for MG and, Stokes reasoned, if Costello could sandwich in the more bulky V8 beneath an MGB bonnet, the Abingdon engineering staff could do as well if not better. A more compact exhaust manifold, a different oil pump and other minor modifications allowed installation, in altered engine compartments, in otherwise nearly standard MGB GTs. Curb weight was 2,427 pounds ready to roll.

Brake horsepower was rated 137 at 5,000 rpm, less really than the MGC, but the torque (193 pounds foot at 2,900 rpm) would have won the "Battle of Britain's Exports" had the venture not run afoul of the federal regulations of 1973–1974. When the MGB V8 was introduced to the motoring press in August 1973, the plan was to produce 100 cars per week, with half of them slated for export to the USA. Press releases claimed 121.8 mph top speed, with acceleration to 60 mph in under 7 seconds. Published reports verified the claims. Gear speeds—first, second and third—were 39, 62 and 97 mph, respectively, and over-all roadability equaled that of the 1,798 cc. 4-cylinder MGB.

Abingdon was ready, willing and able to meet the production schedule, but none of the V8s were exported to the States and fewer than 2,600 were built. Though pollution standards were subtly blamed (along with a shortage of the Rover engines), corporate politics is the more likely cause of MG not being allowed to field a sports car, in quantity, which would have been a tremendous winner. Cancellation of the MGB V8 in 1976 was followed, a short three years later, with the Triumph TR-7 V8, which turned out to be a loser in the marketplace everywhere. Had the MGB V8 been turned loose in the USA, there would have been precious few across-the-counter sports cars, or "sporty" domestics, in its price range and under 6-litres displacement, able to hold a candle to this car. Perhaps the ill-fated MGB V8 was prophetic. After all, MG had always outstripped Triumph, along with all others in the sales race. But by the mid-1970s, the old Triumph rivals were choreographing the dance in BLM at MG's expense.

The final six years began with the introduction of the MGB Mark IV in the October

1974 Motor Show in London. Most enthusiasts were appalled at what they saw. Washington, D.C., had dictated some rather strict bumper requirements and a host of other regulatory nonsense. These regulations necessitated raising the overall height by an inch (the bureaucrats cared nothing about decreasing roadability by raising the center of roll, and gravity) and the bumper stipulations resulted in the plastic nose and tail.

The "rubber-nosed" MGB Mk.IV was a sight to behold. Cries of anguish were heard wherever the faithful gathered. (Now the Mark IV looks good alongside the trivia being produced domestically to the designs of the Feds!) Pollution restrictions strangled the 1,798 cc. engines, on which carburetion was changed to a single Zenith-Stromberg 175CD5T carburetor. Additional detuning included de-

creasing the compression ratio to 8.0:1. The strangling tended to cause the engines to "run on after shutting off"—an happenstance called "dieselizing." The output was decreased to 82 bhp at 5,400 rpm. Acceleration suffered due to decreased low end torque and so did fuel mileage.

British Leyland, per se, cannot be blamed for the steadily increasing emission standards, which caused a gradual decrease in output to a mere 67.3 bhp at 4,900 rpm according to the 1978–1979 factory specifications.

Demand remained high; dealers continued to sell every MGB they could lay their

In 1975 an MGB Mark IV rubber-nosed two-seater ran the London to Land's End Trials route as a 50th Anniversary commemoration. The same year MG passed the one million production mark. (Courtesy: British Leyland Motor Corporation, Ltd.)

The 1980 MGB "Limited" owned by Steve Hendricks and Laura Chandler. (Joseph H. Wherry photo)

MGB "Limited" of 1980 was the final series production from Abingdon, all black with gunmetal gray stripes and a spoiler to go with the rubber nose.

Sic transit gloria mundi, a final view of the final MG, the very limited MGB "Limited" of 1980. (Joseph H. Wherry photos)

hands on. Everyone who knew the enjoyment of driving a genuine *Safety Fast!* fun car longed for the return of the beautiful GT, which had been withdrawn from the American market very early in 1975.

After more than a half-million MGBs had been built by Abingdon, production ended late in 1980. The grand total of the "sports car supreme," all types and models, was 1,112,740—give or take a few. The last MGB exported to the United States was the "Limited" of 1980. Appropriately all black, the "Limited" was identified with plastic gunmetal-gray stripes.

What might have been MG's future had management fully understood the unsatisfied demand for the "sports car supreme" right down to the bitter end, for the *marque* that had outsold sporting competitors in every price and performance range?

A brief look will suffice, and then we'll let "Mr. MG" have the last word.

Epilogue

Chapter XV

Many specialist shops are restoring MGs throughout the English-speaking nations. This line-up of mostly T-Type Midgets are awaiting final detailing at Octagon Motor Group, Ltd., in Vancouver, British Columbia. (Joseph H. Wherry photo)

According to Webster, an *epilogue* is "a concluding section employed to complete a work" or something of the sort. As automobiles go, however, there probably has never been a *marque* as capable as the MG of accomplishing its own conclusion in concert with its global band of owners.

Dealers and customers had every right to expect new models by 1970, rather than cosmetically updated versions. Hopes were raised, in the ranks of the faithful, and rumors were fanned by automotive journalists who, themselves, were as anxious to see "all new" MGs as were the merchants, sales managers and hundreds of thousands of owner/drivers.

Late in 1968, British Leyland Motor Corporation, Ltd., informed MG Car Club chairman John Thornley that corporate support was being withdrawn. The Club had eight Centres in the United Kingdom and 43 Centres abroad. Determined to survive, the Club became independent and *Safety Fast*, the monthly journal, became the property of the Club.

When the *Zanda* became the British Leyland centerpiece in the 1970 auto shows in the United Kingdom and overseas, enthusiasts were justified in expecting—as a matter of faith based upon MG tradition—that a "new MG" was in the works.

When federal regulations in the United States became more restrictive for the 1975 and subsequent seasons, MGs kept right on selling briskly. MG, in fact, kept British Leyland thriving in that nationalized corporation's largest marketplace, the USA. Simultaneously, interest in vintage MG types boomed; specialized Registers for groupings of technically related models began organizing in England and around the world.

Long before the ax fell, collecting MGs became the prime objective of enthusiasts—and car collectors in general, for that matter—and by 1975 almost any well-preserved MG open sports car, a mere decade old, was worth at least as much as when new. When the forewarning of eventual closure was announced in 1979, prices zoomed on many models almost overnight.

What might have been? John Thornley told the story in the best possible way in the December 1980 issue of *Safety Fast*. Readers can do no better than to affiliate with the MG Car Club if they are anxious to preserve the traditions established by Kimber's creation. Jaguar dealers can facilitate contact with regional MG clubs. Club information and the current addresses of regional Centres also can be obtained by writing to:

The General Secretary and Office
MG Car Club
67 Wide Bargate
Boston, Lincolnshire
United Kingdom PE21 6LE

(Enclose adequate International Postal Response Coupons.)

Parts and service will continue to be made available by Jaguar dealers, according to a current communication from British Leyland's headquarters for the USA in Leonia, New Jersey.

Widespread use of MG engines by builders of other sports car marques has not been limited to some models of the T.V.R. and Marcos illustrated herewith. The Elva Courier of the late 1950s was powered by MGA engines. From 1953, the Gilbern GT, manufactured in

Centerpiece of British Leyland's display in the 1970 New York International Motor Show was the Kamm-backed *Zanda*. The overhead MGB GT and Midget signs made enthusiasts' mouths water and prompted a spate of rumors. A similar wedge shape was lavished on Triumph but the best-selling MGBs and Midgets of Abingdon, Berkshire, soldiered on into their second decade with scant corporate regard. (Joseph H. Wherry photo)

The respected, limited-production T.V.R. sports cars, made in Blackpool, used MGA and MGB engines in some models during 1960—1970. The 1970 Vixen in the New York Show.

A grand assortment of *Safety Fast!* types in various stages of restoration in Octagon's shop. Run on! (Joseph H. Wherry photos)

Another of many limited-production quality sports cars to use MG engines during the post-war years was Marcos. Built in Bradford-on-Avon in Wiltshire, this is the 1970 GT.

Fire left most of the metal but the hardwood body frame will have to be replaced in this unfortunate MG TD Midget, which was about to receive the attention of Octagon Motor Group's craftsmen. (Joseph H. Wherry photos)

An octagon craftsman restores a T-Type facia to perfection. (Joseph H. Wherry photo)

Llantwit, Pontypridd, Glamorgan in Wales, used MGB engines in some models—as did the Tuscan Mk. IV GT in the late 1960s, and the Ginetta. Even some models of the coveted Lotus have been series-produced with MG engines; the well-known Mark VIII of 1954 utilized 1,497 cc. units.

Adventurous motor sports enthusiasts might be interested in an event being organized for mid-1982. In 1907, the famous Peking-to-Paris race took place. The winner was an American car, the Thomas Flyer. As this volume goes to press, several vintage MGs have been entered—T-Types, an MGA or two, a prewar WA and others. The 8,000-mile ordeal will be known as the 1982 Peking-to-Paris Marathon. From Peking, the course will cross the Gobi Desert and Mongolia, continue through Siberia, cross the Ural Mountains, traverse Russia to Moscow and continue on to Berlin and Paris, a rather decent trial for MGs.

Quite possibly, the MG will be rising, like the mythical Phoenix, to a renewal of some sort by the time this title is released. The survival of the octagon *marque* is being promoted and new rumors arrive with the regularity of new moons.

In any event, there are at least a half-million MGs loose in the world and a large percentage of them are in North America. Latch on to one, and run on with the car that brought modern motor sports to America.

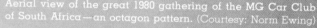

A *concours d'elegance* of vintage MGs in Somerset West, RSA. Right foreground, C-Type Montlhéry Midget. Top left, TA Midget showing production slab fuel tank. CFM-3409 and CA-9602 are TC Midgets, and at far right is a 1¼-Litre Series Y Saloon. (Courtesy: John Watts)

Aerial view of the great 1980 gathering of the MG Car Club of South Africa—an octagon pattern. (Courtesy: Norm Ewing)

Afterword

The traditional birthmarks of the Abingdon thoroughbred—lubrication fittings on outside edge of firewall, octagon on aluminum alloy gearbox housing—in an MG F.1 Magna made in 1931, the same year JWT joined the works staff and helped found the MGCC. (Joseph H. Wherry photo)

MG Car Club badges from three continents. (Courtesy: the Centres and Registers illustrated)

Fitting in every respect as the closing words of this volume are those written by Mr. MG himself, Lieutenant Colonel John W. Thornley, OBE.

The following letter, graciously supplied by JWT, along with a letter expressing his good wishes for the success of this venture, was rushed "To all MG Dealers in the U.S.A."

JWT spent a half-century closely associated with the *marque* MG, as an employee from 1931 to July 1969 and as General Manager from 1952. In his various roles, JWT was as instrumental as any (and more so than most) in seeing MG become synonymous with sports cars worldwide.

JWT was one of the founders of the MG Car Club, which thrives on six continents. Even after retiring from the works scene in Abingdon, JWT continued to live nearby. Active in the MGCC, JWT finally resigned as chairman in November 1980 and withdrew from the limelight.

"I have turned my back on motor cars ('they' having destroyed *my* factory) and directed my energies and consideration towards my wife, my dog, my music and my garden" he wrote the author in the spring of 1981.

Apologizing for the lack of historic photographs ("... almost everyone has written to me for pictures, such that I now have no pictorial memorabelia left—none at all ..."), JWT's cordial letter exemplified the rapport he has always displayed when communicating to the faithful about the object of their automotive affection.

"I wish you well with your venture," he wrote. The author trusts that Mr. MG will enjoy this volume—the first off the press is reserved for him.

Now JWT's letter to MG dealers in the United States; John W. Thornley has the last and well deserved word:

22 Norman Avenue,
Abingdon-on-Thames,
OX14 2HQ
England

13th September 1979

Dear MG Dealer,

This will, I hope, prove to be one of the most important letters to come to you for some time, so please read it carefully. But first let me explain myself. I worked at MG, Abingdon from 1931 to 1969 and was in charge there from 1952. I am now retired. Of *course* I have a personal interest in this: nobody can stand idly by and watch his life's work being poured down the drain; but that is not what I am writing about. This letter concerns *your livelihood*—together with that of a few thousand other people.

You will have heard that the MGB is to cease production by next July, 1980. You have been—or will shortly be—told that 50,000 TR7/8 vehicles will be shipped to North America next year. The production of these, recently transferred from Speke to Canley, (you will doubtless remember the shortage of TR7s which this caused) has so far struggled up to 700 per week, but is again to be uprooted and transferred to Solihull. This morning's Press carries the news that the BL plant at Castle Bromwich—which makes the Jaguar and Rover bodies—is to be closed and the manufacture of those bodies transferred elsewhere *without loss of production!*

There are a whole lot more changes, but let us just consider these, which directly affect you. Let us be realistic and get away from the theory, bearing in mind that the declared intention to reduce the BL labour force by a further 20/25,000—necessary though it be—will have put the workers, and 'organized labour', in a ferment.

To start with, MGB production cannot be maintained at present levels through to cut-off point. The well-behaved labour force at Abingdon has just been kicked in the teeth and anyone who is any good—which includes most of them—will be off seeking employment elsewhere. Replacement, in the present climate, will be virtually impossible.

Clearly, the estimate of 50,000 TR7/8s is wildly optimistic. To build them at Solihull will require the recruitment of labour, and what

chance *that* will have so soon after the completion, last week, of a redundancy programme is anyone's guess. (As I write, news reaches me that Solihull has gone on indefinite strike over a manning dispute.) Anyway, I know as well as you do that the TR is not a market interchange for the MGB.

Does anybody really believe that production of the Jaguar body can be moved without loss? There is bound to be a fall-off, particularly in the short term.

So, taking it all together, it is fairly obvious that, in the not far distant future, you are going to start to have a very thin time of it. And, knowing some of you as I do, it wouldn't surprise me if you—perhaps most of you—felt you had had enough of British Leyland and went off to sign up with the Japanese or the Italians. That would be a pity, because it would spell the end of Leonia and British Leyland's foothold in the US. This, in turn, would be the end of JRT, and where would BL be then?

Your own Benjamin Franklin wrote "For the lack of a nail, a shoe was lost; for the lack of a shoe, a horse was lost . . . " What we are now talking about is not so very different except that the 'nail' is rather large—an MGB.

To stay alive as a Dealer, you *must* have MGBs, and, of all the links in the chain, this is the easiest for BL to put right. The engineering programme for 1981 is advanced and going well. It needs only a word from the Chairman.

You can ensure that he says that word. When you have made up your mind where you stand, write and tell:

Sir Michael Edwardes,
Chairman,
BL Ltd.,
41—46, Piccadilly,
London,
W1V 0BD,
England.

Please do as I say. And quickly. This is a very urgent matter. I am convinced, as I said at the beginning, your livelihood with British cars depends on it.
Good luck to you.
Sincerely,

John Thornley

To all MG Dealers in the U.S.A.

The *marque* MG might have been spared the ax if the dealers in the United States had taken strong and unified action. Some protested, but John Thornley's prophecy came true. The author knows, for certain, that some sales managers and key people in many dealerships never saw Thornley's letter. Not enough was done to counter the "programme" of British Leyland, which had become a nationalized enterprise in the mid-1970s.

Dwayne Anderson at speed in MGB in which he won the 1980 Southern California Sports Car Championship. (Courtesy: Motor Racing Graphics and British Leyland Motor Corporation, Ltd.)

1980 SCCA National Champion and MGB mount in their natural habitat. (Courtesy: Motor Racing Graphics and British Leyland Motor Corporation, Ltd.)

As Thornley predicted, the ball was badly fumbled.

Now Triumph and Rover are also gone.

Happily, there are sub-rosa indications that MG will be revived as a *marque* in its own right.

Meanwhile the MG Car Club is alive and well. MGs are in demand.

True to form, may every MG enjoy tender, loving care and run on.

Run on, MG. Run on!

The MG Car Club
Combined Southern African Centres

The NEW ENGLAND 'T' REGISTER, LTD.

THE CHESAPEAKE CHAPTER

Specifications

MGB two-seaters on assembly line as the end drew near in Abingdon. (Courtesy: British Leyland Motor Corporation, Ltd.)

Type	Production Period (approx.)	Cylinders	Bore and Stroke (mm.)	Valves	Displacement (c.c.)	Compression Ratio (-- to 1)	Carburetors
14/28 MG Super Sports (Bullnose)	Late 1924 through 1926	4	75 × 102	Side	1802	5.0	1 SU Solex or Smith
14/28 MG Super Sports (Flat Rad)	Late 1926 through 1929	4	75 × 102	Side	1802	5.0	1 Solex hor.
14/40 MG Super Sports Mark IV	through 1929	4	75 × 102	Side	1802	5.0	1 Solex hor.
12/12 Midget	mid 1928	4	57 × 83	OHC, vert dyno	847	5.4 probably	2 SU
M Midget	late '28 to mid '32	4	57 × 83	OHC, vert dyno	847	4.5	1 SU
18/80 MG Six Mark I	late '28 to mid '31	6	69 × 110	OHC, chain	2468	5.8	2 SU hor.
18/80 MG Six Mark II Type A	late '29 to mid '33	6	69 × 110	OHC, chain	2468	5.8	2 SU hor.
18/100 MG Six Mk. III Type B	1930	6	69 × 110	OHC, chain	2468	6.9	2 SU hor.
C Montlhéry Midget	March '31 to mid '32	4	57 × 73	OHC, vert dyno	746	5.8 / 9.0	1 SU / 1 SU
D Midget	Oct 1931 to May 1932	4	57 × 83	OHC, vert dyno	847	5.4	1 SU
F.1 Magna F.2 F.3	Oct 1931 to Dec 1932	6	57 × 83	OHC, vert dyno	1271	5.7	2 SU
J.1 Midget J.2	July 1932 to Jan '34	4	57 × 83	OHC, vert dyno	847	6.2	2 SU
J.3 Midget	same	4	57 × 73	OHC, vert dyno	746	5.2	1 SU
J.4 Midget	same	4	57 × 73	OHC, vert dyno	746	5.5	1 SU

NOTE: Dimensions employed throughout SPECIFICA-TIONS (decimals, fractions, Metric and English systems) are listed as officially employed in MG factory materials.

Brake Horsepower @ RPM	Transmission Speeds	Gear Ratios and alternates	Rear Axle Ratio	Tires	Wheelbase (inches)	Tread front/rear	Production numbers
28 (approx.)	3	1.00 1.72 3.20	4.42	19×4.95 Tourer 20×4.95 Saloon	102 1924 108 '25/26	48	400±
28 (approx.)	3	1.00 1.72 3.20	4.42	19×4.95 Tourer 20×4.95 Saloon	106-1/2	48	200±
35/4000 est.	3	1.00 1.72 3.20	4.42	19×4.95 Tourer 20×4.95 Saloon	106-1/2	48	700±
27/4500	3	1.00 1.83 3.50	4.89	19 ×4.00	78	42	5 + reps
20/4000	3	1.00 1.83 3.50	4.89	19×4.00	78	42	3235
60/3200 est.	3	1.00 1.55 3.10	4.25	19×5.00 and 19×4.95	114	48	500
60/3200 est.	4	1.00 1.306 2.00 3.42	4.27	19×5.00 and 19×4.95	114	52	236
83-96/4300	4	1.00 1.306 1.84 3.42	4.27	19×5.00 or 19×4.95	114	52	5
52.5/6500 s'charged 44.0/6400	4	1.00 1.36 1.86 2.69	5.375 5.50	19×4.00	81	42	44
27/4500	3 alt 4	1.00 (n/a) for 1.83 later 3.50 4-speed	5.375	19×4.00	84 early 86 late	42	250±
37.2/4100	4	1.00 1.36 2.00 4.02	4.78	19×4.00	94	42	1250
36/5500	4	1.00 1.36 2.14 3.58	5.375	19×4.00	86	42	380 J.1 2083 J.2
various	4	same	4.780	19×4.00	86	42	22
72.3/6000 supercharged	4	1.00 1.36 1.86 2.69	5.375	19×4.50	86	42	9

Type	Production Period (approx.)	Cylinders	Bore and Stroke (mm.)	Valves	Displacement (c.c.)	Compression Ratio (-- to 1)	Carburetors
K.1 Magnette 4-seat	Oct 1932 to July '33	6	57 × 71	OHC, vert dyno	1087/KA	6.4	3 SU
	Feb-July 1933				1087/KB	6.4	2 SU
L.1 4-seat L.2 2-seat Magna	Jan 1933 to Jan 1934	6	57 × 71	OHC, vert dyno	1087/KB	6.4	2 SU
K.2 Magnette 2-seat	Feb-July 1933	6	57 × 71	OHC, vert dyno	1087/KB	6.4	2 SU
K.3 Magnette 2-seat racer	Mar 1933 to Sept '34	6	57 × 71	OHC, vert dyno	1087	6.2	1 SU
K.1 Magnette 4-seat	July 1933 to Mar '34	6	57 × 83	OHC, vert dyno	1271/KD	6.4	2 SU
K.2 Magnette 2-seat	July-Dec 1933	6	57 × 83	OHC, vert dyno	1271/KD	6.4	2 SU
KN Magnette 4-seat	Fall 1934 to Sept 1935	6	57 × 83	OHC, vert dyno	1271/NA	6.1	2 SU
PA Midget	Jan 1934 to July '35	4	57 × 83	OHC, vert dyno	847	6.2	2 SU
PB Midget	Sept 1935 to May 1936	4	60 × 83	OHC, vert dyno	939	6.8	2 SU
NA, NB, ND Magnette	Mar 1934 to Nov 1936	6	57 × 83	OHC, vert dyno	1271	6.1	2 SU
NE Magnette	mid 1934	6	57 × 83	OHC, vert dyno	1271	9.8	2 SU
Q Midget racer	May 1934 to Oct 1934	4	57 × 73	OHC, vert dyno	746	6.4	1 SU
R Midget racer	Apr 1935 to end June '35	4	57 × 73	OHC	746	6.2	1 SU

Brake Horsepower @ RPM	Transmission Speeds	Gear Ratios and alternates	Rear Axle Ratio	Tires	Wheelbase (inches)	Tread front/rear	Production numbers
39/5500 41/5500	4 4	1.00 1.36 2.00 3.40	5.78	19×4.75	108	48	71±
41/5500	4	1.00 1.36 2.14 3.58	3.58	19×4.50	94-3/16	42	486 L.1 90 L.2
41/5500	4	1.00 1.36 2.14 3.58	5.78	19×4.75	94-3/16	48	15± some KA engines
120/6500 supercharged	4	1.00 1.36 2.32 4.18	5.78 4.89 4.33	19×4.75	94-3/16	48	33
48.5/5500	4	1.00 1.36 2.00 3.40	5.78	19×4.75	108	48	80±
54.5/5500 Valve timing different than in K.1	4	1.00 1.36 2.00 3.40	5.78	19×4.75	94-3/16	48	5±
56.6/5700	4	1.00 1.36 2.32 4.18	5.78	19×4.75	108	48	201±
36/5500	4	1.00 1.36 2.32 4.18	5.375 or 5.125 5.875	19×4.00	87-5/16	42	1973
43/5500	4	same as PA	5.375	19×4.00	87-5/16	42	526
56.6/5700 NA/B various ND with/ w-out supercharger	4	1.00 1.36 2.32 4.18	5.125 5.375 NA/NB 4.875 ND	18×4.75	96	45	738± NA/NB 40 ND
74.3/6500	4	1.00 1.36 2.14 3.58	4.875	18×4.75	96	45	7
113/7200 supercharged	4	1.00 or 1.00 1.36 1.31 2.00 1.84 3.40 3.097	4.50 or 4.875 4.125	18×4.75	94-3/16	45	8
110/6500 supercharged	4	1.00 1.31 1.84 3.097	4.125 or 4.50 4.875	18×4.75	90-1/2	46-3/8 45-1/2	10

Type	Production Period (approx.)	Cylinders	Bore and Stroke (mm.)	Valves	Displacement (c.c.)	Compression Ratio (-- to 1)	Carburetors
SA 2-Litre	Oct 1935 to Sept '39	6	69 × 102 early 69.5 × 102 late	OHV	2288 early 2322 late	6.5	2 SU
TA Midget	July '36 to April '39	4	63.5 × 102	OHV	1292	6.5	2 SU
TB Midget	May to Sept 1939	4	66.5 × 90	OHV	1250	7.3	2 SU
VA 1-1/2-Ltr.	Apr 1937 to Sept 1939	4	69.5 × 102 73 × 102	OHV	1548 1707 Police Engine TPDG	6.5	2 SU
WA 2.6-Litre	Oct 1938 to Sept '39	6	73 × 102	OHV	2561	6.5	2 SU
TC Midget	Fall 1945 through '49	4	66.5 × 90	OHV	1250	7.25	2 SU
YA 1¼ Ltr. Saloon	Apr 1947 to 1952	4	66.5 × 90	OHV	1250	7.2	1 SU
YB 1¼ Ltr. Saloon	1952 through 1953	4	66.5 × 90	OHV	1250	7.4	1 SU
Y 1¼ Ltr. Tourer	1948 into '50	4	66.5 × 90	OHV	1250	7.25	2 SU
TD Midget	Oct 1949 through 1953	4	66.5 × 90	OHV	1250	7.25	2 SU
TD Midget Mark II	1951 – '53	4	66.5 × 90	OHV	1250	8.0	2 SU
TF Midget	Oct 1953 to March '55	4	66.5 × 90	OHV	1250	8.0	2 SU
TF 1500 Midget		4	72 × 90	OHV	1466	8.0	2 SU

Brake Horsepower @ RPM	Transmission Speeds	Gear Ratios and alternates	Rear Axle Ratio	Tires	Wheelbase (inches)	Tread front/rear	Production numbers
78.5/4200	4	1.00 1.38 2.13 3.76	4.75 alt. 4.455 5.273	18×5.50	123	53-3/8	2738
52.4/5000	4	1.00* 1.00 1.42 1.32 2.20 2.04 3.715 3.454 * to Eng. No. MPJG 683	4.875	19×4.50	94	45	3003
54.4/5200	4	1.00 1.35 1.95 3.38	5.125	19×4.50	94	45	379
55/4400 n/a for TPDG Eng.	4	1.00 1.35 1.95 3.38	5.22	19×5.00	108	50	2407
95-100/4400	4	1.00 1.418 2.155 3.646	4.78	18×5.50	123	53-3/8 56-3/4	370±
54.4/5200	4	1.00 1.35 1.95 3.38	5.125	19×4.50	94	45	10000±
45/4800	4	1.00 1.385 2.07 3.50	5.143	16 × 5.25	99	47-3/8 50	6158
48/4800	4	1.00 1.355 2.07 3.50	5.143	15 × 5.50	99	47-3/8 50	1301
54.4/5200	4	same as YB	5.143	16 × 5.25	99	47-3/8 50	877
54.4/5200	4	1.00 1.355 or 1.385 2.07 3.50	5.125 or 4.875 4.555	15× 5.50	94	47-3/8 50	29664 combined
57/5500 and 60/5500	4	1.00 1.385 2.07 3.50	same as TD	15 × 5.50	94	47-3/8 50 wire: 48-3/16 50-3/4	
57/5500	4	1.00 1.355 2.07 3.50	4.875 or 5.125 4.55	15×5.50	94	same as TD MkII	6200
63/5500	4						3400

Type	Production Period (approx.)	Cylinders	Bore and Stroke (mm.)	Valves	Displacement (c.c.)	Compression Ratio (-- to 1)	Carburetors
ZA Magnette	Oct 1953 to Oct 1956	4	73.025 × 88.9	OHV	1489	7.15	2 SU
ZB Magnette	Oct 1956 to late '58	4	73.025 × 88.9	OHV	1489	8.3	2 SU
Magnette Mk. III	1959 to late '61	4	73.025 × 88.9	OHV	1489	8.3	2 SU
Magnette Mk. IV	Late 1961 to early '68	4	76.2 × 88.9	OHV	1622	8.3	2 SU
1100 Mk. I/II	Fall 1962 into 1967	4	64.58 × 83.72	OHV	1098	8.8	2 SU
1300 Mk. I/II	Mid-1967 to 1971	4	70.63 × 81.33	OHV	1275	8.8	1 SU 2 SU
MGA 1500	Sep 1955 to May 1959	4	73.025 × 88.9	OHV	1489	8.3	2 SU
MGA Twin Cam	Apr 1958 to Apr 1961	4	75.414 × 88.9	Dual OHC, chain drive	1588	9.9	2 SU
MGA 1600 Mk I	May 1959 to Apr 1961	4	75.414 × 88.9	OHV	1588	8.3	2 SU
MGA 1600 Mk II	June '61 to June '62	4	76.2 × 88.9	OHV	1622	8.9	2 SU
Midget Mk I GAN. 1	June 1961 to Oct 1962	4	62.9 × 76.2	OHV	948	8.3 9.1	2 SU 2 SU
GAN. 2	Oct 1962 to Oct 1964	4	64.58 × 83.72	OHV	1098	8.9	2 SU
Midget Mk II GAN. 3	Oct 1964 to Oct 1966	4	64.58 × 83.72	OHV	1098	9.0	2 SU
Midget Mk III GAN. 4 GAN. 5	Oct 1966 to Oct 1974	4	70.61 × 81.28	OHV	1274.86	8.8	2 SU
Midget 1500 (Mk IV)	Oct 1974 to mid-1979	4	73.7 × 87.5	OHV	1493 (Triumph Spitfire engine)	7.5	1 Zenith Strom-CD4T
MGB Mk I	Oct 1962 to mid-1967	4	80.26 × 88.9	OHV	1798	8.8	2 SU
®GT (same all Mks)	Oct 1965 to mid-1979						

Brake Horsepower @ RPM	Transmission Speeds	Gear Ratios and alternates	Rear Axle Ratio	Tires	Wheelbase (inches)	Tread front/rear	Production numbers
60/4600	4	1.00 1.374 2.214 3.64	4.875	15 × 5.50	102	51	12754
68/5500	4	1.00 1.374 2.214 3.64	4.55	15 × 5.50	102	51	23846
66.5/5200	4	1.00 1.37 2.21 3.64 Mk. IV opt automatic	4.55	14×5.60	99-3/16	48-9/16 49-7/8	15676
68/5000			4.30	14 × 5.60	100-1/4	50-5/8 51-3/8	13738
55/5500	4	1.00 1.41 2.17 3.63 (automatic optional 1967/68)	4.13 Front Drive	12 × 5.20	93-1/2	51-1/2 50-7/8	116827
65/6000 70/6000							26240
68/5500 72/5500			4.3	15 × 5.60			58750
108/6700	4	1.00 1.374 2.214 3.64	4.3	15 × 5.90	94	47-3/8 49	2110±
80/5600			4.3	15 × 5.60			31501
93/5500			4.10	15 × 5.60			8719
46.4/5500 50/5500		1.00 1.357 1.916 3.20	4.22 Alt: 3.73 4.55 4.88 5.12 5.38	13 × 5.20	80	45-3/4 44-3/4	16080
55/5500	4					46-5/16 44-3/4	9601
59/5750	4	1.00 1.357 1.916 3.20	4.22 alts. as Mk I	13 × 5.20	80	46-5/16 44-3/4	26601
65/6000	4	1.00 1.357 1.916 3.20	4.22 alts. as Mk I	13 × 5.20	80	46-9/16 45	86650±
66/5500	4	1.00 1.433 2.112 3.412	3.909	13 × 4.5J 145SR × 13	80	46.56 45.0	72000 (approx)
95/5400	4	1.00　0.85 1.37　Over- 2.21　drive. 3.63	3.91	14 × 5.60	91	49 49-1/4	Total MGB/GT produced: see under Mk IV below.

Type	Production Period (approx.)	Cylinders	Bore and Stroke (mm.)	Valves	Displacement (c.c.)	Compression Ratio (-- to 1)	Carburetors
MGC GT	Oct 1967 to Sept '69	6	83.34 × 88.9	OHV	2912	9.0	2 SU hor.
MGB GT V8	Aug 1973 to early '76	8	88.9 × 71.12	OHV	3528.08	8.25	2 SU hor.
MGB/GT Mk II	From mid 1967	4	80.26 × 88.9	OHV	1798	8.8	2 SU
MGB/GT Mk III	From Oct 1971						
MGB/GT Mk IV	Oct 1974 to 27 Oct '80	4	80.26 × 88.9	OHV	1798	8.0	1 Zenith-Stromberg

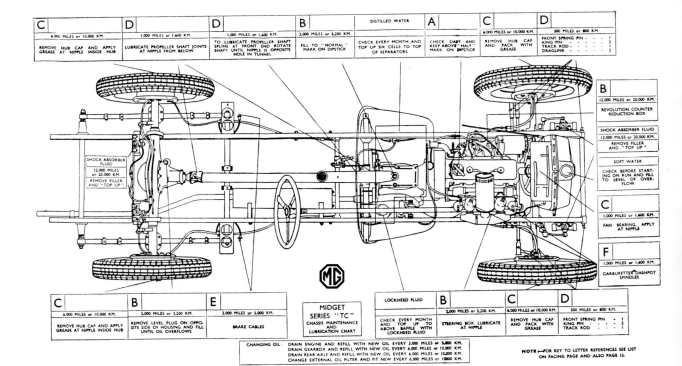

MIDGET SERIES "TC"
CHASSIS MAINTENANCE AND LUBRICATION CHART

Brake Horsepower @ RPM	Transmission Speeds	Gear Ratios and alternates		Rear Axle Ratio	Tires	Wheelbase (inches)	Tread front/rear	Production numbers
145/5250	4	1.00 1.38 2.17 3.44	0.82 Over-drive	307 3.307 Overdrive	15 × 5J 165 × 15	91	50 49-1/4	8999
137/5000	4	1.00 1.259 1.974 3.138	0.82 Over-drive	3.07 3.307 Overdrive	175HR × 14	91.125	49 49.25	2550+ (under 2600)
95/5400	4	1.00 1.37 2.21 3.63	0.85 Over-drive	3.91	14 × 5.60	91	49 49.25	see below.
92/5400							49.3 49.3	
82/5400 eventually 67.3/4900 (see text)	4	1.00 1.40 2.21 3.3	0.85 Over-drive	3.91	14 × 4.5J 165SR×14	91.25	49.5 49.75	Total MGB/GT 500000±

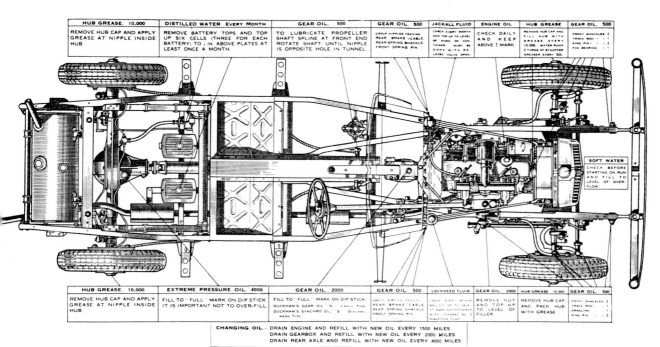

NORTHWEST REGISTER

THE BONNET

Index